God in a Single Vision

In the ancient conversation between Western philosophy and Christian theology, powerful contemporary voices are arguing for monologue rather than dialogue. Instead of these two disciplines learning from and mutually informing each other, both philosophers and theologians are increasingly disconnected from, and thus unable to hear, what the other is saying, especially in Anglo-American scholarship. Some Christian philosophers are now found claiming methodological authority over doctrine, while some Christian theologians even deny that philosophy has its own integrity as a separate discipline. Against these trends, David Brown has argued over the past thirty years that philosophy and theology are both necessary in order to grapple with the reality of divine mystery and Christian faith. Neither discipline can be reduced to the other, and each has its own contribution to make for a full understanding of what Brown describes as 'a single vision' of God. In this volume, Brown addresses some key topics in philosophical theology, including the created order, experience and revelation, incarnation and redemption, and heaven and our communal destiny. Combining analytic clarity, doctrinal substance, and historical depth, this volume exemplifies Brown's project of truly integrating philosophy and theology. It thus provides an ideal introduction to this vital conversation for undergraduate and postgraduate students, as well as a connected argument of interest to specialists in both disciplines.

David Brown is Emeritus Professor in the School of Divinity at the University of St Andrews. Ever since the publication of *The Divine Trinity* in 1985, he has been recognized as one of the leading philosophical theologians of Great Britain and an important international voice in the conversation between philosophy and theology. He is a priest in the Scottish Episcopal Church, a Fellow of both the British Academy and the Royal Society of Edinburgh and a previous President of the Society for the Study of Theology.

Christopher R. Brewer is Manager of Church Partner Development at The Colossian Forum on Faith, Science and Culture in Grand Rapids, Michigan, USA, and Visiting Scholar at Calvin College. He is the editor of *Art that Tells the Story*.

Robert MacSwain is Associate Professor of Theology at the School of Theology of The University of the South in Sewanee, Tennessee, USA. The author of *Solved by Sacrifice: Austin Farrer, Fideism, and the Evidence of Faith*, he has edited or co-edited five other volumes, including *Theology, Aesthetics, and Culture: Responses to the Work of David Brown.*

God in a Single Vision

Integrating Philosophy and Theology

David Brown
University of St Andrews, UK

Edited by Christopher R. Brewer and Robert MacSwain

Routledge
Taylor & Francis Group

LONDON AND NEW YORK

First published 2016
by Routledge
2 Park Square, Milton Park, Abingdon, Oxon OX14 4RN

and by Routledge
711 Third Avenue, New York, NY 10017

Routledge is an imprint of the Taylor & Francis Group, an informa business

British Library Cataloguing in Publication Data
A catalogue record for this book is available from the British Library

Library of Congress Cataloguing in Publication Data
CIP data has been requested.

ISBN: 9781472465566 (hbk)
ISBN: 9781472465597 (pbk)
ISBN: 9781315585239 (ebk)

Typeset in Bembo
by Out of House Publishing
Printed and bound in Great Britain by
Ashford Colour Press Ltd, Gosport, Hampshire

Contents

Editor's Introduction

Robert MacSwain

Although David Brown's first book was an essay in Anglican moral theology,[1] he established his primary reputation as a philosophical theologian with his second volume, *The Divine Trinity*.[2] Born in Scotland in 1948 and originally trained as a classicist at Edinburgh, Brown then pursued a joint degree in philosophy and theology at Oriel College, Oxford, followed by a doctorate in moral philosophy at Clare College, Cambridge, co-supervised by Elizabeth Anscombe (1919–2001) and Bernard Williams (1929–2003). After training for ordained ministry at Westcott House, Cambridge, Brown returned to Oxford in 1976 as Fellow, Chaplain, and Tutor in Theology and Philosophy at Oriel, and then subsequently University Lecturer in Ethics and Philosophical Theology. In keeping with the heritage of Oriel, Brown deliberately identified his work with two of the college's most prominent past members: Joseph Butler (undergraduate, 1715–1718) and John Henry Newman (fellow, 1822–1845).[3] However, Brown was also associated closely with two successive Nolloth Professors of the Philosophy of the Christian Religion who were also fellows of Oriel, Basil Mitchell (1917–2011) and Richard Swinburne.[4] He was thus generally affiliated with the analytic movement in contemporary Anglo-American philosophy of religion, and his early work was in this mode primarily.

Brown remained at Oriel until 1990, when he became Van Mildert Professor of Divinity at Durham University and Residentiary Canon of Durham Cathedral. At Durham his primary conversation partner was Ann Loades – now Professor Emerita of Divinity – and in collaboration with her his teaching and research expanded to include sacramental theology and the dialogue between theology, the arts, and human culture.[5] In 2007 he thus returned to Scotland as Wardlaw Professor of Theology, Aesthetics, and Culture at the Institute of Theology, Imagination and the Arts (ITIA) based at St Mary's College, the School of Divinity of the University of St Andrews.[6] A Fellow of both the British Academy and the Royal Society of Edinburgh, Brown formally retired from teaching and supervision in September 2015.

When he published *The Divine Trinity* thirty years earlier in 1985, Brown sought to produce a creative fusion of patristic studies, historical-critical biblical scholarship, systematic theology, and analytic philosophy. Despite the continued growth and development of analytic philosophy of religion, this is not even now a common combination, as at least one of these four elements is usually missing.[7] This fusion is, however, representative of a certain type of Oxford Anglicanism, and Brown stands squarely – and indeed, somewhat defiantly – in a philosophical and theological tradition that includes not only Butler and Newman but also, more recently, Austin Farrer (1904–1968) and Basil Mitchell.[8] *The Divine Trinity* divided readers along broadly disciplinary lines, with philosophers appreciating it and theologians more dubious; but much of the negative response often seemed as much impatience with Brown's whole school of thought as with this book in particular.[9] This tradition might be called 'Critical Catholicism': instead of seeking to go beyond (or around) 'secular' reason, it accepts native British empirical standards in both philosophy and history, does not object to metaphysics and natural theology in principle, sees special revelation as building upon general revelation, and rather than isolating Christian faith in a protected world of its own seeks to integrate it fully with what is known in other fields of human inquiry. At the same time, such 'Critical Catholicism' takes seriously the basic contours of Nicene Christianity and works as much as possible within those parameters, adjusting them only when it seems absolutely necessary in light of new knowledge.[10]

The volume currently being introduced brings together some of Brown's most significant philosophical and theological essays published in the three decades between the publication of *The Divine Trinity* in 1985 and his retirement in 2015, as well as some new material that reflects his current positions on certain topics. Although remaining both 'Catholic' and 'critical', Brown's thought has changed considerably in the last thirty years, and this volume thus bears witness to development as well as continuity. Brown introduces the chapters in the Introductions to the four Parts, and so my goal here is simply to provide a broader context for readers new to his work, which by comparison with much contemporary writing in philosophical and systematic theology is distinctive in several respects.[11]

First, Brown's consistent pursuit of the Anglican *via media* means not only that he positions himself intentionally between the disciplines of philosophy and theology, but that in *philosophy* he positions himself between analytic and Continental approaches, and in *theology* he positions himself between both liberal/conservative and Protestant/Catholic polarities. He thus remains in conversation with as many perspectives as possible.[12] Second, Brown is an unusually hospitable thinker who genuinely allows various disciplines to be themselves, and so even in his engagements with other fields such as history, literature, classical studies, or anthropology he seeks to *learn* from them rather than fit them into some overarching scheme, agenda, or narrative.

Third, in pure philosophy of religion, Brown does not offer original theories dealing with metaphysics, epistemology, or language, but rather works within a broadly analytic framework to make critical interventions in current debates. He typically seeks to offer a more holistic or historical perspective on a given issue, drawing on a wider range of references and considerations than his interlocutors. He does, however, defend the truth of certain positions, such as the value of religious experience and the validity of metaphorical discourse. Fourth, in philosophical and systematic theology, Brown has made original and widely discussed contributions in his non-punitive theory of purgatory, his defence of specific versions of social trinitarianism and kenotic christology, his distinctive theory of divine revelation as mediated fallibly through both tradition and imagination, and his proposals regarding a pervasive sacramentality discerned in nature and human culture alike.[13] As with his work in philosophy of religion, here too Brown seeks to revitalise options and open pathways that are often neglected by more dominant approaches.

To conclude, in an academic world of increasing hyper-specialization, Brown is a rare example of a scholar who remains in careful conversation with biblical studies, analytic philosophy, Continental philosophy, Protestant theology, Roman Catholic theology, and secular religious studies. He has also deliberately cultivated expertise in a wide range of historical eras, for example contributing important studies of the twelfth-century Anselm as well as the eighteenth-century Butler. Brown's work does not exhibit the type of formalist precision currently in philosophical fashion,[14] but his compensating virtues of disciplinary breadth and historical depth are augmented by an illuminating acuity of insight. Although he has never repudiated his early analytic training, Brown's journey since 1985 might be titled 'Escaping Flatland' – that is, avoiding a preoccupation with logical issues to the exclusion of the three-dimensional world in which we live.[15] It is a journey towards a single vision of integrating philosophy and theology that readers are invited to travel along while reading this volume – and perhaps beyond.

Notes

1 David Brown, *Choices: Ethics and the Christian* (Oxford: Basil Blackwell, 1983).

2 David Brown, *The Divine Trinity* (London: Duckworth; LaSalle, IL: Open Court, 1985).

3 See the Preface to Brown, *The Divine Trinity*, vii. Brown subsequently published several studies of both Butler and Newman: see, for example, David Brown, 'Butler and Deism', in *Joseph Butler's Moral and Religious Thought: Tercentenary Essays*, ed. Christopher Cunliffe (Oxford: Clarendon Press, 1992), 7–35; and the introduction to David Brown, ed., *Newman: A Man for Our Time* (London: SPCK, 1990), 1–18.

4 Brown contributed essays to the Festschriften for both Mitchell and Swinburne, and wrote Mitchell's biographical memoir for the British Academy. For details see David Brown, '"Necessary" and "Fitting" Reasons in Christian Theology', in *The Rationality of Religious Belief: Essays in Honour of Basil Mitchell*, ed. William J. Abraham and Steven W. Holtzer (Oxford: Clarendon Press, 1987), 211–230; David Brown, 'Did Revelation Cease?', in *Reason and the Christian Religion: Essays in Honour of Richard Swinburne*, ed. Alan Padgett (Oxford: Clarendon Press, 1994), 121–141; and David Brown, 'Basil George Mitchell', *Biographical Memoirs of Fellows of the British Academy*, XII (2013), 303–321.

5 See their co-edited volumes, David Brown and Ann Loades, ed., *The Sense of the Sacramental: Movement and Measure in Art and Music, Place and Time* (London: SPCK, 1995); David Brown and Ann Loades, ed., *Christ: The Sacramental Word: Incarnation, Sacrament and Poetry* (London: SPCK, 1996); and Brown's contributions to Natalie K. Watson and Stephen Burns, ed., *Exchanges of Grace: Essays in Honour of Ann Loades* (London: SCM Press, 2008). For a comprehensive later tribute to the cathedral where he served for seventeen years, see the massive volume, David Brown, ed., *Durham Cathedral: History, Fabric and Culture* (New Haven and London: Yale University Press, 2015).

6 For an engagement with this aspect of Brown's work, focusing on five volumes published by Oxford University Press, see Robert MacSwain and Taylor Worley, ed., *Theology, Aesthetics, and Culture: Responses to the Work of David Brown* (Oxford: Oxford University Press, 2012). Some of Brown's essays in this area are forthcoming in a companion volume to this current one, *A Generous God*, also published by Routledge.

7   For various interpretations, critiques, and defences of this movement, see William Wainright, ed., *God, Philosophy, and Academic Culture: A Discussion Between Scholars in the AAR and the APA* (Atlanta: Scholars Press, 1996); Harriet A. Harris and Christopher J. Insole, ed., *Faith and Philosophical Analysis: The Impact of Analytical Philosophy on the Philosophy of Religion* (Aldershot: Ashgate, 2005); Oliver D. Crisp and Michael C. Rea, ed., *Analytic Theology: New Essays in the Philosophy of Theology* (Oxford: Oxford University Press, 2009); and Andrew Davison, ed., *Imaginative Apologetics: Theology, Philosophy and the Catholic Tradition* (London: SCM Press, 2011; Grand Rapids, MI: Baker Academic, 2012).

8   For Brown's engagements with Farrer, see David Brown, 'God and Symbolic Action', in *Divine Action: Studies Inspired by the Philosophical Theology of Austin Farrer*, ed. Brian Hebblethwaite and Edward Henderson (Edinburgh: T & T Clark, 1990), 103–122, now reprinted in Robert MacSwain, ed., *Scripture, Metaphysics, and Poetry: Austin Farrer's* The Glass of Vision *With Critical Commentary* (Farnham: Ashgate, 2013), 133–147; and David Brown, 'The Role of Images in Theological Reflection', in *The Human Person in God's World: Studies to Commemorate the Austin Farrer Centenary*, ed. Douglas Hedley and Brian Hebblethwaite (London: SCM Press, 2006), 85–105.

9   American analytic philosophers of religion such as William P. Alston and Eleonore Stump responded positively to *The Divine Trinity*, whereas British theologians such as Colin Gunton, Nicholas Lash, and Kenneth Surin were negative, with British figures such as Sarah Coakley and Rowan Williams being somewhere in the middle. The Scottish Dominican Fergus Kerr's later assessment is more irenic: see Fergus Kerr, 'Trinitarian Theology in the Light of Analytic Philosophy', in *The Oxford Handbook of the Trinity*, ed. Gilles Emery and Matthew Levering (New York: Oxford University Press, 2011), 339–345, discussion on 340–342.

10 The term 'Critical Catholicism' is obviously inspired by Edward Gordon Selwyn, ed., *Essays Catholic and Critical: By Members of the Anglican Communion* (London: SPCK, 1926), and is meant to conjure both comparison and contrast in relation to the 'Liberal Catholicism' of Charles Gore and *Lux Mundi* (1889), the 'Affirming Catholicism' movement in the Church of England, the 'Radical Orthodoxy' of John Milbank and his associates, and the 'post-liberal' theology that emerged from Yale Divinity School in the 1970s and 1980s. I am not at all suggesting that 'Critical Catholicism' is a distinct movement, nor that it is uniquely associated with Oxford, only that it aptly describes the specific tradition of Anglican theology within which Brown situates himself.

11 For a comparison of Brown with two other significant Anglican theologians writing today, see Benjamin J. King, Robert MacSwain, and Jason A. Fout, 'Contemporary Anglican Systematic Theology: Three Examples in David Brown, Sarah Coakley, and David F. Ford', *Anglican Theological Review* 94 (2012), 319–334.

12 See, for example, his volume *Continental Philosophy and Modern Theology: An Engagement* (Oxford: Basil Blackwell, 1987). In the introduction Brown writes, 'Despite the fact that my own background is in analytic philosophy, I have sought to resist the temptation common among English-speaking philosophers of regarding continental philosophy as "shallow" simply because it is in general more accessible and less technically argued. For the issues it raises are clearly important ones' (xii).

13 Most of these topics are treated in this current volume, with the focus on sacramentality included in *A Generous God*.

14 See, for example, his brief review of the volume *Analytic Theology* (cited in note 7 above), 'Is Clarity Always a Virtue?', *The Expository Times* 121/5 (February 2010), 254–255.

15 Edwin A. Abbott's satirical parable *Flatland* was published in 1884: see the critical edition with notes and commentary by William F. Lindgren and Thomas F. Banchoff (Cambridge: Cambridge University Press, 2010). The 'three-dimensionality' of Brown's work is even stronger in his writings on sacramentality and the arts, but my focus here is on his contributions to philosophical and systematic theology: see notes 5 and 6 above for this other aspect of Brown's work.

Part I
The Created Order

Introduction

This volume would not have emerged at all had it not been for the insistence of the volume's editors, two former research students of mine, who volunteered to facilitate the process; and for all the work they subsequently expended on the project I am profoundly grateful. Perhaps inevitably, somewhat different visions emerged. Should a collection of essays that touched on philosophical concerns freeze the point at which I had reached, 'greatest hits' so far, as one of them put it? Or should it also address some obvious gaps, as the other editor suggested? Or should there perhaps be some attempt to produce a connected volume, one in which one essay flowed naturally on from its predecessor (my own preference)? The resultant compromise has attempted to achieve all three objectives, and so what follows does tell a story, with offerings both from the distant and more immediate past.

Overall, as is indicated by the volume's title, *God in a Single Vision: Integrating Philosophy and Theology*, my concern over the years has been to value the contribution of both disciplines. Historically, demarcation lines were once clear, with philosophy of religion a matter of arguments for and against the existence of God, the coherence of the classical divine attributes, and so forth, with theology then taking over to treat of the deliveries of revelation. However, as I began my teaching career in the 1970s, analytic philosophy began to spread its net more widely, and indeed one of my own books, *The Divine Trinity* (1985), could be seen as part of that process of encroachment on theology. Although many theologians regarded the results with suspicion, my own view was that the boundaries between natural and revealed theology were to a great extent artificial in any case, and so such cross-disciplinary fertilization could be immensely fruitful. However, a word of caution needs to be sounded, and that is reflected in this volume, for just as it is implausible to claim that Christian revelation can be understood apart from the wider culture into which it was once delivered and within which it is now set, so philosophers could not assume either an unchanging deposit in the nature of the Christian faith nor that their own discipline was not subject to the possibility of various potential distortions of Christianity as a result of the more common contexts in which it was deployed. There is not the space to develop such themes here; a few examples must suffice. As I indicate in the essays on Scripture, there is a worrying tendency for analytic philosophers to assume a simplicity to the text that in my view cannot be sustained, and that in turn leads them to deploy understandings of the incarnation that are no longer historically defensible. Then, on the question of potential distortions from the discipline itself, I would cite the desire for clear-cut arguments that dispense with the complexities of figurative language, including the full richness of metaphor and analogy. This is not to deny the presence of excellent books on such subjects,[1] but it is to suggest that the full implications are seldom drawn, as I attempt to indicate here when writing in detail about the atonement and *en passant* on the Trinity. It is surely after all no accident that theologians have invariably opted to express their ideas about the human condition in the language of continental philosophy, and not in that deriving from the English tradition. Phenomenology and existentialism, and even deconstructionism, offered avenues of exploration and questioning that were less readily available within analytic philosophy.[2]

More immediately, some of these points can be observed in the three chapters that follow in this Part. Thus in the first chapter, 'Why a World at All?', answers from both philosophy and theology are considered but in a way that takes very seriously the fact that 'creates' is itself a metaphor. Much twentieth-century theology rightly sought to make us more aware of the subtleties of the image of God as Father and its potential dangers. Yet even as deep a thinker as Karl Barth could go badly wrong, and so it is important to recognize that while the qualification 'ex nihilo' ('out of nothing') protects the term from any suggestion of the use of antecedently existing material – which many (including myself) would see as fundamental to what we mean by God: the source of all that is, itself, dependent on nothing (technically known as divine aseity) – there are deeper questions that also need to be faced.[3] 'Create' after all remains very much an anthropomorphic image, suggesting the need for decision, application, and effort, none of which can be made to yield sense in relation to an almighty or omnipotent deity. More pertinent is the way the image suggests some interest in what emerges, some connection with what is created, as is true in every human act of creativity. It is the nature of that interest that is pursued in the first of the chapters that follow, in which the legitimacy of the question is accepted at the same time as the constraints imposed by aseity.

God as Creator is such a fundamental article of the Creeds and of Christian doctrine that it is all too easy to suppose the implications of the term self-evident and as such necessarily in conflict with alternative ways of expressing the divine's relation to the world. In pursuing that question in the next chapter, 'Creation and its Alternatives', it is noted how many of the apparently different approaches depicting that relation are not necessarily as far apart as is usually supposed, at least once they too are also seen to involve metaphors. Thus with terms such as emanation, pantheism, panentheism, and transcendence it is more a matter of how precisely these images are applied rather than their basic meaning as such which will determine how distant or close particular conceptions or interpretations are to the orthodoxies of Christian doctrine. So, for example, in practice some versions of pantheism do succeed in retaining a strong sense of divine independence from the world (contrast Stoicism and Process Theology),[4] while to use the metaphor of all things flowing out of God as in emanation need not necessarily lead either to an exaggerated sense of the divine character of the world nor to a turning away from divine transcendence (witness Neo-Platonism).[5] Although I have most to say about how these terms have been used in the western tradition, it is worth noting that greater conceptual clarity on such matters could have important implications for inter-faith dialogue and perhaps also allow greater flexibility in the re-conceptualization of the divine relation to the world within Christianity itself.

Then, in the final chapter, I turn to the problem of evil in the world, or theodicy, as it is sometimes more technically known. Here, my aim was to integrate philosophical and theological considerations, as well as their location in historical context. My suggestion is that the typical philosopher and theologian of the present day are alike both wrong: the theologian in denying that there is any fundamental logical challenge that needs to be answered; the philosopher in supposing that answering that challenge can ever constitute a complete response in itself. The term 'solution' is not, therefore, wrong on the lips of the philosopher, but its limited applicability must be acknowledged. Equally, the theologian must avoid appearing to suggest that an adequate response lies solely in the cross of Christ. Rather, such an appeal can only be seen to be of help if it is allowed to work indirectly through being brought alongside other cases of suffering, to illumine how God as creator and Saviour responds to issues of the quantity of suffering and the unique particularity of each individual.

Notes

1   Janet Martin Soskice, *Metaphor and Religious Language* (Oxford: Clarendon Press, 1985) has rightly acquired a definitive place in reading on the topic, while Martha Nussbaum through several books, including *Love's Knowledge* (New York: Oxford University Press, 1990) has done much to broaden analytic philosophy's horizons.

2   For a much-praised example of the use of deconstructionism, see Kevin Hart, *The Trespass of the Sign* (Cambridge: Cambridge University Press, 1989).

3   In *Credo* the meaning of Father is virtually identified with power: (London: Hodder & Stoughton, 1964), 19–27, esp. 19, 22. So it comes as no surprise that in the *Church Dogmatics* creation and fatherhood are seen as a single revelation: (Edinburgh: T & T, Clark, 1975), I/1, 390–391. But what such footwork ignores is that both terms have a range of antecedent meanings. Thus, so far from escaping natural theology, all Barth is in effect doing is accepting one cultural understanding of 'father' to which questions of power are central over against other meanings that in more recent times have assumed greater prominence, for example love.

4   Although Process Theologians in general identify the divine with the mental aspect of the world, it is an aspect that is profoundly affected by the material. Indeed, that vision of interaction and interdependency is often viewed as one of Process Theology's great strengths. While by contrast there is within Stoicism no element that is not material, the divine creative Fire (or the later Spirit of Chrysippus) is portrayed as inherently directive rather than dependent or interdependent on other forms of matter. See further M. Lapidge, 'Stoic Cosmology', in *The Stoics*, ed. John M. Rist (Berkeley: University of California Press, 1978), 161–185.

5   Although some contemporary commentators such as Lloyd Gerson want to downplay the importance of Plotinus's mystical experiences, the more common view remains that, while asserting divine immanence in the world, it is experience of the One as

transcendent to that world which brings us closest to understanding the nature of divinity. See Lloyd P. Gerson, *Plotinus* (London: Routledge, 1994), 218–224; for a contrary view, A. Hilary Armstrong, 'The Apprehension of Divinity in the Self and Cosmos in Plotinus', *Plotinian and Christian Studies*, ed. A. Hilary Armstrong (London: Variorum Reprints, 1979), XVIII, 187–198.

1   Why a World at All?

Though my title may suggest yet another re-run of the cosmological argument, what I want to consider in this chapter is the reasons that have been adduced within the Christian tradition for God creating the world, and their relative plausibility. Five principal categories may be distinguished, and so we shall examine each of these in turn. These five are: (i) a biblically or experientially based argument that it is inappropriate to look for a reason; (ii) the suggestion that it is to be found in an act of pure divine will; (iii) that it is a matter of divine need, for instance a need for, or to give, love; (iv) that it is part of the meaning of divine goodness, and (v) an aesthetic variant, that creativity is natural to God. I shall argue that the last two present the least difficulties. None the less, it is instructive to consider, if only to reject, the earlier possibilities because of what they tell us about the nature of theological argumentation.

Reasons as Inappropriate

First then, the argument that it is wrong to seek for such a reason. Both Schleiermacher and Barth take such a view, but for very different motives. For Schleiermacher theology has no proper basis other than in experience and so to ask a question about God that steps beyond our experience is to violate the Kantian limits to our knowledge: it is to ask a transcendental question that in the nature of the case can have no answer. Indeed that is why for Schleiermacher the heart of the doctrine is not some original act of creation of which we can have no knowledge, but the experiential certainty of our preservation and that of the world in existence at this and every particular moment of our lives, our feeling of absolute dependence for our existence on something other than ourselves.[1]

By contrast, Barth seeks to justify his own rejection of this search for an ultimate reason, not in the limits of experience but on the alleged constraints he finds in the biblical witness. For him covenant is the central biblical category and creation is only to be interpreted in its light. While unlike Schleiermacher he thinks that this allows him to pronounce at length on the subject of creation (much space is devoted to the doctrine in his *Church Dogmatics*),[2] he remains adamant that all this is to be inferred from the covenant and that nothing can be said apart from that context. Thus, when in the following quotation Barth speaks of the creation being for our benefit one should not think of him as giving God's ultimate reason but only the reason to be inferred from the covenant; indeed he goes on to warn against any attempt to raise the question except in this way.

> We cannot understand the divine creation as otherwise than benefit …. That God's creation has the character of benefit derives everywhere … from the fact that its fundamental purpose lies in the covenant between God and man …. But doubt falls on this character in proportion as we dissociate covenant and creation … seeking either a particular knowledge of creation alongside or outside the Christian knowledge of the covenant[.][3]

But the arguments of neither Barth nor Schleiermacher are persuasive. The difficulty with Barth is that his analysis of the biblical revelation has been superseded by the work of subsequent biblical scholars. For so long as the work of Gerhard von Rad was taken as normative it did appear that for the Bible Exodus was, as it were, subordinate to Genesis; that is to say, that a belief in creation was derivative from, and thus subordinate to, belief in the covenanting God. Even Deutero-Isaiah was interpreted in this light. As von Rad writes, 'at no point in the whole of Deutero-Isaiah does the doctrine of creation appear in its own right … it performs only an ancillary function …. It is but a magnificent foil for the message of salvation, which thus appears as the more powerful and more worthy of confidence'.[4] It is, von Rad claims, only through influence from the Egyptian wisdom tradition that in late psalms such as 19 and 104 that creation first appears in its own right, and not just as supportive of covenant theology.[5]

But such an analysis has been fundamentally undermined, not to say disproved, by more recent scholars such as Claus Westermann and H.H. Schmid. In response to von Rad's observation that creation fails to appear in Israel's historic credo in Deuteronomy 26:5–9, Westermann makes the telling point: 'Creation was not an article of faith because there was simply no alternative …. They had no need expressly to *believe* that the world was created by God because that was a presupposition of their thinking.'[6] It was thus this assumed wider backdrop against which the doctrine of covenant was developed, a backdrop which Israel shared with its Canaanite neighbours and whose chaos mythology lies demythologized just beneath the surface of the biblical text at a number of points, for instance in the enthronement psalms identified by Mowinckel.[7] Schmid carries the argument further by suggesting that the basic assumptions of covenant theology could only have been generated from a creation theology. This is because its pattern of reward and punishment presupposes a God automatically able to bring about such effects in nature, but how could this be possible unless he were already a God of nature and not just a God of covenant history?[8]

Sufficient has perhaps now been said to indicate the way in which Barth's exegesis of Scripture might be undermined. But, though this removes the objection that Scripture precludes the search for a reason for creation, it does not necessarily mean that Scripture can of itself provide us with such a reason. The most obvious place to look would be the first chapter of Genesis. Though in the history of Christian thought there has been frequent appeal to the recurring phrase, 'And God saw that it was good', it is doubtful whether in its historical context any such answer was intended.

Writing in the late nineteenth century against the background of the discovery of the Babylonian creation account *Enuma Elish*, Hermann Gunkel not only argued for dependence but that the apparently innocent reference to 'good' might also need to be understood against the background of the original account's story of the struggle to impose order.

> Here also lies in the background an originally strong anthropomorphism: the possibility of failure. God considers each act of creation, testing how it has turned out: he finds each to be 'good', which is to say successful. These are considerations, which P certainly did not come up with on its own, and which it perhaps hardly even understood. And yet, such considerations lie behind his words.[9]

While not denying the roots of the story in pagan mythology, this particular claim I find difficult to believe, since the present narrative contains no indication of struggle. Much more likely, it seems to me, is that the explanation lies in the reassurance the repeated phrase can give to the reader: God's purposes for this world are good. In other words, though the thought is put in the mind of God, the real intention of the narrative is to say something to us: the world is not a battleground between the gods as in the original Babylonian myth (Marduk defeating Tiamat), but one under the care of a God who always creates what is good. But, if that is so, the passage can be of no help to us in answering the more basic question we have posed ourselves: why create at all?

Schleiermacher's objection to raising the question may be dealt with much more briefly than Barth's. Certainly it must be conceded that to raise such a question is to pose an issue beyond our experience, but that cannot of itself undermine its legitimacy. For basic to the traditional understanding of creation is a claim that God's existence is intelligible apart from, and not reducible to, that of the world, but if that is so, the nature of the connection between God and the world is not given in itself but has first to be sought. Schleiermacher cannot conceive of such a response precisely because he has tied the meaning of God to an experience that indissolubly links them both, this feeling of absolute dependence, and that is what in the end draws him nearer to pantheism than to the traditional doctrine of creation. Of course, a fully adequate reply to Schleiermacher would also need to face the more fundamental question of his acceptance of the Kantian, experiential limit to our knowledge. But that is too large an issue to tackle here. Suffice it to say that Schleiermacher's rejection of the search for a reason cannot be justified on experiential grounds alone. A claim that something is known only through experience cannot of itself foreclose the intelligibility of conceptual questions then being raised which are not themselves based upon, or answerable in terms of, experience. Such a position only follows when combined with a contentious Kantian metaphysics, which there seems to me good reason (at least in this instance) for deeming false: the question is in itself intelligible and generates no obvious antinomy.

An Answer in the Divine Will

But even conceding the legitimacy of the question, need the reason be anything other than divine fiat, God's will that it should be so? Here we have the second type of response which I said I would consider. First, let me mention one obvious pointer in its favour. If, as in the cosmological argument, God is seen as the source of all that is, it would seem puzzling to suggest that he act for any other reason than simply his will; for would that reason not then exist outside of God, and so not after all have its source in the source of all that is? Such considerations came to dominate later medieval thought and the Reformation, but the gist of the idea is already in Augustine:

> If the will of God has a cause, it is something that precedes the will of God, which is an outrage to believe. Therefore, to him who says, Why did God make heaven and earth, we must respond: because he willed it. For the will of God is the cause of heaven and earth, and thus the will of God is greater than heaven and earth. He then who asks, why then God willed to make heaven and earth, seeks something greater than the will of God: but nothing greater can be found.[10]

But, though the idea is thus clearly in Augustine, it would be wrong to suppose the notion central to his thought. Its presence, however, did give the Reformers the justification they were seeking to allow it to assume central stage in their own writings, particularly the writings of Calvin. For Augustine was of course *the* theologian par excellence for Luther and Calvin. But, as is increasingly being acknowledged, the immediate antecedents of many of their ideas lie in the later Middle Ages, and this stress on the divine will is no exception.

One major, perhaps the major, contrast between earlier and later medieval philosophy is a changed conception of God, from God conceived of primarily in terms of intellect to a God defined by will. Determining the range of factors which helped bring about this change is not easy, but certainly a major impetus was given by the late thirteenth-century reaction to Aquinas and rationalist theologians like him, as reflected in the Bishop of Paris's famous condemnation in 1277 of 219 propositions. The rejection of two of them is of particular significance, no. 34, 'that the first cause cannot make many worlds', and no. 163, 'that the will necessarily pursues what is firmly believed by reason, and that it cannot abstain from that which reason dictates'. The denial of the second proposition seems to imply that rationality is no necessary guide to the conduct of God, while the denial of the first, though capable of a traditional interpretation, came to be taken to imply that there were no limits to the sort of world God might create.

It was this view which came to dominate the thinking of later Franciscan philosophers such as Duns Scotus and William of Ockham. Scotus for instance uses an argument of Augustine's to endorse such a conclusion: 'Such an ultimate end [i.e. God] cannot be caused in any other way. This is proved from the fact that it cannot be ordained for another end, otherwise it would not be ultimate.'[11] A little later Ockham does not hesitate to draw the conclusion that this means that God may change the content of morality, for example, make murder right, at his own whim. But it is perhaps in Calvin that this obsession with God as power shines through most clearly. Sometimes he seems to reveal an admiration for naked power itself: 'With what clear manifestations his might draws us to contemplate him! Unless perchance it be unknown to us in whose power it lies to sustain this infinite mass of heaven and earth with his Word; by his nod alone sometimes to shake heaven with thunderbolts, to burn everything with lightnings, to kindle the air with flashes.'[12] But more commonly the references are softened somewhat by talk of the divine glory: 'Although God lacks nothing, still the principal aim in creating men was that his name might be glorified in them.'[13]

William Bouwsma in his fascinating study of Calvin suggests that this pre-occupation with divine power very much reflects Calvin's own psyche.[14] Disillusioned with the humanist attempt to gain self-control through the power of reason, he saw the only solution as invasion of the individual by a still greater power, that of God. On perhaps the most common analysis what power signifies is freedom, and so it is perhaps not surprising that in the following century Descartes makes this central to his analysis:

> As for freedom of will, it is in God in a way far different from the way it is in us. For it is repugnant to the will of God not to have been indifferent from eternity to all that has taken place or ever will take place, because nothing good or true, nor nothing that is to be believed or done or omitted can be imagined, for which the idea will have been in the divine intellect before God's will decides that it be of that kind as a result .... Certainly, to give an example, he did not thus will to create the world in time because he saw it to be better thus than if he created from eternity .... On the contrary, because he willed to create the world in time, it is thus better so than if he had created from eternity.[15]

So much for history, what of assessment? My sympathies on this issue at least are very much with early medieval rather than later medieval or Reformation thought. Three reasons for this may be given.

(a) The later tradition operates with an inadequate notion of freedom. Certainly freedom as range of possible action is a significant notion for us human beings who are still in the process of self-creation, determining by our actions what we wish to be, but what sense can such a notion make in the case of God who has existed from all eternity? Putting it somewhat anthropomorphically, will he not have long since determined who he is? So will absence of choice not rather be what characterises divine freedom? That is to say, having already in the first 'moment of his existence', as it were, determined who he is, freedom will be constituted by perfect conformity to what he already is, perfect conformity to his nature. In other words, freedom for God will be the joy of a perfect match between action and nature rather than choice in determining that nature. God's freedom would then be like our freedom in heaven. For having chosen our nature in this life, our freedom will consist in the next life in the spontaneity of doing what we have already chosen, not in the continuing theoretical possibility of an alternative decision.

(b) Secondly, a related point is how we should understand divine power. The later tradition understands power as pure potentiality. But which is the greater power, a power as yet unrealized or a power carried into effect? For the earlier tradition it is undoubtedly the latter; potentiality is seen as inferior to act, and so God is defined as pure act, as completed self-realization.

(c) Finally, it is arguable that the cosmological pressure to make God the source of all that is points in a quite different direction to that which we have observed Scotus implying in his use of Augustine. What I have called the cosmological pressure leads one to define God as the source of all, as that upon which all else depends, himself dependent on nothing. The technical term for this is aseity. But for God to possess this, not to be dependent upon anything, he must be self-contained. Yet, if God is defined solely in terms of will or power, then he has nothing really in himself until that power is exercised, no internal resources upon which he can draw to delight himself. Thus, so far from possessing aseity, he is desperately dependent upon what he has not yet willed into existence. It is no doubt for this reason that the earlier tradition insisted upon an already existing perfection in the divine life, a richness of the actuality of intellect rather than an ultimately dependent potentiality of power.

A Matter of Divine Need

But it is not that earlier tradition that contemporary theology has in the main chosen to follow. Instead, the dominant line has been to make God yet more dependent, whether we take process theology as our example from the United States or the writings of Dorothee Sölle or Jürgen Moltmann as illustrations from Germany. Both nationalities appeal to both biblical and conceptual considerations to justify their case. Suffice it for us to observe here that, though Process theology makes the stronger case – it argues that divine action makes no sense unless the divine is like us embodied – precisely because of that stronger claim it can offer no reason for God choosing to create – on this scenario he just has no choice. Sölle and Moltmann at least concede the choice, but Sölle in particular insists that the God who is revealed is a God who needs the other and so, as she memorably put it on one occasion, 'God did not create out of nothing; he created out of love'.[16] Moltmann is, on the whole, more concerned to be loyal to the Christian tradition and indeed explicitly affirms *creatio ex nihilo*, but even so there are quite a number of occasions on which he seems also to identify need as the motive for creation. For instance in *The Trinity and the Kingdom of God* he writes: God 'expects and needs love; this world is intended to be his home. He desires to dwell in it.'[17]

Such appeals to love as a divine motive in the creative process are of course by no means new. Indeed, Calvin ends that same section I quoted earlier, in which he describes the divine power immanent in nature, with an appeal to the divine love;[18] or consider the following passage, again from the *Institutes*: 'God has ordained all things to our profit and salvation, and in order to contemplate his power and grace in ourselves … thereby to incite us to trust him, to call upon him, to praise and love him.'[19] But there remains a clear difference from Moltmann. Calvin did not intend to suggest that God needs either to give or receive love. Love remains a mediate, not an ultimate cause. That is to say, God having decided to create humanity exercises love in the process, but love is not the ultimate motive; in Calvin's case it remains an act of will.

But might Moltmann none the less be right? I think not, for two reasons. First, the suggestion undermines divine aseity, and that remains for me the primary clue to understanding what we mean by the term 'God'. His existence and nature are not just brute facts, a being who just happens to appear on the canvas of revelation, as Moltmann's approach suggests, but definitive to understanding the nature of reality, because he is the source of all reality. Augustine puts it well in his allegorical interpretation of Genesis 1:2: 'Needy and unsatisfied love is naturally subject to the things it loves …. The Spirit of God in whom we apprehend his holy benevolence and love is said to "move over" the waters, lest God be thought to love the works he should create through the compulsion of need than through the overflow of benevolence.'[20]

Secondly, any suggestion that God needs to give or receive love is in any case contradicted in the Christian revelation by the doctrine of the Trinity. God already has within himself a complete community of love, an argument brilliantly employed by Richard of St Victor in the twelfth century to answer the very point that Moltmann now wants to make to justify his view of creation, that love needs another.[21] Admittedly, Moltmann wants to add that even given the Trinity complete love is missing because this involves filling a lack in the beloved. But that seems to me quite untrue even in the human case. Think of the pleasure of a friend's company over a meal or on a walk, where no need seems to be supplied.

An Overflow of Goodness and Beauty

And so at last I come to the two versions of the divine motivation which I am prepared to accept. First, there is the claim that it was a good thing to do. Nowadays most people are only familiar with Leibniz's version of this claim, that this is the best of all possible worlds. But it is not this version I wish to defend; apart from how good in any case one might view this world there are too many difficulties in making coherent the notion of a best possible world. Yet this is not to say that there is no sense in Leibniz's basic starting point: the definition of God as goodness. For instance, he offers a very effective and succinct summary of what is wrong with the will approach: 'In saying that things are not good through any principle of goodness, but solely through the will of God, one destroys without thinking of it, it seems to me, all the love of God and his glory. For why praise him for what he has done if he would be equally praiseworthy in doing everything to the contrary?'[22]

However, rather than pursue Leibniz's ideas any further, it makes sense to go back to the roots of this notion of goodness as the divine motivation in the patristic and early medieval view that the world exists because it is natural for goodness, as it were, to overflow into further goodness. Inevitably to the modern mind this image must initially appear rather strange, but it repeatedly occurs in patristic and medieval writing, and indeed is even to be found in theologians who have abandoned the approach in favour of the will model. For instance, Scotus can write: 'Communicating the rays of your goodness most liberally, you are boundless good.'[23] This is an echo of a recurring theme, particularly prominent in Pseudo-Denys among others,[24] of good of its very nature being diffusive of itself. Aquinas not only alludes to the principle on a number of occasions but also takes it as self-evident from this, given the nature of God as goodness itself, that the world must therefore also exist.[25]

What the claim in effect amounts to is the conviction that it is of the nature of goodness to share and so, if God is good, he must also share his being with others. Note that this is not at all the same as saying that God needs to share, as in the love argument we noted earlier. Rather, what is envisaged is pure gift, pure grace, if you like. God does not create the world because he needs something from the world or even because he needs to give something to the world, but rather the world comes into existence because on this analysis of goodness there can be no perfect goodness that is not defined by generosity, by giving without requiring a return. Now of course to make sense of this notion one must assume that what is given is itself a good, but that is precisely the claim that the earlier tradition makes, by asserting that existence of itself is good. God as perfect Being and perfect Goodness imparts to the world some of that existence, some of that goodness, and nothing is lost from him thereby because he is infinite Being, infinite Goodness.

Certainly the underlying metaphysics of this is highly complicated. All I can do here is draw attention to five elements that may help to make it more readily acceptable. First, unlike the will analysis, which denies content to divine goodness (this exists only subsequent to the divine will), or the need analysis which denies divine aseity, both divine goodness and divine aseity are maintained. Though on first reading aseity may appear to be denied, it is not: the world comes into existence not because God in any sense needs the world to perfect his existence but because his already perfect existence is such that it necessarily generates further goods. Second, it is based on a very simple and not easily contested assumption, that it is of the nature of goodness to share. Third, it avoids the anthropomorphic idea of God needing to make a decision about whether or not to create the world. The world exists simply in virtue of the fact that he is what he is, namely perfect goodness. Fourth, though it thus makes the emergence of something other than God inevitable, it does not rob God of all choice: some world was inevitable, but not necessarily this particular world. An element of choice thus remains. Finally, contrary to the traditional contrast between nature and grace, this approach implies that grace is intrinsic to the creation itself as part of the divine generosity that defines God as goodness itself.

Though it might be truer to say that there is not much discussion at all in contemporary theology regarding the reasons for the divine creation, certainly in such discussion as there is this kind of answer is seldom mentioned. Indeed the only example that readily springs to mind is the American philosopher, Norman Kretzmann.[26] However, an aesthetic variant on this approach lies at the heart of one recent major theology; so let me end with that, namely Hans Urs von Balthasar's *Glory of the Lord*. Central to his argument is that modern theology has lost one of the great strengths of its past, the vision of God as beauty that finds its reflection in the biblical phrase, 'the glory of the Lord', and it is that beauty which naturally overflows into a world of beauty.

Augustine does not hesitate to speak of 'the workman's art' but rebukes Plato for suggesting that the creator could have any 'joy in the beauty of the universe'.[27] As a result one is left wondering how seriously he really took the notion of God as beauty. Tillich at least is unequivocal: 'From the point of view of the creator, the purpose of creation is the exercise of his creativity, which has no purpose beyond itself because the divine life is essentially creative.'[28] But that is but a passing phrase compared to Balthasar's extensive use:

> Nothing is richer and fuller than Being in its incomprehensibly glorious and absolute victory over nothingness … and yet this fullness can unfold absolutely only once: in God. But since there is nothing against which it must assert itself (for nothingness is nothingness) it does not need, holding on to itself, to enclose itself in the casing of an entity in order perhaps to break out from this and communicate itself beyond its borders (which it does not have). Rather, fullness as such is pure power from whose potency all that is potential proceeds as rich abundance, which is thus pure freedom and, as freedom does not hold on to itself (or gather itself into an entity), is also pure gift and love.[29]

It is now beauty rather than goodness which has become diffusive. His point is that a being of such infinite richness as God will inevitably flow out of himself into correspondingly varied and rich veins of creativity. Whether in the human artist or the divine, beauty cannot remain a pure idea: it must be a reality. Once more the talk is of inevitability, but please note two points in conclusion. It is an inevitability that stems from the nature of God, not from something other than himself (Balthasar holds beauty like goodness to be an essential attribute of God). Secondly, let me reiterate, it is only the inevitability of some world emerging, not necessarily exactly this one; so some notion of divine choice is maintained.[30]

Notes

1 Friedrich Schleiermacher, *Der Christliche Glaube* (Berlin: Walter de Gruyter, 1960), 195–204 and 272–301; *The Christian Faith* (Edinburgh: T & T Clark, 1928), 149–156 and 206–228.

2 Volume III of the *Church Dogmatics* has the general title of 'The Doctrine of Creation'. Its four volumes contain 2,237 pages in the English edition.

3 Karl Barth, *Church Dogmatics* III.1 (Edinburgh: T&T Clark, 1958), 332–333.

4 Gerhard von Rad, 'The Theological Problem of the Old Testament Doctrine of Creation', in *The Problem of the Hexateuch and Other Essays*, trans. E.W. Trueman Dicken (Edinburgh and London: Oliver and Boyd, 1966), 134.

5 von Rad, 'The Theological Problem', 140.

6 Claus Westermann, *Creation* (London: SPCK, 1974), 5.

7 According to Mowinckel the so-called enthronement psalms (47, 93, 96–99) were sung at an autumn festival which celebrated YHWH's victory over the waters of chaos at creation; hence the appositeness of verses such as 93:3–4 or 98:7–9. Cf. Sigmund Mowinckel, *The Psalms in Israel's Worship* (Oxford: Basil Blackwell, 1962), 1, 106–192; and 2, 222–258.

8 H.H. Schmid, 'Creation, Righteousness, and Salvation: Creation Theology as the Broad Horizon of Biblical Theology', in *Creation in the Old Testament*, ed. Bernhard W. Anderson (London: SPCK, 1984), 102–117, esp. 106–110.

9 Hermann Gunkel, 'The Influence of Babylonian Mythology upon the Biblical Creation Story', in *Creation in the Old Testament*, ed. Bernhard W. Anderson (London: SPCK, 1984), 30.

10 My translation: Augustine, *De Genesi adversus Manicheos*, 1, 2, 4.

11 My translation: Duns Scotus, *De Primo Principio*, 3, 31–32.

12 John Calvin, *Institutes of the Christian Religion*, trans. F.L. Battles (Philadelphia: Westminster, 1960), 1, 59 (I, 5.6).

13 John Calvin, *Opera omnia* (1863), 8, 293; quoted in François Wendel, *Calvin*, trans. Philip Mairet (London: Collins, 1965), 171.

14 William J. Bouwsma, *John Calvin: A Sixteenth-Century Portrait* (Oxford: Oxford University Press, 1988), esp. 162–176.

15 René Descartes, *Reply to Objections*, VI, section 6: *The Philosophical Works of Descartes*, vol. 2, trans. E.S. Haldane and G.R.T. Ross (Cambridge: Cambridge University Press, 1968), 248.

16 The remark was made at the 1984 WCC Klingenthal consultation: quoted in P. Lønning, *Creation: An Ecumenical Challenge?* (Macon, GA: Mercer University Press, 1989), 101. But one finds similar comments in Sölle's book *To Work and To Love: A Theology of Creation* (Philadelphia: Fortress, 1984), e.g. 14.

17 Jürgen Moltmann, *The Trinity and the Kingdom of God* (London: SCM Press, 1981), 99.

18 Calvin, *Institutes of the Christian Religion* (I, 5.6) 'Furthermore, if the cause is sought by which he was led once to create all these things, and is now moved to preserve them, we shall find that it is his goodness alone. But this being the sole cause, it ought still to be more than sufficient to draw us to his love, inasmuch as there is no creature ... upon whom God's mercy has not been poured.' Such a statement may appear to contradict my claim that for Calvin the explanation for the creation lies in the divine will alone. But two points need to be borne in mind. First, like Scotus or Augustine he gives more than one answer, and so the key question becomes where the primary stress lies. Secondly, it is arguable that where Calvin speaks of the divine goodness or love he has our perspective in mind (i.e. as recipients) and not a formal analysis of the divine nature and its motivation.

19 Calvin, *Institutes*, 1, 14, 22; Wendel, *Calvin*, 181.

20 Burnaby's translation: Augustine, *De Genesi ad Litteram*, 1.13.

21 Richard of St Victor, *De Trinitate*. For a modern version of Richard's argument, see Richard Swinburne, 'Could there be more than one God?', *Faith and Philosophy* 5/8 (1988), 225–241.

22 G.W.F. Leibniz, *Discourse on Metaphysics, Correspondence with Arnauld, Monadology*, ed. Paul Janet, trans. George R. Montgomery (La Salle, IL: Open Court, 1980), 4–5.

23 Scotus, *De Primo Principio*, 4, 84.

24 E.g. Pseudo-Denys, *De divinis nominibus*, 4,20: 'perfecta bonitas, quad per omnia se diffundit'.

25 Cf. e.g. Aquinas, *Summa contra Gentiles*, 1,37 or 3,24.

26 Norman Kretzmann, chapters 8 and 9 in Scott MacDonald, ed., *Being and Goodness: The Concept of the Good in Metaphysics and Philosophical Theology* (Ithaca, NY: Cornell University Press, 1991), 208–249.

27 Augustine, *De Civitate Dei*, 11,21.

28 Paul Tillich, *Systematic Theology*, vol. 1 (London: Nisbet, 1953), 293.

29 Hans Urs von Balthasar, *The Glory of the Lord*, vol. 5 (Edinburgh: T & T Clark, 1991), 625–626.

30 This is one of five papers given at the University of Utrecht in March 1992 as part of an Erasmus exchange with my then home university of Durham. I would like to thank all those who took part for their helpful comments and criticisms, particularly my host Professor Vincent Brümmer. First published in *Nederlands Theologisch Tijdschrift* 47 (1993), 37–45, it is reproduced here with permission.

2 Creation and its Alternatives

In the second of his volumes on comparative theology, Keith Ward, the former Regius Professor of Divinity at Oxford, tackles the theme of creation.[1] In that work he contends that incoherence results from the type of interplay between freedom and necessity employed by some contemporary theologians.[2] If I understand him aright, Ward's own position is that, while there remains a divine openness to the future that leaves many of the world's specific forms as yet undetermined, Christianity may well need to concede a necessity in the divine nature that leads to the initial creative act as such.[3] Rather than engaging directly with Ward's own position or his criticism of others, what I would like to do here is examine the terminology commonly employed by Christian theologians to discuss creation and its alternatives. My hope is to illustrate how in general the contrasts are not nearly as sharp as often supposed, and thereby provide some indirect confirmation for Ward's more limited moves in this direction.

In rough, the conventional Christian claim can be characterized as the contention that the world originated from divine will without necessity, and it is a world that is therefore wholly distinct from him, and upon which he is in no sense dependent. Emanation, pantheism, monism, and immanence are all thought to threaten such a contention in one way or another. But how far is this so? In my view modern discussion usually stops too soon, as though each of the terms had a single, precise sense, whereas in fact their varied historical applications suggests not only a quite different account of the matter but also significant overlaps with what are often portrayed as uniquely Christian emphases. Inevitably, given my competence, most of my examples will come from the western tradition.

Creation and Emanation

'Emanation' stems from the Latin verb *emanare*, which means 'to flow' or 'pour out'. Here God is conceived of as somewhat like a bubbling cauldron of infinite being, so rich in abundant existence that he overflows into progressively lesser levels of being until the lowest possible level of such reality is reached. A serious competitor to Christianity in the later patristic period, the Neo-Platonism of Plotinus (d. 270), envisaged the divine One flowing out into the Divine Mind and that in turn into the World Soul and so the material world being eventually generated. Although the extent of the influence of such a triadic structure of divinity on the doctrine of the Trinity can be contested, what cannot be disputed is that at least within the Godhead Christianity developed a notion closer to emanation than to creation, and so it would be wrong to see emanation as an entirely alien notion. Likewise, the later influence of Neo-Platonism ensured that emanation also played a role within Islam and Judaism. If Avicenna (Ibn Sina) provides an example from Islam in the eleventh century, a famous example from Judaism is the thirteenth-century Kabbalistic document, the Zohar. Here the world is depicted as a flame from the divine coal and as the divine garment beneath which God will be found. If the imagery could be read as pantheistic, attention to the wider context indicates that it is emanation which is being explored.

So far as contrasts with creation are concerned, these may be considered under three heads: the necessity of the process, the connected theme of the absence of a personal dimension, and the alleged negative consequence of divinizing nature. Necessity in this context is, I think, often misunderstood. For, though emanation certainly implies the necessity of the world, it does not in fact make it necessary to God's existence. That is to say, the world only exists in virtue of the fact that it has flowed out of God, but God himself (or the One) is held to be complete even apart from this overflow. God's perfection is held to be infinite and so nothing is lost through the overflow: a finite sum taken from an infinite still leaves an infinite sum. An analogy sometimes used (though the physics is erroneous) was that of the sun and its rays: light pours out, but takes nothing away from its source. It would certainly, therefore, be unfair to criticize the view on the grounds that it detracts from the aseity or independence of God and so undermines the traditional definition of him as that upon which all else depends, himself depending on nothing. It is worth observing that in this respect at least emanation is quite unlike pantheism or even the proposal of many modern Christian theologians who posit some requirement on God's part to create the world based on reciprocal notions such as love or expressiveness.

Even so, some find the kind of necessity postulated less than satisfactory. In the course of suggesting that making and emanation should be treated as complementary models of creation, John Macquarrie sums up what he sees as emanation's principal advantage and disadvantage: it avoids the impression that creation could be considered like an arbitrary act, but it does this by moving too far in another direction and suggesting that creation is like a natural process.[4] But can the issue be decided quite so summarily? Is there not something distinctly mythic in the Christian assumption that God might have to make a decision about such a matter? Even in the human case we think that there is something defective in a person's character or goodness if he has to think before he does some good deed – for instance, tell the truth. With God that oddness would seem still further heightened, not least because the most obvious reasons for legitimate hesitation in our case, uncertainty about the quality of the end or the best means to achieve it, are clearly absent in his case. Again, pure generosity is usually polluted in our case by the need to resolve to act (to let down our self-defences), whereas God surely has no such need to steel his resolve. So, if it is good that the nature of one's being should be shared, one might argue that it is not only natural but even inevitable that it should be shared. Indeed, so plausible is this argument that, so far from patristic theology rejecting it, it was actually accepted but confined to within the Godhead itself in accounts of the Trinity, though with one key modification in the claim that the effects (the Son and the Spirit) could be as great as their cause.

Some, though, may protest that I am still missing the heart of the issue, which is the absence of a personal dimension as compared with the stress on will in the creation model, however mythically this may be expressed in terms of actual decision-making. By way of response two key factors must be stressed. The first is that, although historically emanation has tended to exclude the personal, its application to the Trinity shows that this is not inevitable, while even where the personal is excluded it should be noted that (as in Neo-Platonism) this is because it is believed that there is a higher form of reality than the personal beyond the divisions and pluralism of decision-making. So from that perspective the problem only arises because Christianity is too anthropomorphic in the way it customarily speaks. Then, secondly, emanation presents itself as appealing to a higher justification than any need for reciprocal or experiential love. If personalized, the ground lies in the generosity of pure gift; if expressed impersonally, in the overflowing riches of the inexhaustibility of divine being. So there is no lack that needs filling as in so much contemporary Christian exposition; instead, a fulfilled being gratuitously shares its being.

Finally, we come to what is often regarded as the crunch objection, that emanation divinizes the world. This is an objection that will need to be considered in more detail when we turn to pantheism. But for the moment two observations may be made. The first is that, though in confining emanation within the Godhead there were undoubted gains in securing human independence and responsibility within this world, Christianity also paid a price in that it raised the very question of the intelligibility of God's relation to matter, if it is indeed something totally other than himself. Significantly, in trying to circumvent this difficulty, Karl Rahner seems to come close to an emanationist model: 'Theologians proceed from the assumption that absolutely everything that is not God is created by one and the same God .... Materiality must be understood as the lowest stage of this spirit .... Otherwise, materiality cannot be conceived as originating from an absolute spirit, since this spirit cannot create something that is absolutely disparate from itself.'[5] If Christian theologians are seldom quite so explicit, the more common focus on divine expressiveness in matter betokens a similar kind of anxiety.

If such concerns argue for matter not being totally other than God, equally nothing necessarily follows which requires matter to be of great religious significance, far less divine. For, if Plotinus was as a result led to defend the goodness of the material world, this certainly did not prevent him from according it a very lowly status.[6] Indeed, it is worth observing that emanation of itself tends to generate a quite different kind of spirituality from pantheism. For it declares that, though the world derives from the being of God, the best clue to his nature involves, not as in pantheism turning towards the world in awe and wonder, but rather away from that world and towards the higher levels of divine existence, not in themselves constituted by the world. So, instead of celebrating the presence of God in a flower, for instance, the recommendation becomes that one should try to strip off the world, to retreat into one's own spiritual core, so that thereby one can achieve identity with what God is most like when unencumbered by the world, and so we have Plotinus's famous phrase describing what is involved – 'the flight of the alone to the Alone.'[7]

Pantheism and Panentheism

Rather surprising to relate, 'pantheism' as a term originated during the deist controversy. One leading advocate of the deist, non-interventionist God, John Toland, first used the word in 1705 in one of his lesser works: *Socinianism Truly Stated*. Four years later it was taken up by one of his critics, and henceforth the term passed into common use, Toland himself in 1720 publishing a work entitled *Pantheisticon*, a pagan celebration of the identity of God and the world. Literally the term means 'all is God' or 'God is all', but to use the term in that wide sense would, I think, fail to draw out significant differences which exist between what is now most commonly acknowledged as pantheism, a celebration of the world as divine as in Toland's original use, and variants such as emanation, where 'God is all' but by no means confined to the world. Under such a narrower definition – the equation of God and the world – perhaps the most obvious modern example would be New Age theology's equation of our world with the goddess Gaia or 'Mother Earth'. But of course the phenomenon is much older than this. The Romantic poets and the early Schleiermacher, with their ready equation of the Universe, the All and God, must also be seen in the same light, as must the philosopher whose rediscovery by Lessing ensured the popularity of pantheism in the late eighteenth and early nineteenth century, namely Spinoza. His famous formula, *Deus sive Natura*, could scarcely be more unequivocally pantheistic, the Latin *sive* as distinct from *aut*, indicating the absolute indifference of whether we refer to Nature or God, both alike having extension and thinking predicated of them. Stoicism (rather than Platonism in any of its forms) then becomes the most obvious classical version.

Widely adopted in contemporary theology as a response is the notion of panentheism, so it is worth noting its earlier history. First coined by a now-forgotten theologian K.C.K. Krause (1781–1832), to describe his own system, the term was intended to imply that (compatible with pantheism) the being of God includes and penetrates the whole universe, so that it all exists in him, but that (incompatible with pantheism) nonetheless the divine being is more than and not exhausted by the universe. Putting it at its simplest, the universe is part of God but not the whole of him. It is a term which has been enthusiastically adopted by process theologians to describe their own approach, and clearly it does this quite well, as one of their favourite analogies is to suggest that the world should be viewed as God's body, distinct from but interacting with the divine mind. However, with so many modern theologians abandoning the classical attributes of God which guaranteed his independence of the world it is clearly a term capable of much wider applicability.

It is a conception with which, for instance, John Macquarrie declares that he 'has a good deal of sympathy',[8] but Jürgen Moltmann is perhaps the best example of a contemporary theologian employing the term. In *God in Creation* Moltmann explicitly endorses its use while attacking the process theologians's denial of *creatio ex nihilo*.[9] Even so it is not clear that he has completely disengaged himself from his earlier Blochian Hegelianism in *The Theology of Hope*, according to which focus on the created order was seen as an endorsement of the status quo, and so God's involvement had therefore to be tied exclusively to the world's future rather than its past.[10] In an intermediate work he had declared: 'If God is love, then he does not merely emanate, flow out of himself; he also expects and needs love; his world is intended to be his home. He desires to dwell in it.'[11] If Moltmann is more cautious in his choice of language in *God in Creation*, the same basic sentiments continue,[12] and it is significant that even in more recent work it remains unclear in what sense God is really independent of the world, since God's trinitarian life is held to be intimately bound up with the future of the world, and that world, it is held, will, though transformed, never in fact end.[13]

It is therefore all the more surprising that he is so severe in his criticisms of both process theology and Schleiermacher, for what seems in dispute is a matter of degree and not kind, in as much as all three abandon divine aseity for some notion of divine dependence on the world. In the case of Schleiermacher, it is often suggested that the later *Christian Faith* represents a decisive move away from the earlier pantheism of the *Speeches*.[14] Certainly, gone are the more explicit use of the 'Universe', the 'Whole', and 'the All' of the earlier work. Yet creation is still in effect reduced to preservation,[15] while the relevant divine attributes are analysed as expressive simply of the way the world is. So, for instance, omnipotence is cashed out purely in terms of the actual causal laws of the universe rather than the potentiality of God to do otherwise: 'since divine omnipotence can only be conceived as eternal and omnipresent, it is inadmissible to suppose that at any time anything should begin to be through omnipotence; on the contrary, through omnipotence everything is already posited which comes into existence through finite causes, in time and space.'[16] Again, omniscience is analysed out into what he calls 'the absolute spirituality of divine omnipotence', by which he appears to mean that, so far from there being ascribed to God knowledge of all potentialities and their implications, it is a matter of believing that the actual totality of causes in the world is not just a matter of 'a lifeless and blind necessity'.[17]

Yet, if we turn to ask what it is that might make the panentheism of Moltmann acceptable and the pantheism of Schleiermacher not, it is hard to see what it is that really divides them, apart of course from the more sympathetic use of the latter word by Schleiermacher. To illustrate how Moltmann's objections reduce to caricature, let me measure them against a very early version of pantheism: Stoicism.[18] Moltmann objects that pantheism 'makes everything a matter of indifference' because all things become God; he suggests that 'if there is no creation in the beginning, there cannot be a new creation either'; and he objects to the resultant 'divinisation of the world'.[19] Like Schleiermacher, Stoicism in fact claimed a larger, decisive significance for the pattern of natural causation as a whole, detecting in it certainly a necessity but a necessity based on an inherent divine principle, the Logos or Reason, and indeed its advocates were prepared to go rather further than Schleiermacher in a 'panentheistic' direction in their insistence that the activity of the Logos should not be too closely identified with this present world but rather with a number of such recurring worlds (or new creations). One notes too that the resultant spirituality can scarcely be said to have led to the worship of nature. Rather, respect was due to all nature as part of a cosmic design, with, however, some aspects more closely reflecting the Divine than others, in particular human beings. Even human beings, though, were expected to accept a cosmic purpose larger than themselves. It is thus possible to speak of a transcendent dimension to Stoicism, and indeed this is reflected in its most famous religious work, Cleanthes's 'Hymn to Zeus'.[20]

One suspects that in contemporary theological writing there is a tendency to equate pantheism too quickly and too readily with popularized forms of the sort found in Romantic poetry or New Age writing. The reality, I suggest, is otherwise, with pantheism and panentheism not only on a sliding scale, but with the latter sometimes further from classical Christianity than the former. Intriguingly, Moltmann himself elsewhere uses the terminology of divinization for his own views,[21] while at times one finds him speaking of a degree of divine dependence on the world that would be rejected in at least some versions of pantheism: 'from eternity God … wanted to communicate himself to the one who is other than himself …. That is why the idea of the world is already inherent in the Father's love for the Son.'[22]

Monism and Dualism

Monism might seem initially too remote from the concerns of Christian doctrine to merit consideration here. Why very much the reverse is so will emerge shortly, but first some brief remarks on the history of the term. It was invented in the eighteenth century by Christian Wolff, the popularizer of Leibniz, as a way of characterizing the two opposed theories of idealism and materialism, that is to say the view that everything is mental and the view that everything is material. It then came to be widely used of the *Identitätsphilosophie* of Schelling and Hegel in the next century, with their claim that matter and mind are ultimately identical, Schelling for instance describing matter as 'congealed spirit'. Put like this it need not of course be a religious claim at all; thus Marx's turning of Hegel's philosophy on its head could equally be described as monism, though in his case it is the reduction of all reality to matter. As such Marx and Hegel, despite the enormous religious difference between them, could philosophically be set on one side as monists with Descartes on the other as a typical dualist, someone who believes that the mental and material are fundamentally two different kinds of reality.

But in considering the range of options regarding God's relation with the world, it will be more helpful to narrow the definition somewhat. We may say that religious monism is the view that nothing exists except a single (non-dual) divine reality; in other words, we have a monism that not only chooses between mind and matter but also insists that all of the one or the other is God. On such an analysis most forms of pantheism would not in fact be monistic since their exponents are content to speak of the world as exhibiting the features of both spirit and matter. There would, however, be some exceptions. Thus Spinoza would certainly emerge as a monistic pantheist since on his view all reality is reducible to a single substance, matter which thinks. Similarly, this would hold for Stoicism, since on its view only matter exists, though with the proviso that only one form of matter is quintessentially divine (fire).

So there will be an overlap with pantheism. Nonetheless, the analysis does offer a great gain. For in general monism does suggest a very different form of piety from pantheism. Thus while Schelling in his writings did take nature seriously, it is hard not to detect in Hegel's analysis the conviction that it is just an insignificant element on the way to the true realization of *Geist* or Spirit, as this works itself out in the history of the human consciousness. It is a contrast which emerges with equal force if we turn to an eastern variant in the ninth-century Hindu philosopher Sankara. Brahman is the only true reality, in relation to which the plurality of material phenomena must be seen as illusory. To use his analogy, we perceive what we take to be a serpent, but it is in fact a rope. Clearly none of this is compatible with according a high value to the variety of the world in which the typical pantheist so often takes delight.

Much the same might be said of Muslim versions. Since in the following passage Sufism is analysed as monism yet distinct from pantheism, it is worth quoting:

> The basic doctrine of Islamic mysticism, which later came to be termed Oneness of being, and which western scholars term monism, is implicit in the divine name al-haqq (truth, reality) .... If God alone is absolutely real, God alone *is*, whence the term Oneness of Being. But this does not mean that God is the sum of all existing things .... That would be pantheism, whereas on the contrary ... the doctrine of the Oneness of being means that appearances are deceptive and that each apparently separate object is, mysteriously, nothing other than the indivisible plenitude of the absolute, infinite, and eternal truth.[23]

I hasten to acknowledge that such an analysis does not apply to all versions of Sufism, al-Ghazali's bridge to orthodoxy being for instance very different from the position of al-Hallaj or Rabi'a.

Nowadays hostility to dualism is a common theme in Christian theology. What is meant, though, is not dualism in general but the perceived negative influence of Platonic dualism in diverting historical Christianity from the biblical view of human beings as psychosomatic unities and towards a narrow emphasis on soul that despised enmattered reality. I have not the space to indicate why I think such an account unfair to Platonism.[24] More relevant in any case to note here is the way in which such discussions usually bypass a far more important issue, namely the principal reason why Plato and his successors moved in that direction. Because of the not implausible Greek principle that like can only know like, it was thought essential to place human beings at least in part on the side of divine and thus of immaterial reality. Nor has Christianity been immune from such considerations in its later history. One might think of the philosophies of Berkeley or Malebranche, or indeed the way in which both Protestant and Catholic theology moved towards giving dogmatic endorsement to belief in the immortality of the soul.[25]

Nor has this principle been absent in materialistic monism. If Tertullian is a rare example of a Christian theologian willing to think of God as material, Stoicism adopted the principle wholesale. It is all too easy to give short shrift to their notion of the divine as fire and forget the neurons firing in our brain that make such a thought possible. Like Plato, it was an attempt to ensure continuity and thus connections between the human and the Divine. So, when engaging in dialogue in the modern world with eastern religious systems that are monistic, our first thought should not be that crucial distinctions are dissolved (though sometimes this is so), but rather the importance of that underlying religious motivation, the desire to make links possible between ourselves and the Divine.

Transcendent and Immanent

The above reflections can perhaps be most conveniently brought together under the contrast between transcendent and immanent, for contemporary theology often uses these two words to demonstrate what is supposedly unique about Christianity, that it portrays God as both transcendent and immanent. But no less than the terms discussed above, these too are in fact quite slippery. Literally, they should mean that God is 'beyond the world' and that he 'remains within it', yet as an immaterial being he clearly does not quite do either, being equally related to all places as to none. So in talking of the Christian God's transcendence to the world one must guard against supposing that really more has been said than is in fact the case, for, as I have tried to indicate above, without endorsing *creatio ex nihilo*, emanation through its hierarchy of divinity offers a greater sense of transcendence than Christianity, while without having a God beyond the world both pantheism and monism can still sometimes succeed in ensuring the transcendence of deity, in the directional control of the whole over its parts.

As that last sentence indicates, though, meaning can still sometimes be conveyed without explicit definition. But it is important to note that the process often conceals hidden ambiguities. Thus in this case if the transcendence of emanation is one of lack of involvement (the world is not the result of any 'interest' on the part of the One), clearly with pantheism this cannot be so; rather, in the nature of the case there is inevitably considerable interaction, but still with the divine element remaining in overall control (at least in versions such as Stoicism). But, equally, immanence should not be assumed to entail some sort of dependence simply because the Divine is now portrayed as being 'within' the world. So, for instance, however widely believed in the past, all would now agree that the immanence of eucharistic presence should not be seen as subject to human control. Indeed, given our own situatedness within the world, any knowledge of a transcendent reality will inevitably be heavily dependent on immanent action. A purely interventionist model may well sometimes be appropriate (as in a conventional reading of miracles), but its very occasionalism would force God to the margins if left on its own. So, not surprisingly, other sorts of appeal are often commonly made, but what is seldom noted is their heavy prior dependence on immanence. Take, for example, appeal to conscience summoning the individual to a radically new and challenging form of conduct, or to the experience of wonder before the majesty of an awe-inspiring landscape.[26] Conscience is in fact an 'inner' prompt, while even mountains and seas only function in this way in virtue of the immanent reality they are. Apart from the inevitably highly episodic intervention, any acknowledgement of transcendence would seem, therefore, to be inescapably parasitic on a prior immanence. So the fact that the Transcendentalism of mid-nineteenth-century America turns out to constitute a strong claim to immanence is not as absurd or paradoxical a notion as it may first appear. Mediated through Kantian 'transcendentals', it simply carries further Kant's insight into the extent to which all experience is conditioned by the way the world is.

Conclusion

Long before process theology, J.R. Illingworth had suggested that we get our sense of immanence and transcendence from our own relation to our bodies, as both intellectual spirits and active through matter. In his case the suggestion was deployed as a means of offering a curt dismissal to deism, pantheism, and monism.[27] But the way in which half a century later process theology could use the same image to justify its panentheism illustrates well how slippery all these terms can be. None of this is intended to argue for rejection of the traditional Christian doctrine, but it is to suggest that contemporary theologians often 'win' the discussion too easily, forgetting that others with quite different views can be no less subtle than themselves. It is the great strength of Keith Ward's own innovative work on comparative theology to insist that great care should be taken not to misrepresent rival views, and instead due acknowledgement should be given of the vitality and complexity of positions different from characteristically Christian options, yet sometimes much closer than an initial, casual look might suggest.[28]

Notes

1 This chapter's starting point alludes to the fact that the essay was commissioned to mark Keith Ward's retirement, and appeared as part of a Festschrift, *Comparative Theology: Essays for Keith Ward*, ed. T. W. Bartel (London: SPCK, 2003), 56–65. It is reproduced here with the publisher's permission.

2 Keith Ward, *Religion and Creation* (Oxford: Clarendon Press, 1996), 177–179 (criticizing Paul Fiddes).

3 For the former, see ibid., 236–238, 257–261; for the latter, ibid., 224–225 and, more tentatively, 319–321 (cf. esp. 320).

4 John Macquarrie, *Principles of Christian Theology* (London: SCM Press, 1966), 200–205, esp. 201.

5 Karl Rahner, *Theological Investigations*, vol. xxi (London: Darton, Longman and Todd, 1988), 34–35.

6 See Plotinus, *Enneads*, II, 9 for the former (his attack on the Gnostics); for the latter, e.g. *Enneads*, II, 4, 16.

7 Ibid.,VI, 9, 11.

8 John Macquarrie, *In Search of Deity: An Essay in Dialectical Theism* (London: SCM Press, 1984), 54.

9 Jürgen Moltmann, *God in Creation* (London: SCM Press, 1985), 72–103, esp. 78–79, 98, 103.

10 Jürgen Moltmann, *The Theology of Hope* (London: SCM Press, 1967), 42–45, 84–94. What worried Bloch and Moltmann was the type of natural theology that seemed to imply a given, unalterable blueprint.

11 Jürgen Moltmann, *The Trinity and the Kingdom of God* (London: SCM Press, 1981), 99; cf. 58.

12 Moltmann, *God in Creation*, 79–86.

13 Jürgen Moltmann, *The Coming of God* (London: SCM Press, 1996), 267–279.

14 For Schleiermacher's own hesitant comments, see *The Christian Faith*, ed. H.R. Mackintosh and J.S. Stewart (Edinburgh: T & T Clark, 1928), 38–39 (§8, postscript 2); for a strong assertion of the counter-view, making good use of the *Dialektik*, see Richard Brandt, *The Philosophy of Schleiermacher* (Westport, CT: Greenwood, 1941), 232–252.

15 Schleiermacher, *The Christian Faith*, 142–156 (§§36–41) and 170–184 (§§46–47), esp. 143 (§36,2).

16 Ibid., 212 (§54,1).

17 Ibid., 219 (§55,1). While both passages could be read in a manner compatible with classical theism, this seems to me unlikely as an interpretation, for not only does Schleiermacher nowhere use the language of the traditional formulae, it is also part of his overall strategy to ensure experiential understandings of all aspects of Christian doctrine.

18 For an excellent collection of relevant texts in both Greek and English, see A.A. Long and D.N. Sedley, *The Hellenistic Philosophers*, 2 vols (Cambridge: Cambridge University Press, 1987), §§43–55 in both vols.

19 Moltmann, *God in Creation*, 78, 79, 103.

20 For both the original Greek and an English translation, see Constantine A. Trypanis, ed., *The Penguin Book of Greek Verse* (London: Penguin, 1971), 283–285.

21 Moltmann, *The Coming of God*, 272–275.

22 Moltmann, *The Trinity and the Kingdom of God*, 108.

23 Trevor Ling, *A History of Religion East and West* (London: Macmillan, 1968), 295, emphasis in the original.

24 For discussion of the varieties of Platonism, see my *God and Enchantment of Place: Reclaiming Human Experience* (Oxford: Oxford University Press, 2004), 61–79.

25 It was declared a dogma of the Catholic faith at the Fifth Lateran Council in 1513, while it was also included in the Calvinist Westminster Confession in 1646.

26 In *Painters of Faith: The Spiritual Landscape in Nineteenth-Century America* (Washington, DC: Regnery, 2001) Gene Edward Veith interprets nineteenth-century American landscape in artists such as Thomas Cole and Frederic Church as a Calvinist expression of divine transcendence at the opposite pole to the immanent mediation of saints and miracles in Catholic Baroque, forgetting that the landscape is no less a mediator: cf. 13–34, 82–83.

27 J.R. Illingworth, *Divine Immanence: An Essay on the Spiritual Significance of Matter* (London: Macmillan, 1898), 65–72.

28 I am grateful to Tom Hamilton and Ann Loades for help with an earlier draft of this chapter.

3   The Problem of Pain

Why Philosophers and
Theologians Need Each Other

Lux Mundi, published in 1889, was intended as a response from Anglicans in the Catholic tradition to developments in nineteenth-century thought, including biblical criticism. As such the book marked a move away from the intense conservatism that had characterized Pusey's and Liddon's view of Anglo-Catholicism. The original *Lux Mundi* article that shared my main title was written by J.R. Illingworth, the person in whose vicarage the meetings of the group were held and whose influence on the group as a whole was in fact considerable, despite his withdrawal from Oxford to the country living of Longworth on grounds of ill health.[1] Indeed, though Gore's essay was to become the most famous, with its developmental view of inspiration, it too can be seen as breathing something of the strongly progressive, Hegelian outlook of Illingworth, despite the predominance of Platonic ideas elsewhere in Gore's writings. Intriguingly, the author of the entry in *The Oxford Dictionary of the Christian Church* describes Illingworth as 'a philosopher rather than a theologian'.[2] That his background was predominantly in philosophy, with a strong influence from the Hegelian T.H. Green, is of course true,[3] but the comment is unfair if it is intended to imply that he did not take theological issues seriously. His already noted ill health meant that the problem of pain was more than just an academic issue to him, and his essay is in fact an impressive attempt to combine the insights of natural and revealed theology. Perhaps, therefore, the best tribute that I can offer him a century later is to continue that typical Anglican tradition and attempt to explore the relation between philosophical and theological approaches to the problem of evil.

While in general there continues to be no sharp distinction drawn in Anglican writing, as is well illustrated by the two best known popular writings on the subject of the last half-century, C.S. Lewis's *The Problem of Pain* and Austin Farrer's *Love Almighty and Ills Unlimited*,[4] increasingly one is aware of hostility to philosophical approaches in German theology and of the way in which this is in turn influencing the attitudes of English-speaking theologians, most notably of late perhaps in Kenneth Surin's *Theology and the Problem of Evil*.[5] Likewise analytic philosophers, when they read someone like Moltmann, express surprise at how any of this could be thought of relevance in offering a 'solution' to the problem of evil. The result is that philosopher and theologian view one another across a divide of mutual incomprehension, and that is a pity since both have useful things to say and the approach of each is impoverished by their failure to take the other's questions seriously. Indeed, what I want to argue in this chapter is that the problem arises precisely because each fails to appreciate adequately the true nature and limits of the question that is their own proper domain. That is, I shall argue that the philosophers err when they think that they have anything of importance to say to a specific case of human suffering, the theologians when they deny that there is any general problem of pain to be answered, or, putting the matter more positively, it is the philosopher's task to deal with the general problem, the theologian's with the specific case. To show how this is so, I shall look first at the philosophical issue, and then at the theological.

The Philosopher's Contribution

The first thing to note is that the philosophical problem in its classical form is essentially a logical problem, that is of showing that there is no contradiction involved in holding together the following three propositions: (1) that God is all-good, (2) that God is omnipotent and (3) that evil exists in the world. Thus this is the way in which the problem was seen as early as Epicurus,[6] and the way in which it continues to be seen by America's most distinguished philosopher of religion, Alvin Plantinga.[7] I stress this point for two reasons: first because, as we shall see, the problem is being viewed rather differently in England in the writings of Richard Swinburne and second, and perhaps more importantly, it explains why despite the protests of many theologians it is none the less entirely appropriate to speak of a 'solution' to the problem. Far from representing any lack of sensitivity to the issues, all such talk represents is the claim that the purely logical problem of the apparent contradiction in the Christian simultaneously holding these three beliefs is in fact resoluble.

To show that this is so is Plantinga's strictly limited aim, and it is important that this should not be lost sight of, amid all the complexities of the argument in terms of 'possible worlds' and 'transworld depravity' that have resulted from his debate over the issue with the atheist J.L. Mackie.[8] The structure of any possible solution is in fact quite simple. Since omnipotence is bound by nothing save the laws of logic, the only way out of the dilemma must be to argue that the existence of evil is a logically necessary concomitant of the existence of some good that is willed by the Creator, whether the concomitant be as a consequence of or as a means to that good.[9] Plantinga's version is of the former kind, and his argument is that, if God wished to give his creatures the good of freewill, then as a logically necessary consequence of this must come the possibility of them doing moral evil. Where possible worlds then become relevant is in Plantinga's further claim that it is possible that in every conceivable world which God might have created with creatures enjoying such freedom, its misuse would have occurred. For if that is so, then God in surveying the possible worlds that might have been created would have seen that, whatever choice were made, human beings would do wrong. In other words, 'transworld depravity' exists, and, so even God could not avoid a world with evil in it. Mackie responds by arguing that a world with free, perfectly good human beings is easily conceivable, but significantly, he has to change the definition of freedom in the process, to one in which it is compatible with determinism.[10] So it is perhaps worth stressing that this so-called 'free will defence' is only intelligible in terms of a contra-causal view of freedom, one in which, though many factors may incline us in particular ways, nothing ultimately causes our actions except our own free decisions.

The extent to which Plantinga views the problem as a purely logical one is particularly highlighted by his willingness to use precisely the same sort of strategy to deal with natural evils (disease, earthquakes and so forth) which do not appear to have their origin in any moral evil. For here he resorts to an explanation in terms of fallen angels, who like men have misused their freedom. Significantly, however, he adds the comment: 'The Free Will Defender, of course, does not assert that this is true; he says only that it is *possible*.'[11] His point is that, to show that there is no contradiction involved in holding the three propositions, all one need do is establish their compatibility, not make the means of that compatibility plausible.

Where Philosophers Err

It is perhaps not very surprising that philosophers in general have not been content to have their role so narrowly circumscribed. One of many such examples is his fellow American, Stephen Davis, who after discussing 'the logical problem of evil' goes on to tackle what he calls 'the emotive problem of evil' (EPE),[12] which he introduces thus: 'But even if it is true that theism is logically consistent, there is another difficulty that remains, namely, what I call the EPE .... To show that "God is omnipotent and God is good and evil exists" is possibly true does not show that it is true or even probably true, i.e. it does nothing to show that people should believe in God's omnipotence and goodness.'[13] Davis then goes on to make just such an attempt, and, though he has no doubts about the existence of Satan, he is honest enough to admit 'that Plantinga's luciferous defense may be both true and theologically satisfactory, but at least it is not clear that it is'.[14] Certainly it is an explanation which the once Anglican, and now Orthodox, philosopher, Richard Swinburne, is careful to eschew, his own suggestion being that the existence of natural evil is logically necessary if we are to be free agents in a world where the consequences of our actions matter.[15] He describes this as 'the argument from the need for knowledge' and points out that, since we learn inductively, there could be no acquiring of knowledge unless consequences of good and bad kinds regularly followed specific sorts of actions in accordance with natural laws. He develops this argument at considerable length, compared to another, better known argument that also makes a logical point, that evil is a logically necessary condition for the occurrence of certain virtues.[16] Thus, for example, the notion of courage makes no sense unless there is something bad to be feared, compassion no sense unless there is suffering to be alleviated, and so on.

Personally I find this latter argument a powerful one. Admittedly sometimes it is objected that compassion, courage, and so forth only have value because the world is the way it is, and that in the absence of suffering they would never have been accorded such independent value. But such an objection seems to me a mistake. For there are surely other obvious reasons for valuing, for example, compassion, than simply the relief of pain which is involved. To give an illustration from the original essay *Lux Mundi*, compassion helps build up a strong sense of human solidarity or, if this is thought to reflect too strongly Illingworth's Hegelianism, one might mention the more general point that such virtues are thought to produce the type of character that fits us for heaven, and yet, though that character will no doubt be exercised there in numerous ways, none of them will have anything to do with the relief of pain.

However that may be, as already noted Swinburne devotes more attention to another argument, his so-called 'argument from the need for knowledge'. This is to be explained by the way he conceives of the problem of evil. For him the issue is not merely a logical one; it is also a question of probabilities. Can the fact of evil be accommodated within his cumulative, probabilistic case for theism? This is why he is concerned both with the quantities of evil in the world and with specific cases, and not just with the purely logical point with which he begins. It is thus this that leads him to say in respect of the amount of evil in the world: 'There must be naturally occurring evils … if men are to know how to cause evils themselves or are to prevent evil occurring. And there have to be *many* such evils, if men are to have sure knowledge, for as we saw, sure knowledge of what will happen in future comes only by induction from many past instances.'[17] Again, as an illustration of his willingness to consider specific instances we might take the following: 'Actually seeing a friend have to have his arm amputated as a result of standing too close to a dangerous machine in a factory and getting his arm trapped in it is rightly going to deter me from standing too close to the machine much better than is a notice which says "Dangerous."'[18]

It is comments like these that have led to some of the harshest criticisms one is ever likely to read in the contemporary philosophy of religion. Thus D.Z. Phillips remarks of another of his examples that it is 'a sign of a corrupt mind … to ask of what use are the screams of the innocent',[19] while Surin comments on Swinburne's reply as follows: 'This incapacity to acknowledge that a particular reality is mind-stopping betoken an irremissible moral blindness, in less serious cases it testifies to a real lack of moral imagination, to an unshakeable moral coarseness. But in all cases the failure to lend a voice to the cries of the innocent (and there can be few more glaring instances than the willingness to construct a divine teleology out of innocent suffering) is to have lost the capacity to tell the truth.'[20] His fellow academics in the Oxford Theology Faculty, of whom I was once one, would readily perceive the gross unfairness of such accusations. Nevertheless it does seem to me that Swinburne, admittedly in common with many others, has made a serious error of judgment in going beyond the purely logical problem into considerations of quantity and specific cases.

Taking quantity first, consider one of Newman's more controversial utterances: 'The Church holds that it were better for sun and moon to drop from heaven, for the earth to fail, and for all the millions who are upon it to die of starvation in extremest agony … than that one soul … should commit one single venial sin, should tell one wilful untruth though it harmed no one, or steal one poor farthing without excuse.'[21] My point in quoting this particular utterance is not to endorse it, but simply to draw attention to how far removed traditional Christian morality is from any utilitarian calculus, any attempt to weigh good and evil in the same balance. Yet very often responses to the problem are phrased in ways which, whatever the intention, can easily admit of a utilitarian reading. For example, Davis, in discussing the amount of evil in the world, sees the issue in terms of whether 'this freedom has turned out to be cost-effective', whether we have 'the best possible balance of good over evil'.[22] Likewise, Swinburne responds to the objection that 'the game ... is not worth the candle' by an admission that seems to concede that such weighing is the heart of the problem: 'This is, I believe, the crux of the problem of evil. It is not the fact of evil or the kinds of evil which are the real threat to theism; it is the quantity of evil.'[23] It is little wonder therefore that, when theists themselves speak like this, their opponents also inevitably express the issue in terms of whether the good outweighs the evil it involves.[24]

But, if we take this hint from Newman, what we shall see at stake is not at all the quantity of evils in the world but a different system of values. That is, the existence of evil in the world should simply be seen as a tragic consequence of certain goods being valued by God, not something that has to be weighed in the same balance as them. As Christians we attach supreme worth not to the creation of happiness, nor any attempt to balance out good and evil, but find it instead in the radical freedom that God has given us to shape our own destinies, including a type of character and virtues that simply would have no intelligibility, no meaning in the absence of pain. Thus it is just not the case that the argument with the non-believer takes place within a shared system of moral values. Rather, the heart of the debate lies in the fact that the Christian has opted for a different moral universe, one in which freedom, compassion, sympathy, courage and so forth exist. This is not to say that non-Christians never attach a similar high worth to these values, only to draw attention to the extent to which Christian as well as non-Christian can be infected in the modern world by utilitarian assumptions in making the issue of quantity primary.

But to this it may be objected that I have ignored one vital fact, that God can foresee the future and so must have had the choice between various possible worlds, some of which had more evil than the present one, some less, and so, even if he was not concerned with weighing evil against good, he still had the option of creating a world with less evil in it than at present and so quantity of evil remains a relevant issue, even if we are only comparing it with other possible levels of evil rather than with the good *per se*. Some contemporary philosophers would argue that, since God can only know what it is logically possible to know, he cannot know future, free human action since this remains undetermined until the individual makes his decision.[25] That would be one way of responding, but even if we take the traditional account of omniscience, it still remains unclear to me how we can make any objective assessment of the quantities of evil in the world. It is a commonplace in modern theology to speak of the need for a post-Auschwitz theology and indeed it is also a theme in contemporary philosophy, but I quite fail to see the point. God infinitely values each one of us and the tragic dimension of suffering would seem to me just as acute, whether we were to envisage just one individual suffering or millions. Here C.S. Lewis is more astute than many a modern writer: 'We must never make the problem of pain worse than it is by vague talk about the "unimaginable sum of human misery" .... Search all time and space and you will not find that composite pain in anyone's consciousness. There is no such thing as a sum of suffering, for no one suffers it. When you have reached the maximum that a single person can suffer, we have, no doubt, reached something very horrible, but we have reached all the suffering there ever can be in the universe. The addition of a million fellow-sufferers adds no more pain.'[26]

Since questions of quantity can enter consideration of the problem of evil in a number of different ways, it is perhaps worth pausing at this point to clarify what it is that is being affirmed and denied within the Christian tradition, as reflected in the writings of Newman and Lewis. As I understand it, the relevance of quantity is being denied in two specific ways. First, in contrast to those who think the argument is just about arithmetic, about what the total balance of pleasure and pain is, the claim is that the disagreement is in fact much more fundamental, there being no shared calculus in which to measure quantities, no sufficiently shared system of values. Secondly, given the traditional Christian stress on the unique, irreplaceable worth of each individual, the claim is that total quantity of pain in the world cannot be the issue, since that would be to suggest that persons were somehow dispensable in relation to a larger whole. Rather, the key issue must be the maximum amount of pain suffered by any particular individual. Of course, in a sense there is more tragedy in more suffering simply because more are suffering but the tragedy lies in what each suffers, not in some mysterious total summation of suffering. That being so, the only proper question of quantity must be whether God was justified in allowing the maximum quantity of suffering that can happen to the human condition to befall some particular individuals among us. There is thus no global question of quantity, only the tragic conflict between the moral value of freedom and the virtues and the maximum pain that any of these particular persons of infinite value could suffer.

Should someone still object that I have ignored one issue which remains crucial for them, namely that too many suffer this individual maximum of pain, my response would be that, once one has conceded that it is legitimate for God to let that happen to one individual, no further moral question can arise about the legitimacy of letting it happen to more than one. That one was already of infinite value in God's eyes, and so the tragic dimension in the divine decision is already present and in no way significantly increased by many others also suffering in this way. This is not to say that God would not try to keep the number who suffer to a minimum. But it is to claim that with free will there is no way of effectively controlling this and that the really important moral issue must be expressed in terms of the legitimacy of allowing just one individual to suffer, not by means of an irrelevant introduction of numbers.

The reference to Auschwitz may also be used to illustrate the other main failing in contemporary philosophical approaches, the appeal to specific cases. Part of the problem is that discussion of whether pain could serve some point in a particular case can easily lend credence to the idea that what is at stake is whether or not that particular pain was engineered by God to serve that point. In other words, by discussing particular cases it is very easy for a major shift of perspective to occur without its full implications being realized. For from the fact that God allows pain to occur as part of the general divine purposes, it by no means follows that such pain befalls this particular individual also as part of God's plan. The system is such that it is inevitable that some individual will suffer, but this does not mean that God has deliberately chosen a world in which it is this specifiable individual. Rather, it is entirely arbitrary whether the pain befalls A or B. That is to say, if the goods that God wants are to be realized, then tragically pain has to be part of the world, but who bears that pain is irrelevant. For the same results can be achieved, whoever it is. It is thus a logical mistake to discuss specific instances, because the philosophical 'solution' requires only that some individuals suffer, not that any actually uniquely identifiable individual should do so.[27]

The main reason why this conclusion is resisted is, I think, because of the desire of philosopher as much as theologian for a total explanation. He thinks that there must be a reason why one individual suffers rather than another, and so wants to give that reason. Again, equally he may feel that it is incompatible with omnipotence to admit that any evil could finally frustrate the divine purpose and so all evil must ultimately be caught up to serve the good. Thus, for example, Nelson Pike tells us that omnipotence can only be safeguarded if God succeeds in shaping all the evil that exists to ultimate divine purposes,[28] while, to give a theological example, Barth expresses himself in very similar terms with his emphatic declaration that God 'would not be God if he were ... restricted in his actions' and so he has no hesitation in concluding: 'The effect of the creature is in the hands of God .... It is wholly subordinated to the contexts of his wider purposes.'[29]

That I just cannot believe. If God has given free will to human beings, this must have introduced a radical indeterminacy to the world, which even God cannot fully control. So if one accepts the free will defence there just is no avoiding the admission that there is an incurably tragic dimension to the creation, both in the sense that not everyone *may* be redeemed, since that is ultimately in our hands, not God's, and in the sense that not every event in our lives can now be used for the good, since the opportunity for that to be so has passed, and here again God has no power to alter the nature of time.[30]

Where Theologians Err

But, if philosophers err by attempting too much, so too do theologians. If the philosopher's mistake is to search for reasons everywhere, even where none are to be found, as on the questions of quantity and the pain of specific individuals, the theologian's characteristic error is to suppose that everything can and must be given a christological reference. Traditionally Anglicanism has avoided this mistake by accepting the Catholic distinction between natural and revealed theology, but that it is under threat is evident from the increasing influence of Lutheranism noticeable even among some of the contributors to the 1989 volume of which this chapter was originally part. Certainly it is from Germany, in the writings of people like Dorothee Soelle, Jürgen Moltmann and Eberhard Jüngel, that the strongest attack on the sort of position that I have so far outlined has come. For them only the cross can offer an answer to the problem of evil, and indeed Jüngel in particular wants to go further in not only seeing philosophical approaches as an irrelevance but as positively responsible for the rise of atheism in the modern world. What is wrong with his argument I have tried to point out elsewhere.[31] So here perhaps it will suffice to draw attention to the need to take seriously the fact of the cross as a 'scandal of particularity'. For that very particularity must surely mean that it can only provide answers to questions set by humanity already situated in its particularity, not to questions that are prior to any particularity, the very sorts of questions with which we have been dealing in the first sections of this chapter. One cannot help in fact wondering whether much modern theology is not based on a pious conceptual confusion between a logically necessary and a logically sufficient condition. For, while of course since Christ is the source of our salvation, and the final end of the creation finds its point in him, his role must be an indispensable one, it by no means follows from this indispensable role that in many areas of thought his role will not still be very remote and not as it were centre stage, as in the purely logical issue of the consistency of our beliefs with which this chapter began.

The Contribution of Theology

But where then does the contribution of revealed theology lie? The answer must surely be in the very particularity which Christ came to share. But, that said, one finds the writings of contemporary theologians on the subject sadly disappointing. Perhaps because of the christological assumption to which reference has already been made, they seem to assume that it suffices to say that God himself entered into human suffering in Christ and leave the matter at that, without trying to make the precise nature of the connection explicit. Yet surely we must make it so, since the fact of another's suffering of itself does nothing to reduce the tragedy of an individual's suffering, even if that other be God himself. Two wrongs never of themselves make a right. Let me therefore draw attention to the two ways in which it seems that the cross can deal with the scandal of particularity that it shares, the arbitrariness of the particular case.

The first thing to note is the arbitrariness of the form of Jesus' death. Had he lived a few centuries earlier and lived in a different land it might have taken the relatively painless form of drinking hemlock, as with Socrates. Again, were it to have taken place this century in some of the countries of Latin America, it could well have been much more gruesome still – years of torture producing a wasted body that is finally just dumped in an anonymous grave. Indeed, depending on one's theory of atonement, one might even be prepared to go further, and question whether the story had to end brutally. For it is not so much the fact of the suffering itself that produces its impact on us, as the way in which Jesus responded to the diverse actors in the story as the drama unfolded.

Now of course such reflections are appropriate only to a limited degree, since there comes a point at which it becomes problematic whether we are still talking about Christianity, so much is our religion bound up with a particular story set in the framework of a particular prior religious tradition. But what they surely can be allowed to do is to emphasize the way in which God's involvement with suffering in Christ is an involvement with that most frightening aspect of suffering, its essential arbitrariness. There is no providential reason why one of us will die in his forties of cancer, while another will enjoy a ripe old age; no reason why a Mother Teresa of Calcutta lives universally honoured by almost all, while a fellow believer languishes in a Soviet psychiatric hospital, forgotten even by his fellow Christians. It is this which makes Christ's cry of dereliction from the cross the cry of all sufferers – Why me? Why has God abandoned me to this fate? Of course, the cry had been heard before, most poignantly of all perhaps in Psalm 88 with its unrelieved gloom. But here in Jesus we have God himself endorsing that cry, the tragic element in his creation that each new sufferer must discover for himself, that there is no reason why it has befallen him rather than another. Many a hospital chaplain has commented on the need for patients to let their anger loose against God. In the incarnation we have God taking part in the tragic element in his creation by railing against himself.

But that in itself would serve little point unless the incarnation had also brought with it a way beyond and out of the suffering into its creative transformation and redemption. I find myself fully persuaded by Moltmann's view in *The Crucified God* that the incarnation implies God's involvement in suffering to a degree that cannot be adequately described, if the patristic doctrine of the divine impassibility is maintained.[32] All analogies for God are inadequate, but the following may be of some help. Some children have the misfortune to be born without the ability to experience pain, and so unless they are educated in time about the consequences of their actions they end up by doing themselves permanent damage, even accidentally killing themselves. However, if they survive to adulthood, then they will have acquired a good knowledge of the consequences of pain, but even so they will remain without any experiential knowledge of what it feels like to be in pain. Similarly it seems to me with God. Of course, without the incarnation God already had perfect knowledge of the consequences of pain, but only the incarnation could have brought divinity knowledge of what it feels like to be one of us.

But more important for our argument here is not the difference the incarnation makes to God, but the difference it makes to us, and here Moltmann is disappointing. The connection he makes is largely through a modified penal theory of the atonement,[33] whereas the more interesting question seems to me to be how through this suffering God can help us in all our suffering, not just where it bears some connection with our sins. Dorothee Soelle's stress on God's solidarity with us in our suffering initially sounds more promising, but on examination it turns out to be a case of God in Christ as one of the oppressed identifying with the oppressed rather than effecting its creative transformation.[34] So let me offer an alternative account.

The key problem in pain seems not to be its physiological level, but what is happening psychologically. Thus it is a fact well known to doctors that the same level of physiological pain can lead one individual to take early retirement, another to have frequent absences off work and yet others to show no apparent traces in their conduct at all. Again, a large part of the rationale for the hospice movement has been that patients' attitude to the pain is very heavily a function of the background environment against which it is set, that is whether it is a caring and loving one or not. Requests for euthanasia in hospices are in fact almost unknown. In other words, it is the question of meaning that is primary in pain, not its degree.

But when we address that question to Christ's suffering, what we discover is that God in Christ experienced pain at its most apparently meaningless and yet brought good out of it. The Epistle to the Hebrews tells us that Jesus experienced temptation from the inside.[35] But to that we can also add guilt. For, simply in being born a Jew feelings of social guilt must have been inevitable, given the numerous occasions on which the nation had failed God, and so, though objectively Jesus had no guilt, to baptism he went to purge that guilt. Now dying, he finds himself abandoned by all and so enters that most painful human experience of them all, the assigning to one's life by others of a label one cannot accept – to the Jewish authorities a blasphemer, to the Romans a common criminal and, worst of all, to his own disciples a failure. Here we have the story of Job relived, because, of course, Job's tragedy was not that he was innocent but that his friends believed him to be other than he was. The answer that book gives is not entirely satisfactory,[36] whereas in the case of Jesus we do clearly see meaning emerging out of the meaninglessness. This is most conspicuously so in the case of Luke and John. But even Mark twice implies the acquiring of a meaning. Most obviously is this so in the judgement of the centurion in that it suggests that there must have been something in the manner of Jesus dying to evoke this comment, while it does not seem too fanciful to suggest of the cry of dereliction that Mark intends us to recall the confident note with which the Psalm ends, from which the quotation is taken.[37]

So it is a God who has entered into the most awful pain of all, the pain of meaninglessness, who offers us his aid in giving our pain a meaning. It is surely here that special providence enters the picture. It is no part of the divine plan that any specific individual suffer pain. But because pain is a tragic consequence of the values the creation embodies, God has chosen to enter into our pain at its most acute and now is always available to help creatively transform whatever befalls us as one who knew pain at its worst and potentially most destructive.

Perhaps I should add that in speaking of such creative possibilities both for the sufferer and for others in his environment I should not be taken as referring to anything that can be measured. It is not for us to judge how people use their opportunities. A smile may require heroic effort; the gift of a large cheque the vapid movement of a languorous hand. God alone knows how easy or how difficult is the exercise of our free will in terms of our antecedently formed character.

Thus my conclusion is that current approaches in both philosophy and theology err in claiming too much and in despising the other. Anglicanism's *via media* of accepting both natural and revealed theology is surely right. For it is only from the former that we can learn why pain in general exists in the world (because pain is the tragic price that has to be paid for the realization of certain values), while it is only from the latter that we can obtain a response to the specific suffering individual (that it is a God who has fully entered into pain at its most arbitrary and threatening who now comes to our aid to help give that pain a meaning, if we will allow this). Goodness and tragedy are thus inextricably linked not just in the crucifixion but in the nature of creation and thus in the nature of God, and it is to that one and the same reality that both natural and revealed theology point.[38]

Notes

1 The nature of his illness seems to have been more psychological than physiological. Thus his wife speaks of a 'delicacy of body and nerves' inherited from his mother (Agnes Louisa Illingworth, ed., *The Life and Work of John Richardson Illingworth: As Portrayed by His Letters and Illustrated by Photographs* [London: John Murray, 1917]), while Henry Scott Holland too refers to 'nerves' and 'incessant physical trouble under any mental strain', though his death seems to have been caused by a combination of eczema and blood poisoning (ibid., 318 and 322). However, the *Church Times*'s obituary movingly asserted that 'pain was the secret of his power' (ibid., 315) and we know that it gave him particular pleasure that his essay was reproduced as a pamphlet for use during the First World War in the year of his death (1915).
2 F.L. Cross and E.A. Livingstone, ed., *The Oxford Dictionary of the Christian Church*, 3rd ed., s.v. 'Illingworth, John Richardson' (Oxford: Oxford University Press, 1997), 819.
3 Such was the influence of Green on Illingworth and others associated with *Lux Mundi* that Mark Pattison was led to remark: 'Green's honey goes to the ritualistic hive' (Illingworth, *The Life and Work of John Richardson Illingworth*, 84).
4 C.S. Lewis, *The Problem of Pain* (London: Centenary Press, 1940); Austin Farrer, *Love Almighty and Ills Unlimited: An Essay on Providence and Evil* (London: Collins, 1962).
5 Kenneth Surin, *Theology and the Problem of Evil* (Oxford: Basil Blackwell, 1986).
6 Epicurus is quoted by Lactantius (*Patrologia Latina* VII, 121). Latin and English are conveniently both available in M.B. Ahern, *The Problem of Evil* (London: Routledge and Kegan Paul, 1971), 11n2 (Latin) and 2 (English). Cf. Augustine, *Confessions*, VII, 5.
7 Alvin Plantinga, *God and Other Minds* (Ithaca, NY: Cornell University Press, 1967), chapters 5 and 6; Alvin Plantinga, *The Nature of Necessity* (Oxford: Clarendon Press, 1974), chapter 9; and more popularly, Alvin Plantinga, *God, Freedom and Evil* (New York: Harper and Row, 1974), Part 1.
8 J.L. Mackie, 'Evil and Omnipotence', in *The Philosophy of Religion*, ed. Basil Mitchell (Oxford: Oxford University Press, 1971); J.L. Mackie, *The Miracle of Theism* (Oxford: Oxford University Press, 1982), chapter 9.
9 Moral evil will be an unwanted consequence of the good of free will, while natural evil will be a necessary means to the two sorts of goods mentioned later in the paper, namely the creation of the virtues and the growth of knowledge. If an analogy with the human situation is desired, one might in the latter case think of the way in which the surgeon's infliction of pain was necessary to the restoration of health, and in the former of the sorts of cases covered by the doctrine of double effect, where a good intention is approved despite the consequence of evil that will also follow, for example the death of innocent civilians in what is none the less a just war. Of course in our case the limitation is physical necessity, whereas in God's it is only logical; but logic, as the text shows, can also impose considerable constraints. If, following the analogy with the doctrine of double effect, the objection is raised that despite what I say later proportionality between good and evil is still relevant, my response would be twofold: First, in so far as the introduction of proportionality to double effect is relevant, this seems to me to have more to do with finding an easy way of testing the sincerity of the good intention than with the moral situation as such. Thus if the alleged unwanted effect is radically out of proportion to the intended good effect, this can give good grounds for suspecting the motives of the agents concerned. But secondly, in any case God is faced with a vastly different moral dilemma, not with the preservation of a particular good that, whatever happens, will continue to exist elsewhere but with whether a supreme good can be brought into existence at all.

10 Mackie, *The Miracle of Theism*, 162–176, esp. 166–172.

11 Plantinga, *God, Freedom and Evil*, 58.

12 Stephen T. Davis, *Logic and the Nature of God* (London: Macmillan, 1983), chapter 7.

13 Ibid., 106.

14 Ibid., 113.

15 Richard Swinburne, *The Existence of God* (Oxford: Oxford University Press, 1979), 202–214.

16 Ibid., 214–215.

17 Ibid., 207.

18 Ibid., 206

19 D.Z. Phillips, 'The Problem of Evil', in *Reason and Religion*, ed. S.C. Brown (Ithaca, NY: Cornell University Press, 1977), 115.

20 Surin, *Theology and the Problem of Evil*, 184.

21 John Henry Newman, *Certain Difficulties felt by Anglicans in Catholic Teachings* (London: Burns and Lambert, 1850), Lecture 8, 199. The point of the lecture is to contrast the utilitarian standards of the world with those of the Church. Significantly, a few pages earlier (196) he had already made a comment that could be used to reinforce my point that what matters morally is the individual and not the numbers involved: 'The Church looks and moves in simply an opposite direction. It contemplates not the whole, but the parts; not a nation, but the men who form it; not society in the first place, but in the second place, and in the first place individuals.'

22 Davis, *Logic and the Nature of God*, 110 and 108.

23 Swinburne, *The Existence of God*, 219.

24 E.g. Mackie, *The Miracle of Theism*, 154.

25 E.g. J.R. Lucas, *The Freedom of the Will* (Oxford: Oxford University Press, 1970), chapter 14; Richard Swinburne, *The Coherence of Theism* (Oxford: Oxford University Press, 1977), chapter 10.

26 Lewis, *The Problem of Pain*, 104. The central role given to Auschwitz in the theologies of Soelle, Moltmann, and Metz is usefully summarized and discussed in Surin, *Theology and the Problem of Evil*, 112–132,146–149. Davis mentions the Holocaust (100), and Swinburne, Belsen (*The Existence of God*, 219).

27 Of course with some virtues it is logically necessary that the pain be present in the individual himself. For example, it is only courage present if it is exhibited by someone who himself has reason to be afraid. But with most virtues this is not so and there seems to be no essential link between degree of virtue and the amount of pain experienced by the individual himself in his own life. Swinburne does at one point speak of 'victims of the system' (*The Existence of God*, 210), but he seems to think this of only limited applicability.

28 Nelson Pike, 'Plantinga on Free Will and Evil', *Religious Studies* 15/4 (1979), 472–473. Here he is following Augustine in *Enchiridion*, chapter 100: 'How would a Good Being permit evil to be done except that in his omnipotence he can turn evil into good?' It should of course be noted that many a philosopher has been content with a weaker thesis, namely that all evil must have the potential for good, not that it actually achieves this.

29 Karl Barth, *Church Dogmatics* III/2 (Edinburgh: T & T Clark, 1960), 133, 153–154.

30 In stressing the fact of unredeemed evil, we should not of course lose sight of the other side of the equation, of the considerable degree to which we are what we now are and want to be is only so on virtue of a past history of evils both in our own case and that of our ancestors; for further development of this argument, cf. Robert M. Adams, *The Virtue of Faith and Other Essays in Philosophical Theology* (Oxford: Oxford University Press, 1987), chapters 5 and 6, esp. 65–93.

31 David Brown, *Continental Philosophy and Modern Theology: An Engagement* (Oxford: Blackwell, 1987), 202–203.

32 Jürgen Moltmann, *The Crucified God* (London: SCM Press, 1976), chapter 6.

33 Ibid., chapters 4 and 5. For a brief critique, Brown, *Continental Philosophy and Modern Theology*, 117–119.

34 Dorothee Soelle, *Suffering* (Philadelphia: Fortress, 1975). Soelle is certainly also concerned to argue that Christians must do all they can to eliminate the suffering. But what one misses is any recognition of the transformative power of the pain itself, so violent is her reaction against what she labels 'Christian masochism' and 'theological sadism' (cf. esp. 9–32), admittedly often inadequate and insensitive ways of expressing that point. Indeed, the force of her case seems decisively blunted, if my argument is accepted that one cannot describe as part of the divine plan what happens in the particular case.

35 Hebrews 4:15.

36 Though more satisfactory if one stresses 42:5 with its assurance of God's presence through the suffering rather than 42:3 with its appeal to divine inscrutability. For an indication of the range of possible interpretations, cf. Nahum N. Glatzer, ed., *The Dimensions of Job: A Study and Selected Readings* (New York: Schocken, 1969).

37 This is the view of D.E. Nineham, *Saint Mark* (Harmondsworth: Penguin, 1963), 428. But even if this is not so, Mark's narrative still moves from the meaninglessness of Psalm 22:1 at 15:34 to the centurion's assertion of meaning at 15:39. In this he is followed by Matthew. But Luke and John can also be seen as having a similar progression, the former in his move from his initial stress on Jesus' death between two common criminals (23:32) to his confident handing of his spirit to his Father (23:46), the latter in the transition from the poignant 'I thirst' to the triumphant 'It is finished' (19:28–30).

38 I am grateful for helpful criticisms from a number of individuals, especially David Redhouse, Rod Sykes, and Rowan Williams. This chapter was originally published as part of a centennial volume for *Lux Mundi* in *The Religion of the Incarnation*, ed. Robert Morgan (Bristol: Bristol Classical Press, 1989), 46–59, and is used with permission.

Part II

Experience and Revelation

Introduction

Among Christian theologians there has been a long tradition of opposing creation to all other potential forms of God's relation to the world. The historical justification could scarcely be doubted inasmuch as the doctrine appears to have been first formulated to achieve an independence of the world that other religious perspectives of the time lacked.[1] Even so, as the previous Part sought to demonstrate, such contrasts can all too easily become exaggerated. As with those other terms, 'creation' is a metaphor that legitimates unpacking as much in the direction of involvement as distance. So it was perhaps no accident that the early Barth eventually retreated from his overwhelming stress on divine distance and otherness.[2] In any case it is quite wrong to conflate independence and distance. Just as parents can be close to their children yet independent of them, so might the same be true of God. That is why in the last of the chapters in the previous Part (on theodicy) I felt justified in describing God as committed to both independence and closeness. (Drawing on philosophy) God established general principles in the ordering of the world that observed distance as a way of guaranteeing human freedom while at the same time (drawing on theology) God continually extends the offer of a supporting divine presence to those faced with human tragedy and suffering.

In a similar way in this Part I want to protest against too sharp a distinction between the theological construct (revelation) and its allegedly purely human correlate (experience). Once again, there can be no doubt about how sharp a distinction was once drawn: revelation was God 'unveiling' truths, experience merely human attempts to get at God. However, two centuries of biblical criticism have forced the conclusion that revelation must now be seen, like all other beliefs, to have its basis in experience, and so heavily conditioned by the various settings in which those beliefs first arose. None of this need lead to the conclusion that revelation is untrue, but it does entail recognition that what is true and what is not needs much more careful unpacking than was considered necessary in the past.

The theologian of recent centuries who saw most clearly the new importance of experience was undoubtedly Schleiermacher. Unfortunately, his theology's great weakness was in veering too strongly in one particular direction, towards the side of experience, and a very individual dimension at that. The result was altogether too strong a focus on one particular type of experience, the pantheism popular in the Romantic movement of the time that left little room for the great range of ways in which the divine might in fact be encountered.[3] Equally, despite his pioneering explorations of hermeneutics, there is little sense in Schleiermacher of the corporate shaping of experience, nor its resultant effects for both good and bad.[4]

Both criticisms suggest a complexity to experience that philosophers have tended to reject in favour of relatively simple overarching principles. Indeed, the whole notion of religious experience is often rejected because it is taken to exhibit a conceptual complexity and indeed incoherence that contrasts markedly with the relative simplicity of ordinary human perception. It is that contention which the first of the chapters that follow, 'Realism and Religious Experience', is concerned to challenge: whatever complexity is found in the explicitly religious case will be found to have its parallel in the more ordinary instance. An earlier essay of mine had observed a similar mistake among contemporary Christian philosophers who have denied the possibility of any genuine experience of God.[5] For them the very character of God as infinite, omniscient and so on was taken to preclude any access to such a nature but my response was to point out that even with our experience of other human beings perception is partial and aspectual, with inferences then drawn to a more comprehensive whole.

Just as an aspectual character to religious experience entails that apparently conflicting accounts across the great general range (numinous, mystical, transcendent, immanent, love, fear, etc.) need not therefore be seen as in irreconcilable conflict, so equally, as I note towards the end of that earlier essay, in respect of the more specific claims of the individual religions their conditioned character as set within particular traditions means that not every case of conflict between them is necessarily irresolvable. Experiential claims in such contexts should never be read in isolation but assessed from within those separately developing traditions. When that is done a different conclusion may emerge, as I suggest both in respect of abstract doctrines like plurality within the Godhead and specific stories such as the sacrifice of Isaac. It is not that all conflict is thereby dissolved, but it does mean that there is the possibility of a meaningful dialogue in which both sides can now expect to learn.

Not that this is in any way to propose the abandonment or even the weakening of Christianity's central doctrines, but it is to concede, as subsequent chapters will make clear, the need for new forms of defence, as revelation is discovered to be a much more complex phenomenon than has been acknowledged for most of Christianity's history. Thus, as the immediately following chapters observes, there just is no plausible way of maximizing the meaning of the biblical text such that every verse can be seen to be somehow deliberately intended by God, as some analytic philosophers would still claim. Instead, we need to take seriously how dreadful the human contribution has sometimes been, and not disguise this from ourselves through the use of allegory or other such devices. Indeed, sometimes God is to be discovered in spite of the text and not because of it, as we hear in the Bible's victims unexpected pointers to the divine will. Equally, as the final chapter in this Part insists, we must avoid the too easy claim on the part of some theologians to know a Christ who is Lord over the text and its self-interpreter. Without doubt the genuinely new can emerge from within Scripture and its developing tradition, but even so it does so without ever entirely breaking free of the contingencies of history. Instead, how exactly that Lord and his purposes are to be described must be allowed to emerge, sometimes from developments within the text, sometimes from wider cultural change. Such a position would of course be profoundly unsettling did it entail that all of Christian belief must be constantly subject to revision, but fortunately that is not the way a developing tradition works. Only a few possible changes are in the air at any one time, with the foundations contributing to the debate rather than being undermined by it.

Notes

1   Genesis 1 is usually interpreted as a demythologization of the Babylonian story of the world's origins as found in a battle between the gods, with Tiamat's dismemberment the result. Again 2 Maccabees 7:28 (the first reference to *creatio ex nihilo*) can be read as making possible a strong assertion of bodily resurrection dependent on divine action over against Greek notions of a self-generated immortality.
2   Although it may be unfair to claim that the logical conclusion to early Barth lies in books like Thomas J. J. Altizer, *The Gospel of Christian Atheism* (Philadelphia: Westminster Press, 1966), even the novelist John Updike, himself an admirer of Barth, acknowledged the potential difficulties for faith in such distancing in his comic novel *Roger's Version* (New York: Alfred A. Knopf, 1986).
3   The extent of his pantheism is disputed. For a strong claim to that effect, see Richard Brandt, *The Philosophy of Schleiermacher* (Westport, CT: Greenwood Press, 1941), esp. 96ff.
4   Gadamer neatly sums up his 'original contribution' as 'a psychological interpretation': H.G. Gadamer, *Truth and Method*, 2nd ed. (London: Sheed & Ward, 1979), 164.
5   'Experience Skewed', in *Transcending Boundaries in Philosophy and Theology*, ed. Kevin Vanhoozer and Martin Warner (Aldershot: Ashgate, 2007), 159–175.

4 Realism and Religious Experience

One way of approaching the issue of realism in theology is to explore the explanatory value of its concepts and see how far the principles underlying scientific realism might be stretched to include theology's own rather idiosyncratic type of metaphysical realism. However, rather than engaging primarily with the scientific model, another possibility is to investigate how far parallels with ordinary common-sense realism can be sustained. Here the status of religious experience would seem the obvious question to examine, not least because some of the most influential philosophical treatments of such experience have sought to draw parallels with ordinary perception. Perhaps still most familiar is Richard Swinburne's appeal to what he calls 'the principle of credulity', that how things appear to an observer are good grounds for believing that that is the way they are, whereas its negation needs much more evidence to establish its truth.[1] While still pursuing the parallel with perception, two later writers, William Alston and Keith Yandell, acknowledge a much more complex reality. For Alston, Christian perception needs to be set within the rationality of specific 'doxastic' practices, and so his argument is meant to apply only to the reasonableness of accepting the veridical character of Christian experience, and not religious experience in general.[2] By contrast, Keith Yandell intends his argument to apply to all forms of religious experience but he does so by questioning the coherence of 'enlightenment' experiences of the self in Buddhism and Jainism, and of an undifferentiated ultimate reality in Advaita-Vedanta Hinduism.[3] The result is that the argument is deemed only to hold in respect of certain types of experience across the major religions.

In this chapter, rather than consider such arguments directly, I will instead explore three types of objection that might be raised against the viability of any such project based on parallels with ordinary perception. My immediate goal here is thus rather more modest than Swinburne's, Alston's, and Yandell's, but it may still serve in broad support of their respective approaches. The three types of critique are (1) those based on the unusual character of the nature of the object of perception in this case, (2) the unusual conditions associated with such perception, and finally (3) the oddness of the content of such perception. In each case I shall indicate various ways in which the objections might be countered. As will emerge in due course, 'ordinary perception' is not quite as straightforward a category as it is often taken to be, but for the moment my discussion may proceed by taking as standard perception of material objects and their attributes.

The Oddness of Its Object

There are at least two general features of the divine that make it problematic as an object of perception: first, as the divine is essentially not of this world (transcendent, infinite, etc.) it is hard to make sense of what it might mean to talk of 'perception' of such a reality; second, even if such sense can be sustained, there is the difficulty of indicating, as with other perceptual claims, under what circumstances the divine might be repeatedly perceived. Initially, it might be thought that in this matter God is no different from any other free agent such as human beings. But there is this important difference, that it is possible to predict most of the situations under which a particular human being might be perceptible and also the forms under which they will appear, whereas there has been traditionally ascribed to the divine a much more radical type of freedom that is in no way subject to human whim or expectation. The difference comes from human beings exhibiting marked continuation in appearance and also usually acting in character (e.g. picking up their children each day from school), whereas it is frequently contended that there are no such easily identifiable parallels in respect of God.

Both points – divine non-natural otherness and predictability – merit consideration. I shall begin with what I take to be the weaker of the two contentions, the question of predictability, for it seems to me questionable whether the theological commonplace of such divine freedom actually accords with such evidence as we have of how God has chosen to relate to the world. So, for example, throughout Jewish and Christian Scriptures are to be found promises of divine presence and powers under certain circumstances: in the Temple, where two or three are gathered in Jesus' name, in the power to remit sin, in defending oneself before secular authority and so on.[4]

Again, there is a large body of literature where it is claimed that certain types of music or landscape, for example, will commonly initiate a consistent pattern of experience of the divine – for instance, a sense of the grandeur of God before certain types of landscape. However, against such putative experience of God mediated through nature or arts exhibiting such predictive capacity it is sometimes objected that such a claim cannot possibly be sustained precisely because it can so easily be thrown in doubt by all those people who claim to have no such tendencies towards belief when placed under similar circumstances. But is the counter-evidence really that clear? Is it not more common for objectors to suggest, not that they have experienced nothing at all, but that, although their experience had similar characteristics, none of this necessitates a further inference to belief in God? So, for example, the distinguished music critic, Wilfrid Mellers, in *Celestial Music?*, the last book he wrote, on the one hand did not hesitate to concede that certain forms of music make individuals more open to the infinite, while on the other hand as a non-believer he continued to insist that he wanted to resist that pull.[5] But, if that is so, I take it that the lack of a parallel with the predictability of ordinary perception may be more apparent than real: there is a similar perception even if it is read quite differently.

However, an unsympathetic critic might object at this point that all I have demonstrated is the possibility of similar experience that might be described more neutrally (for example, in aesthetic terms), and the role of God then remains a further questionable inference. But in response I would observe that this is not how such experiences are characteristically described, as though the religious believer identifies a further layer within them. Indeed, Mellers portrays himself as resisting what he sees as in some ways the more natural reading.

Of course, it still needs to be conceded that other types of religious experience would exhibit no such predictive capacity, most obviously where we would like to talk of God interacting with human persons (responding to their prayers, and so on). Here a more personalist or interactionist account would seem more appropriate. However, while certainly not denying that some divine action is best explicated in this way, this is surely not the form of encounter with the divine most easily allied with ordinary perception, since it will indeed be God at the least predictable. That is why I believe it important also to acknowledge an alternative kind of divine relation to the world, through which the sort of religious experience that I have hitherto been delineating also becomes possible.

Unfortunately, there is no agreed terminology, but 'numinous' might be a usable term. One possible way of understanding this kind of relation that is quite distinct from the personalist or interactionist model would be to think that the divine presence always (under certain conditions) is available to the world that it has made, but that it remains at least to some extent up to an individual how that presence (under those conditions) is read. That God might be available in this way should scarcely be surprising, as the divine is by definition ubiquitous (omnipresent) and is also responsible for sustaining all things in existence. Nonetheless, theologians concerned to defend the freedom of God may take particular umbrage at the notion of the divine allowing itself to be experienced and yet individuals allowed to deny that this is the nature of their experience. But to Christianity at least this should present no real difficulty since at its heart lies a claim to similar abuse in the events at the heart of its faith, namely in the crucifixion: God present, yet that presence denied.

To talk thus of experience of the numinous or transcendent makes an easy transition to the other objection I said I would consider in this section, and that is the oddness of talking of the perception of something which is essentially 'beyond' this world. The contrast must seem most extreme to those still influenced by classical British empiricism, and in particular Hume's ideal of simple, clear perceptions, and the more complex form this took in twentieth-century notions of basic sense data.[6] However, none of the various arguments in the latter's favour (to do with certainty, illusion, and the partial character of perception) seems decisive. In fact, even the simplest of perceptions preclude any form of naïve realism, with something like the apparently incorrigible red of the tomato, for example, only appearing so in a particular light. Equally, there is no reason why seeing part of the object should not be described as seeing the object or why seeing it otherwise than it is in reality be taken to indicate that one sees something else instead. That is why it is now widely recognized that perceptions cannot be so easily analysed without artificiality into their constituent parts. Perception of a human individual as loving or intelligent would, therefore, now also be commonly regarded as a no less proper way of talking than of the person being seen to be wearing a red coat. Just as such properties might be viewed as supervening on the purely natural yet be said to be perceptible, so in the divine case it would be a matter of certain natural conditions making possible contact with a numinous reality in virtue of the kind of world in which we live and for which theists believe the divine is ultimately responsible. The point would be that the Creator has so established natural conditions as to mediate such contact into the created order. So, although the causal relations may be quite different, the perception of such immaterial properties in both human and divine can alike be successfully mediated through the material.

But, while these parallels with the range of predicates we are prepared to use of human beings and the mode of their mediation lessens the extent of the contrast with ordinary perception, it may still be objected that no sense can be given to claims to experience something quite so non-natural, and other-worldly as God, precisely because of the sort of predicates claimed for the divine. For what could it mean to experience the totality of what it is to be divine, or even particular attributes such as being infinite, the various conventional attributes that are themselves so qualified (infinitely good and so on), or, more generally, a being quite unlike any particular thing?[7]

These objections can scarcely be answered in a short compass but their force can be greatly lessened when it is noted that the same difficulty occurs with any other complex object or person. In any particular act of perception only some particular aspect of the object or person is perceived, and it is only thanks to other mental faculties that the particular is then brought under some more general heading, thanks, for example, to the work of the memory, the mind's categorizing faculty, or whatever. In a similar way, then, strictly speaking on any particular occasion it is only one aspect or another of the divine that is perceived, and that is indeed something that is recognized in much of the literature concerning such experiences.

Even so, some attributes might seem more difficult to envisage as part of human experience than others, infinity being one. John Ruskin makes a suggestion of how such an experience might occur: 'light receding in the distance is of all visible things the least material, the least finite, the farthest withdrawn from the earth …, the most typical of the nature of God, the most suggestive of the glory of his dwelling place.'[8] It is important to note that he is not proposing an inference from the quality of the landscape to the divine property. Rather, his suggestion is that the perception of one occasions the perception of the other in light of the fact of God as Creator being in any case the source of such infinity in nature. Certain features of the created world, we might postulate, are especially conducive to such an understanding: perhaps, it has been suggested, rather like the way in which a vapour trail in the sky occasions thought of an aeroplane although it is not visible.

Admittedly, this aspectival approach does raise the possibility of such varied experience being interpreted in terms of several different gods rather than a single entity.[9] But that is surely right. It is only some forms of experience that suggest an overall unity to the divine; otherwise an inference to that belief is required. So my conclusion here is that, initial appearances notwithstanding, divinity as the object of perception can be said to be not all that dissimilar from more standard cases. There can at times be the same level of predictability while the sort of attributes experienced and the mode of their perception are not wholly unlike our perception in more complex human cases.

The Oddness of the Conditions of Such Perception

Here the objection is likely to be that there is oddness both in initial and in accompanying conditions. Oddness in initial conditions repeats a point already considered in the previous section, namely whether theological insistence on the total freedom of God would inhibit any of the law-like predictability that characterizes more conventional perception. My answer here would therefore be the same, that God has in fact chosen to operate within certain constraints and so, although all perception of the divine cannot be subsumed under some rule, it can be sufficient for the parallel still to hold with ordinary perception.

It is perhaps, therefore, the oddness of accompanying rather than initial conditions that may present the appearance of greater contrast. This is because an affective element is often thought to be no less important than the epistemological. That is to say, in contrast with ordinary perceptual experience, claims to religious experience would commonly be regarded as deficient were they not accompanied by significant emotions such as awe, joy, sorrow and so on. Were the presence of the affective to be seen as merely a contingent feature of such perception, bearing no essential relation to what is perceived, the matter might be considered as of no great moment. But in fact it does seem that customarily having the requisite emotions is a *sine qua non* for having the full perception in the first place. So, for example, it is hard to see what sense could be made of a claim to have experienced the divine infinite without this also inducing awe and wonder, or again perfect divine goodness without some accompanying sense of guilt or shame, mystic intimacy without joy, and so on.

Alston alludes to 'one nagging worry', which is 'the possibility that the phenomenal content of (mystical) perception wholly consists of affective qualities.'[10] Although conceding that 'subjects speak of ecstasy, sweetness, love, delight, joy, contentment, peace, repose, bliss, awe and wonder',[11] he insists that the heart of the experience lies elsewhere in its cognitive content, and only a passing concession (without further elaboration) is made to the possibility 'that a direct perception of God could be effected through affective qualities.'[12] However, the problem with that response is that in fact the emotions seem much more directly involved, indeed to the extent that some emotions both predispose individuals towards the having of a religious experience and are constitutive to its fulfilment. So, for example, a mind not in the least disposed to awe would be unlikely ever to have an experience of divine infinity or majesty mediated through nature or music, or again an experience of divine forgiveness seems precluded without some prior sense of guilt or of 'sin' needing to be forgiven.

All this may seem to make religious perception far removed from 'ordinary' perception, but, as I sought to argue in the previous section, it is only a particular philosophical tradition that takes something elementary as the model of what all perception is like, and then wrongly so. Equally, it would be quite wrong to suppose that in any particular case it is only one of our five senses that is involved and not also various mental faculties. So, for example, hearing a piece of music is not just a matter of hearing but of interpretation in terms of its harmonic and melodic structures, and so on. Including the emotions in these mental faculties, therefore, does not seem such a huge step as it might initially appear.

Even so, were religious experience unique in assigning such a key role to the emotions, then this might count decisively against parallels with ordinary perception. Increasingly, however, it is being acknowledged that similar issues arise with morals and aesthetics. On the latter Nelson Goodman is quite emphatic: 'in aesthetic experience the emotions function cognitively. The work of art is apprehended through the feelings as well as through the senses.'[13] But in many ways it is the situation with respect to moral insight that is the more interesting. When Hume declared that reason without emotion was powerless, it was questions of motivation that he had in mind; but moral philosophers are now increasingly acknowledging that in issues of cognition the emotions might also play a crucial role.

While Martha Nussbaum's claims about 'love's knowledge' are undoubtedly the best known, it is a pity that she focuses so exclusively on the necessity of narrative expansion in order to make the claim clear, because this would seem to lessen the sense of emotion in its own right acting as an epistemological tool.[14] Here Sabine Döring seems more helpful, in suggesting that an emotion like sympathy can itself trump reason as a form of knowledge, as in Huck's discovery of the value of the slave he decides to hide in Mark Twain's *Huckleberry Finn*.[15] Again, in a book-length consideration of the topic, Mark Wynn observes how emotion can improve understanding, including moral perception, in quite a range of different ways. So, for example (following Graham Nerlich), he observes that 'the grief I feel at the death of another may help reveal the value that they hold for me; and on occasion, this response may reveal more than I could understand by discursive reflection alone.'[16] Or again (following Raimond Gaita), a nun's practical loving care for incurable patients may disclose the value they should bear far better than pronouncements of similar values by senior doctors that may smack of the theoretical and condescending.[17] Further support for such a position is given by Patricia Greenspan, who argues that the moral education of children and their training in emotional response often go hand in hand, and indeed are in no sense simply a ladder which can be dispensed with later.[18]

Wynn makes much of the overlap between such moral cases and the more explicitly religious, as in Newman's insistence that conscience is not only our primary means of experiencing the divine but also 'it is always what the sense of the beautiful is in only certain cases; it is always emotional.'[19] But Newman's rather narrow focus on the moral world would seem to me a mistake, for two other reasons: first, because an objector could always propose a reductionist strategy by suggesting that content in the end reduces to the purely moral; then, second, because even among believers it might court a presupposition that with God as good all religious experience necessarily has a moral component, whereas in fact with all such experience as aspectival there may be no moral content at all.

However, it might well be objected to the above that all I have done is draw parallels with equally problematic areas of perception in ethics and aesthetics. Why after all should we be realists about either? While I personally would not endorse such a challenge, it is important to observe here that emotions also affect other areas of perception. So, for example, animals find sexually attractive others that are likely to be appropriate reproductive partners, or again fear is part of the process of detecting a dangerous predator. Equally, much work in psychology has been done on the way in which disinterested concern in others can only be recognized by the percipients first acquiring some empathy with themselves.

The appropriate response here then, I would suggest, is not to deny the essential contribution of the emotions to religious experience but rather to argue that emotion can equally be one means of accessing the truth, and that this occurs also elsewhere than in the specifically religious situation.

The Oddness of the Content

It is often said that ordinary perception allows relatively easy comparability with what others experience, whereas, irrespective of the precise form the religious experience takes, in so far as the data can be made to engage in dialogue with one another at all, this appears to be frequently in conflict not only across the religions but even within them. Certainly, there are serious difficulties, but these are intensified by failure to distinguish between the two types of experience delineated earlier, what I termed 'numinous' and 'personalist' or 'interactionist' experiences. On the whole, it is the latter interactionist model that presents the most problems especially when set against the sort of detail associated with claims to divine revelation in the various religions. By contrast, claims to experience the divine as loving, infinite, pure, angry, forgiving, gracious, generous or whatever can for the most part be seen to complement one another.

Of course, different initial conditions may generate different emphases. To take the history of Christian architecture as an example, Gothic buildings will tend to generate a sense of God as other and infinite, classical a sense of order and beauty in the divine purposes, Baroque a sense of divine playfulness, and so on. However, despite proponents often insisting that only their particular style properly represents the divine character, there is no need to follow suit in such exclusiveness. Instead, we may speak of them revealing different aspects of the divine. Nor need the fact that the history of Christian architecture and that of no other religion took precisely this character argue against the veridical character of the experiences mediated, for it is possible to detect similar elements emerging in the history of other religions also, despite considerable differences in what architectural forms generate the same sort of ideas and precisely when these occur in the history of the religion concerned.[20]

However, although it is relatively easy to see how those assuming a plurality of gods behind such experience might be led to endorse belief in a single divine reality (on grounds of simplicity and the unitive experiences that some have), it is harder to identify how the conflict between personal and impersonal readings of the transcendent reality might be arbitrated. In a famous essay Zaehner, while accepting the genuineness of both types of experience, argued for the superiority of the personal kind, as that which comes in the surpassing of more unitive experiences that still hark back to nature mysticism.[21] But I doubt whether matters can be resolved quite that easily. After all, there is a long tradition in western thought that argues for the superiority of the impersonal, as in Platonism, with the division between contemplating subject and object of reflection fully overcome.[22] Perhaps the best way forward here is to distinguish between the actual nature of the divine reality and how it is experienced, for it is surely possible to maintain that both ways of experiencing divinity are fully veridical (if incomplete), whatever type of reality ultimately lies behind them. This can after all happen also with human agents, even if in the human case a lack of the 'personal' element is usually a subject for complaint, with, for example, institutional mismanagement or computer programs correspondingly blamed. That would entail arbitrating the issue in respect of the divine on grounds other than experience.

However, in terms of content the strongest objections to any parallel with ordinary perception come not from the data of numinous experience but rather from what I have called interactionist experience. Thus it is commonplace to note how certain visions or auditions of saints only occur within a specific religion, and give conflicting information to that found in other religions or even different parts of the same religion. Similarly, the primary revelations themselves of the major religions appear to contradict one another sharply, with the Qur'an, for example, explicitly rejecting some of the New Testament claims about Jesus, or with Krishna as an avatar of Vishnu holding central place instead in Hinduism's Bhagavad-Gita. Partly in response to such difficulties, some have retreated to antirealism, among them Don Cupitt in England and Mark Johnston in the United States.[23] Others, such as Roger Trigg, continue to advocate a very straightforward form of realism according to which, if the experience is veridical, there is some direct correspondence between the experience and God as understood in fairly straightforward theistic terms.[24] More common among academics, though, is probably some form of critical realism, at the extreme end of which lies John Hick's claim that all religions are equidistant from 'the Real' and so what is experienced is a heavily conditioned form of that ultimate reality.[25]

In these debates Hilary Putnam is of particular interest, as he wrestled with such issues throughout the later stages of his long career, moving from realism to antirealism and then towards the end of his life to what might be called pluralist realism, with the recognition that not only do standards of truth vary from discourse to discourse but also that in some contexts apparently competing accounts of the truth could be simultaneously true.[26] So, for example, there is no reason why the meaning of 'exists' should not vary depending on the types of discourse in which it is being employed (moral or mathematical, for example, rather than empirical), why the number of objects in a field should not vary depending on why they are being viewed (mereological or otherwise), or even why something like the Müller-Lyer illusion should not be allowed to call into question the truth of what we actually see (in our perceptual field the lines are actually of different lengths).[27] In particular, Putnam wanted to resist the idea that intermediate representation in the mind makes all such experience indirect. So far from illusion or hallucination demonstrating the need to postulate mediating sense data for all perception, they merely expose a different kind of relation to external reality in these particular cases.[28] If despite his own Jewish belief Putnam did not specifically apply these insights to religious truth, there seems good reason to believe that such an understanding could also be pursued in the religious case.[29] Thus, adopting such applications would allow us to say that the divine experienced as Allah or as the Christian God does not necessarily entail a distorting lens and thus a less direct experience, but that both could be correct relative to the two discourses in which they operate.

Should religion need to be treated as a special case in all of this, that would of course greatly weaken the force of any Putnam-inspired analysis. But the examples Putnam himself gives could also be greatly extended, given that the content of ordinary perception is in fact much more complex than is ordinarily recognized and is itself in part shaped by competing discourses of interpretation. Thus even across European languages the range of colour perceptions is not divided in exactly the same way, while anthropologists commonly insist that almost every perceptual concept is not universal across cultures, with even the nature of human identity itself a contested concept. The advantage of the Putnam approach is that it is not necessary, for example, to arbitrate on the division of the colour spectrum but instead one may acknowledge that what is seen can still be true, each relative to the cultural schema of which it is part.[30] None of this is to deny that cross-cultural comparisons are possible. It is simply to contest whether they should be seen as the only form of truth, and also to emphasize that by allowing these multiple forms of truth, further insights may prove possible, for example in the reasons grounding why different cultures divide up the world differently.

In religion this also would have advantages. So, for example, from a Judaeo-Christian perspective it looks as though Hinduism is of all the major religions the most idolatrous, with its numerous images of the gods. But by first setting such practice in the context of its own discourse, a new possibility emerges, that it is in effect Hinduism's way of guarding against idolatry, since the very quantity and variety preclude any one from becoming dominant. Indeed, it can provide a way for Hinduism to argue against the Judeo-Christian tradition as itself much more idolatrous, since unlike in Hinduism a particular book is given unconditional authority. So there is at least an argument to be had about which of the two discourses is inherently more idolatrous.[31]

In all of this my intention is not to argue that all differences between the religions can then dissolve as their setting within particular traditions is taken more seriously. It is rather to observe that the contrast so often made between simple agreed perceptions on the one hand in other 'ordinary' perceptions and the hopeless contradicting claims of religion on the other is hopelessly naïve both about the character of ordinary perceptions and about the nature of religion. In respect of the former, such a stark contrast immediately collapses as soon as one ceases to consider interrelated cultures and in particular pays attention to the whole sweep of human history, while in respect of the latter, surface conflict does not necessarily always point to deep underlying conflict. The point can perhaps be made clearer by some examples, but these need first to be set in some sort of wider theological and philosophical context. In brief, the philosophical assumption is that all thinking is to varying degrees contextual or culturally conditioned,[32] while the theological assumption is that the divine also has chosen to work within this context, addressing individuals where they are rather than compelling them in directions beyond their immediate comprehension. Such is the pattern that I believe to be disclosed within the Judaeo-Christian revelation, given the gradual character of some of its key transformations, for example from implicit belief in a plurality of gods to a single God, or from a stress on divine unity in the Jewish Shema to a plurality in which even the divine itself (in Christ) chose to be limited by the ordinary conditions of human existence.[33]

Two rather different examples from the Judaeo-Christian revelation may suffice, the first being the sacrifice of Isaac and the second the Trinity. To take a scriptural passage and a doctrine may seem to carry us far from the topic of religious experience, but this is not so. The doctrine is based in experiential claims and continues to influence other such experiences, while, whether or not Genesis 22 records an actual experience, it is certainly true that its traditions of interpretation have influenced how others have interpreted their own encounters with God.

Certainly, if specific historical details such as place or the name of the son involved are regarded as important, then irreconcilable conflict on Abraham's sacrifice of his son between Bible and Qur'an immediately emerges.[34] There will also be conflict if the interpretation that has dominated Protestant Christianity since Kierkegaard is accepted, that the primary focus is on Abraham's dilemma, since in the history of both Judaism and Islam the primary focus alike moved to a potential self-offering by the son. In Islam's case such a transformation was greatly facilitated by identification of the potential victim as the older son, but Jewish exegesis followed a similar route, in assuming Isaac as a responsible individual chosen to represent the Jewish people in the event that became known as the *Akedah* or 'Binding.' For example, one influential midrash argues that Isaac must have been thirty-seven years old at the time, since Sarah's death is mentioned immediately afterwards and so must have been caused by shock at what had nearly happened, the death of her own son.[35]

But in fact traditional Christian exegesis had moved in precisely the same direction, through seeing the offering of Isaac as a type or foretaste of the sacrifice of Christ. So, for example, as early as Clement of Rome we are told that because 'Isaac knew with confidence what was about to happen, it was with gladness that he was led forth as a sacrificial victim', while Irenaeus urges us to 'take up our cross as Isaac took up his bundle of sticks'.[36] In short, if we are prepared to set the apparently competing versions of the narrative in the context of their respective traditions of interpretation, then surface conflict disappears, to be replaced by an agreed emphasis on the key role in religion of the place of self-sacrifice.[37] Nor need that conclusion be confined to the three monotheistic religions. A similar conclusion might be reached if the examination were extended to the role of the sacrifice of Nachiketas in Hinduism.[38] More controversially, I would also suggest that the point even applies to Aztec traditions of sacrifice in the sense that even in the midst of all their brutality there are indications of an alternative, similar view emerging through aspects of the practices and in the poetry associated with the cult.[39]

It perhaps needs emphasizing that it is no part of my intention to suggest that all potential conflicts between the religions can be resolved in this way, only that some can be once such contextualization is taken into account. Nonetheless, it is important that such claims should be made if any real parallel with ordinary perception is to be sustained. It is simply not the case that religion throws up nothing but irresolvable conflicts. Even in the most apparently intractable of disagreements, there may be some converging elements. That is why I would like to conclude with a brief consideration of the doctrine of the Trinity, commonly cited as a clear case of irresolvable conflict across the religions. Islam customarily treats the doctrine as a gross instance of *shirk*, of an idolatrous collapse into polytheism, no less dangerous than the Hindu belief system. Yet, superficial appearances notwithstanding, two elements of contextualization may be used to lessen greatly that sense of conflict, even if they hardly succeed in dispensing with it altogether.

The first is that, although the Trinity is sometimes treated as a datum of Christian experience,[40] it is now virtually standard practice to treat the doctrine as a deduction from other elements of Christian faith, experiential or otherwise. So, for example, the argument might be based on the need to reconcile the revelatory emphasis in the Hebrew Scriptures on monotheism with the New Testament's assertion of the divinity of Christ and the Spirit. But equally this is what is found in Hinduism: that talk of a plurality of gods is reconciled at the conceptual level in the assertion of a single divine reality, even if there is disagreement over whether this should be conceived personally or impersonally.[41] Again, the intellectual history of Islam is not quite as unqualifiedly monotheistic as its accusations against Christianity might initially indicate, for claims that the Qur'an was a created entity led in due course to the postulation of its holy book as uncreated.[42] So, one way of lessening the appearance of tension is to note that elements of unity and plurality in fact operate within all three intellectual traditions.

It is possible, however, also to construct a similar but more direct strategy in respect of experience of the divine itself. Although Hegel's appeal to the *Trimurti* of Brahma, Vishnu, and Shiva is no longer plausible, with Kali or the feminine principle more generally substituted instead of Brahma, it becomes true that most recorded Hindu experience of the divine would find its place within this threefold categorization. This is not to suggest that the three Hindu figures parallel the three persons of the Trinity, only that there is a similar building from 'plural' experience to an ultimate unity. Equally, within Islam, although there is no talk of experiencing the Qur'an as uncreated, there are claims to similar 'plural' experiences in the Sufi tradition in respect of the names of God. Resolved by al-Ghazali from the ninety-nine in the Qur'an into seven, these were further reduced to three by later tradition (life, knowledge, power).[43] Again, my point is not to claim that essentially the same content is revealed as pertains to the Christian God. My aim is far more modest: simply to observe that contextualization enables one to say that there is enough of an overlap on the theme of unity and plurality for discussions to be had. It will not do for the objector to the parallel with ordinary perception to say that the differences are so great that it is inconceivable that it is in some sense the same object that is being perceived.

Obviously many of the points I have made in this chapter could have been explored at much greater length and indeed would need to be if the parallel with ordinary perception is to be fully sustained. Nonetheless, I hope that I have shown that in principle at least such a strategy is indeed possible.[44]

Notes

1 See especially Richard Swinburne, *The Existence of God* (Oxford: Clarendon Press, 1979; 2nd ed. 2004), 254–271, esp. 254–255. In the 2004 edition, 310–323 is of particular relevance. Our somewhat different treatment of conflict emerges from 316ff.

2 William P. Alston, *Perceiving God* (Ithaca, NY: Cornell University Press, 1991). The use of the term 'mystical' to describe such experience is somewhat unfortunate, as, although he takes some of his examples from the writings of Teresa of Avila, he seems to intend in general what others might call ordinary religious experience.

3 For these critiques, see Keith E. Yandell, *The Epistemology of Religious Experience* (Cambridge: Cambridge University Press, 1993), 279–321. His own preferred type of experience he labels 'numinous'.

4 Exodus 29:44–5; 2 Chronicles 6:1–12; Psalm 68:16; Matthew 18:20; John 20:22–3; Luke 12:11–12.

5 Wilfrid Mellers, *Celestial Music?: Some Masterpieces of European Religious Music* (Woodbridge: Boydell Press, 2002), esp. xi–xv and 307–310.

6 The early empiricists's term had been 'ideas' of sense. It was G.E. Moore who first coined the term 'sense data', though Bertrand Russell was the first to introduce it into print in *Problems of Philosophy* (1912). Although they are often related, claims about sense data and simple perceptions should be treated as conceptually distinct.

7 For a Christian accepting this sort of objection, Brian Davies, *An Introduction to the Philosophy of Religion* (Oxford: Oxford University Press, 1982), 70–76. A related objection can be found in Ben Quash's discussion of my own work in his 'The Density of Divine Address: Liturgy, Drama, and Human Transformation', in *Theology, Aesthetics, and Culture: Responses to the Work of David Brown*, ed. Robert MacSwain and Taylor Worley (Oxford: Oxford University Press, 2012), 241–251; to which I offer a brief reply in 'Response: Experience, Symbol, and Revelation: Continuing the Conversation', in *Theology, Aesthetics, and Culture*, ed. MacSwain and Worley, 271–273.

8   John Ruskin, *Modern Painters* (London: George Allen, 1906), II, 3, v, 45.

9   A point Paul Bloom makes against Plantinga (and Calvin) in his 'Religious Belief as an Evolutionary Accident', in *The Believing Primate: Scientific, Philosophical and Theological Reflections on the Origin of Religion*, ed. Jeffrey Schloss and Michael Murray (Oxford: Oxford University Press, 2009), 118–127.

10 Alston, *Perceiving God*, 49–51, esp. 49.

11 Ibid., 50.

12 Ibid., 51.

13 Nelson Goodman, *Languages of Art*, 2nd ed. (Indianapolis: Hackett, 1976), 248.

14 Martha Nussbaum, *Love's Knowledge: Essays on Philosophy and Literature* (New York: Oxford University, Press, 1990), 281: 'we seem to require no unit shorter than this actual story.'

15 Sabine A. Döring, 'Why be Emotional?', in *The Oxford Handbook of Philosophy of Emotion*, ed. Peter Goldie (Oxford: Oxford University Press, 2010), 283–301.

16 Mark R. Wynn, *Emotional Experience and Religious Understanding: Integrating Perception, Conception and Feeling* (Cambridge: Cambridge University Press, 2005), 83.

17 Ibid., 30–35, esp. 30 and 33n7.

18 Patricia Greenspan, 'Learning Emotions and Ethics', in *The Oxford Handbook of Philosophy of Emotion*, ed. Goldie, 539–559.

19 John Henry Newman, *An Essay in Aid of a Grammar of Assent* (Notre Dame: University of Notre Dame Press, 1979), 100; quoted in Wynn, *Emotional Experience and Religious Understanding*, 18.

20 For further development of this argument, see my 'Interfaith Dialogue through Architecture', *Mediaeval Sophia* 13 (2013), 1–11.

21 R.C. Zaehner, *Mysticism, Sacred and Profane* (Oxford: Oxford University Press, 1957). Given that he discusses Advaita-Vedanta at some length, it is surprising to find that Yandell makes no mention of other forms of unity mysticism that might be seen equally to challenge his 'numinous' account.

22 Influential was Plotinus's claim that awareness of difference between subject and object represented not only division in the divine but also an imperfect focus on the object since even in the human case we are most focused when we are least conscious of what we are doing.

23 With Cupitt, a process that began with *Taking Leave of God* (London: SCM, 1980). With Johnston in *Saving God: Religion after Idolatry* (Princeton: Princeton University Press, 2009): his own preference would probably be to have his position treated as a rather extreme form of critical realism, but so much has gone that antirealism might be a more appropriate term.

24 As e.g. Roger Trigg, 'Theological Realism and Antirealism', in *A Companion to the Philosophy of Religion*, ed. Philip L. Quinn and Charles Taliaferro (Oxford: Blackwell, 1997), 213–220; Roger Trigg, *Rationality and Religion: Does Faith Need Reason?* (Oxford: Blackwell, 1998).

25 Although Hick moved far from orthodox Christianity, his own self-description for his later views is critical realism: e.g. in *An Interpretation of Religion: Human Responses to the Transcendent* (Basingstoke: Macmillan, 1989). My own inclination is to accept this view, though it would be challenged by a strong realist such as Trigg.

26 The transition to antirealism can be seen in works such as *Meaning and the Moral Sciences* (London: Routledge & Kegan Paul, 1978) and *Reason, Truth and History* (Cambridge: Cambridge University Press, 1981). A pluralist but realist position is then found advocated in *Representation and Reality* (Cambridge, MA: MIT Press, 1988) and *Pragmatism: An Open Question* (Oxford: Blackwell, 1995).

27 For Putnam's comments on the Müller-Lyer Illusion (the same length of line with outward facing arrows appears considerably shorter than with inward facing arrows), *The*

Threefold Cord: Mind, Body and World (New York: Columbia University Press, 2000), esp. 159.

28 John McDowell makes a similar claim in *The Engaged Intellect: Philosophical Essays* (Cambridge, MA: Harvard University Press, 2009), 225–256.

29 For one such development, Niek Brunsveld, *The Many Faces of Religious Truth: Developing Hilary Putnam's Programmatic Pluralism into an Alternative for Religious Realism and Antirealism* (University of Utrecht doctorate, 2012). Putnam develops a quite different Wittgensteinian approach to religious issues; for a list of his writings on religion, see Brunsveld, *The Many Faces of Religious Truth*, 192n1.

30 On the colour spectrum, the most notorious examples come from ancient cultures such as the extraordinary range of *purpureus* in Latin. On notions of identity, note Bruno Snell's claim that Homer had a unitary view of neither the human body nor the human soul (Bruno Snell, *The Discovery of the Human Mind* [New York: Dover, 1982], e.g. 19), though the interpretation is challenged by H. Lloyd-Jones in *The Justice of Zeus* (Berkeley: University of California Press, 1971), esp. 9–10. Again, Rom Harré has drawn attention to the way in which Inuit is minimally indexical and so only able to distinguish between Eskimo-here and Eskimo-there: R. Harré, *Personal Being* (Oxford: Blackwell, 1983), 85–89.

31 For some further brief comments on this point, see my *God and Mystery in Words: Experience through Metaphor and Drama* (Oxford: Oxford University Press, 2008), 141–143.

32 'Conditioned' rather than 'determined', for otherwise how could real change be possible? But it is one thing to step beyond the existing assumptions of a particular culture; quite another to extricate oneself from these entirely.

33 For implicit belief in a plurality of gods, e.g. Exodus 18:11; Psalm 82:1; for such kenotic assumptions about the incarnation, see my *Divine Humanity: Kenosis and the Construction of a Christian Theology* (London: SCM; Waco: Baylor University Press, 2011).

34 The Qur'an places the event near Mecca, and identifies the son as Ishmael, the father of the Arab peoples.

35 *Genesis Rabbah* 58:5. Sarah is 127 at the time of her death (Genesis 23:1) and had given birth to Isaac at the age of 90 (Genesis 17:17).

36 Clement, *First Letter to the Corinthians* 31; Irenaeus, *Adversus Haereses* 4.10 (both my translation).

37 These issues are discussed in some detail in my *Tradition and Imagination: Revelation and Change* (Oxford: Oxford University Press, 1999), 237–260, esp. 245–257.

38 In the *Katha Upanishad* Nachiketas offers to substitute himself in place of his father's rather stinting gifts to the gods.

39 See further my essay, 'Human Sacrifice and Two Imaginative Worlds, Aztec and Christian: Finding God in Evil', in *Sacrifice and Modern Thought*, ed. Julia Meszaros and Johannes Zachhuber (Oxford: Oxford University Press, 2013), 180–196.

40 Paul might be a possible starting point, as in Romans 8:15 and Galatians 4:6.

41 Ramanuja offers a personalist approach. Contrast the Advaita-Vedanta or non-dualist, impersonalist approach of Samkara, with 'saguna' or form seen as subordinate to 'nirguna', the 'formless' or 'that which transcends form.'

42 The Qur'an as created was explicitly declared by Caliph al-Ma'mun in 827 but soon challenged by Ahmad ibn Hanbal and by then by Ash'arism more generally. For the history, Michael Iprave, *Trinity and Inter-Faith Dialogue: Plentitude and Plurality* (Bern: Peter Lang, 2003), 216–234. Harry Wolfson suggests the term 'inlibration' to parallel 'incarnation': Harry Austryn Wolfson, *The Philosophy of the Kalam* (Cambridge, MA: Harvard University Press, 1976), 246.

43 Ipgrave, *Trinity and Inter-Faith Dialogue*, 241–256. Part of the argument was that the attributes should not be identified with the divine essence but Al Ghazali's devotional treatise, 'The Ninety-Nine Beautiful Names of God', gave the claim a strong experiential thrust.

44 This chapter was first published by *Religious Studies* 51.4 (2015), 497–512, and is reproduced here with permission of the Editor and its publishers, Cambridge University Press. I am very grateful to a number of pre-publication readers for helpful comments and suggestions, particularly at the universities of Notre Dame and Leeds, among them Robin LePoidevin, Rob MacSwain, Michael Rea, Roger White, Mark Wynn, and Sameer Yadav.

5 Present Revelation and Past 'Problematic' Texts

As its Latin roots imply, the word 'revelation' literally means the 'unveiling' of something otherwise unknown, and so in the context of religion it might apply equally to an experience of God through nature or the arts as through Scripture. In this chapter, however, I want to apply the term solely to the latter, and so face directly one of the major apparent embarrassments that Christians face when reading Scripture, and that is its very uneven quality. For Christians the Bible is of course their indispensable source for knowing about salvation, about the nature of the God who in Christ guides and transforms their lives. Not only that, even the most hostile unbelievers would concede that contained within its pages lie some of the most profound moral teaching and moving stories ever to have been written. Even so, Christians and non-believers alike are also aware of another, darker side. In the past, in order to defend a maximal reading in terms of which all came from God, various alternative strategies were adopted for the problematic passages such as patristic appeals to allegory or in the medieval period the defence from Aquinas of apparently immoral divine behaviour on the grounds that God alone as the source of morality has the right to alter its rules. Even in recent times the latter has been an approach adopted by, among others, Karl Barth and Richard Swinburne.[1]

However, the most characteristic feature of the modern response has been to sever any complete identification of divine revelation with Scripture's actual words. Among theologians this has taken a wide variety of different forms.[2] Meanwhile, philosophers have sought a similar distancing, the most influential in recent years being perhaps Nicholas Wolterstorff's idea of the actual words of the Bible being more like those of an ambassador, someone commissioned or endorsed to speak on God's behalf but not thereby to be identified as a simple siphon.[3] Both Barth and Wolterstorff stand within the Calvinist, Evangelical tradition. Even so, it is only quite recently that there has been a similar trend among conservative Evangelical biblical scholars, especially since the publication of Phyllis Trible's *Texts of Terror* urged the hearing of, and sympathy for, the victims behind biblical texts.[4]

Almost all such discussions, however, seem to me to share a number of serious deficiencies. Quite rightly, the biblical text itself is made subordinate to a relationship with Christ, but unfortunately it is then assumed in the process to be a relatively simple matter to apply some appropriate christological test to determine what in Scripture should be identified as God's word to us today. But, as I shall argue in a moment, there is often no easy direct line from Jesus' words and actions to how a particular passage should be evaluated, or even from the preached Christ of the New Testament as a whole. Equally missing is much serious discussion of why God might have acted thus, in allowing such problematic passages and thus humanity to learn divine truth only very gradually. The most commonly canvassed explanation is that it is simply a function of the fallenness of the human condition.[5] But why should an omnipotent deity allow himself to be constrained by human sin? It was dissatisfaction with that negative explanation that led me in one of my earlier writings to advocate revelation as divine dialogue, God waiting on an adequate human response that fully respects human freedom.[6]

Gradually, however, without ever recanting the model entirely, I did come to the conviction that a much more complex story needs to be told. One obvious issue is how the dialogue model can maintain a value for past stages in the process, including these problematic passages; in other words, how, as in my title, such a past might still mediate present revelation. Another, still more troubling issue is that even the perfect Saviour, Jesus himself, seemed enmeshed in similar concerns. In other words, questions of incarnation and revelation need to be seen as inextricably bound up with one another. From that conclusion further implications were then drawn to which particular exception has been taken by a number of my fellow theologians: among them, my contention that the later Church might legitimately overthrow where the great majority of texts in Scripture seemed to be pointing,[7] as also my suggestion that, while a range of criteria are available, each has to be worked through in the particular case under consideration rather than there being any simple or easy formula such as the commonly quoted instance above of the authority of Christ.[8]

Obviously, this is to depart radically from the simple model of revelation that once dominated Christianity. Even as late as 1893 one can find a pope declaring that every word of Scripture was at the dictation of the Holy Spirit,[9] and that there could be no salvation outside of the Church.[10] Yet, on the positive side it is worth stressing that I am led to the further positions that I advocate here through defence of the divinity of Christ not its undermining, and that to recognize a role from outside Scripture in ascertaining truth can be seen, as I indicated at the beginning of this chapter, as also revelation at work.

The Extent of the Problem

Doubts about the moral adequacy of some passages have of course a very long history. Augustine recommended the allegorizing of the concluding verse of Psalm 137 ('Happy shall he be, that taketh and dasheth thy little ones against the stones'),[11] while Gregory of Nyssa asks of Exodus's account of the killing of the first-born of Egypt: 'How can a concept worthy of God be preserved in the description of what happened if one looked only to the history? The Egyptian acts unjustly and in his place is punished his new born child, who in his infancy cannot discern what is good and what is not. If such a one now pays the penalty of his father's wickedness, where is justice? Where is piety? Where is holiness?'[12] Sadly, though, however useful alternative allegorical readings might sometimes prove in giving a continued use to such passages, they can scarcely of themselves provide a complete answer, since the question remains of why the more obvious literal sense remains the more perspicacious or obvious. So, in short, Augustine's recommendation that we should proceed immediately to allegory when the literal sense causes problems just will not do, nor indeed Swinburne's suggestion that this is 'a very natural interpretation'.[13]

In any case, as Evangelical Christian theologians now also increasingly acknowledge,[14] the difficulties run very much deeper, in that biblical teaching can in fact be blamed to varying degrees for what most of us would now regard as immoral practices. So, for instance, not only is there no unqualified condemnation of slavery anywhere in Scripture, but in the Old Testament harsher treatment is recommended for non-Jewish slaves.[15] So it is simply not true that the modern enslavement of black people, whether in the southern United States or with apartheid in South Africa, was totally without biblical warrant. But rather than slavery, it is attitudes to women and war that are currently seen as the most challenging. In the case of women, the problem is not just the issue of hierarchy. Women's lives are frequently treated as of less value than men's,[16] while contemptuous imagery in the prophets for Israel actually also discloses a real disdain for women.[17]

But equally there is the question of appropriate behaviour in war. In the case of God's endorsement in Deuteronomy (20:16–20) of the sacred *herem* or ban that legitimated the killing of innocent women and children in war, there are at least compensating passages elsewhere in the same book that call for the highest standards of morality. Ironically, a few chapters earlier the Israelites had been commanded: 'Love the stranger, for ye were strangers in the land of Egypt' (10:19). So it is not difficult to postulate that God does indeed speak through the book even if only intermittently. But with the book of Joshua we encounter that earlier voice in its most strident form and over several chapters (6–11), and only fail to notice because we are more naturally attuned to the positive spin that spirituals like 'Joshua at the battle of Jericho' are able to afford. Modern commentators often seek to defend the human author by noting that the work was probably written at the time when there were no more native Canaanites in the land, and so his intention was to provide an analogy for total commitment in circumstances where such physical violence was no longer required.[18] But such a response is scarcely adequate since the analogy still presumes the legitimacy of the conduct indicated by a more literal reading. As James Barr observes, 'the problem is not whether the narratives are fact or fiction, the problem is that, whether fact or fiction, the ritual destruction is commended'.[19] Moreover, there can no doubt that the sentiments expressed in the book were used to authorize other questionable conduct within the canon, and, more worryingly, commonly also in the subsequent history of Christianity. On the former, consider what happens in the book of Esther.[20] On the latter, the examples are legion, Oliver Cromwell's justification of his massacres at Drogheda and Wexford in 1649 being an obvious case in point.[21]

A natural temptation at this point might be to separate canon and revelation and insist, as most twentieth-century theologians have done, that the canon is only a potential medium of revelation, with revelation only occurring when we find ourselves addressed through it in an encounter with the living Christ. But in the first place this is not how the churches in fact treat the canon. Sunday by Sunday we hear passages declared without qualification 'the word of the Lord', a declaration that only survives scrutiny because lectionaries are carefully selected to avoid problematic passages and indeed often edited to stop short where problems begin.[22] More substantially, however, the answer assumes that we have independent access to an adequate christological criterion, whereas any such criterion would need to arise out of the canon itself and as we shall now see, even appeal to the Christ of the New Testament is not without its problems.

The Parallel with the Incarnation

Although this is a simplification, it would not be much of an exaggeration to claim that until the nineteenth century Christianity was dominated by an Apollinarian understanding of the relationship between the two natures in Christ, divine and human. That is to say, the human nature in Christ was seen as providing almost no significant input, with the divine virtually always the source of what was said, even to the extent that the cry of dereliction on the cross was read as Christ speaking representatively on behalf of our sinful human natures rather than the entering of divinity into real suffering and alienation.[23] The rise of biblical criticism gradually challenged all that. While it is true that a small minority of biblical scholars would continue to defend a very high consciousness in Jesus of his own status and significance, most would question the historicity of the speeches in John and use Mark as their primary guide to what Jesus actually thought and said.[24] The fact that this entails that Jesus did not think of himself as divine explains in part why various versions of kenosis became popular from the nineteenth century onwards: the idea, as suggested by Philippians 2, that as part of the incarnation God the Son chose some form of 'self-emptying' or self-limitation, so that he might live fully as one of us, living entirely through a fully human consciousness.[25]

   It is here that the relevance of the incarnation for treatments of revelation becomes apparent. Put positively it suggests that God wanted something more than a perfect and immediate communication of Jesus' status and significance. More important to the divine purposes was complete identification with our humanity in all the contingencies of history, even if this meant a gradual growth in how the disciples and early Church came to understand Christ rather than the traditional account that sees both mother and child at his birth already knowing exactly who he was and why he was on earth: illustrated most clearly in numerous paintings of the Nativity in which Jesus plays with some symbol of the cross while his mother looks sadly on.[26] Applying this kenotic model back to the bible as a whole, it would seem plausible to talk of God likewise accepting the contingencies of history as the canon developed, and so we need not think of any particular book as definitive but rather on its way to a greater Truth. In other words, just as the early church took time to perceive the full significance of Jesus, so we should not be surprised to find various stepping stones along the way in the Old Testament canon: for example, from implicit belief in other gods to monotheism,[27] or again from corporate notions of responsibility to more personal.[28] Not that it need necessarily have been a smooth process of continuous advance. Indeed, there is every reason to think that post-exilic Judaism had in some ways at least a harsher creed than what had gone before, for example on the subject of national identity, as in Ezra's insistence that Jews should divorce their non-Jewish wives.

The downside of such an approach, though, is that any proposed christological criterion for what constitutes truth in biblical revelation will itself clearly come up against similar contingencies in history, that not only was the historical Jesus unaware of his own divinity but also he seems to have endorsed various aspects of contemporary Judaism that do not sit well with what the later or contemporary Church now believes. Thus, for example, despite the many efforts to argue that Jesus did not believe that the world would soon end, this does seem the most natural reading of the evidence.[29] Again, given the response of James and Peter to Paul's Gentile mission, it does look as though Jesus did not foresee such a mission.[30] As a third example, consider the fact that Jesus chose twelve male apostles. The most natural reading is surely to suppose that Jesus shared traditional Jewish views on male hierarchy. Or, finally, to give an intriguing example from an Evangelical scholar, I. Howard Marshall observes of Jesus' treatment of hell that 'we can no longer think of God in this way, even if this is imagery used by Jesus.'[31] So, there are far deeper issues to consider than his attribution of the Psalms to David or the Pentateuch to Moses.[32]

Supporters of the christological criterion could of course respond by arguing that inherent in Jesus' practice or teaching was the position eventually adopted by the later church, as with his comparatively generous treatment of women or Gentiles. That may well be so, but the difficulty is that such a conclusion was unlikely to be reached except through some further stimulus towards change. After all, it would have been entirely possible to continue the way Jesus behaved and stop there, as of course the Church did in fact on women through most of its history, or again through assuming that Jesus' teaching entailed pacifism only in personal relations and so did not abrogate the Old Testament on war. So it is far from clear that a christological criterion can function on its own. Still more problematic is the extreme version of this view that any address by the Spirit or Christ comes as self-validating without any criteria given in advance, a position adopted, for instance, by Alan Torrance.[33] If even Christ had to struggle with the question of what was the right interpretation of God's will, so surely too must we.[34] Indeed, despite Matthew's spiritual interpretation of the name (1:21), it is not inconceivable that Christ had himself to wrestle with the very different conception of his ministry implicit in the Hebrew name that he had been given (Joshua).[35]

Revelation and the Community of Faith

So what I want to pursue now is whether a story of revelation can be told that makes every text of Scripture still worth reading, while at the same time acknowledging that there is development. One feature of traditional accounts that must go if we take how the incarnation happened as our base model is the idea that all that is involved in revelation is God and one human individual interacting. Recent philosophical accounts continue to pursue a variant on that idea, with God commissioning or endorsing the words of some particular individual. But, if even the central revelatory event of the incarnation was culturally conditioned, we may naturally assume the same for the rest of the process; that is, God relating to some individual or individuals within a particular community context, with the context no less essential to understanding the nature of the message. So, while I now believe my earlier model of divine dialogue to have been too rationalistic in its primary stress on respect for human freedom, where those earlier writings were correct was in stressing social context, a dialogue with a developing community and not simply with an individual. The positive side is the immeasurable richness gained for symbols with a history such as 'Lamb of God';[36] the negative side is that some prejudices of the age prove particularly difficult to dislodge.

Equally, though, it is important not to think of the community of those addressed now speaking with a single voice. Indeed, one of the main functions of the prophets and other contributors to the canon was to encourage moves in new directions, even as they built upon existing understandings of the divine nature and will. There is not the space here to develop the point, but undoubtedly one of the great strengths of the canon lies in its diversity, in the way that alternative perspectives are canvassed, as, for example, on more open attitudes to other peoples in Ruth and Jonah as against Nahum and Esther, or again Job's challenge to the certainty elsewhere (e.g. Psalm 37) that merit and reward will necessarily correspond in this life. The Old Testament scholar, Walter Bruggemann, makes very effective use of this fact in some of his writings.[37] While the contrasts may not be as dramatic in the New, there remain significant differences of emphases between the four gospels, as also between the epistles of Paul and the others contained in the canon.

However, even where the communal consensus has moved elsewhere, it is important that those earlier voices are not discarded entirely, which is what allegorical readings are in danger of doing. Much better to hear the literal meaning, as witness to how believers once thought and perhaps sometimes still do. Indeed, there remains the real and important possibility of subversive interpretations: of hearing the voice of the maltreated in the subtext, with a critique thus arising not only of the original perpetrators but also of the contemporary world, including conduct within the Church and ourselves.[38]

Indeed, one might argue that such readings are as desperately needed now as they were in the past. After all, it is as recently as the 1990s that similar conduct to that described in the book of Joshua was perpetrated by two Christian states, Serbia and Croatia. Again, looking at things from the other side, given the almost complete failure of French society to integrate its Muslim population into its central institutions and power structures, the recent violence in Paris was almost certainly borne of alienation,[39] in much the same way as was the book of Joshua's envisaged destruction of everything that seemed to threaten the Jews in the world within which the book came to birth. Equally, texts that assume male hierarchy and female dependency (e.g. Ephesians 5:22–28) need not necessarily now be assumed to have no further meaning in the contemporary world, since children and mentally challenged adults, for example, will remain in such dependency relations, and so such texts may now be heard to speak of the mutuality of respect and care required for them.

In giving this account, I want to differentiate it from any view that God actually planned such texts to work in this way. This is where I think Wolterstorff's notion of the divine authorization of scriptural texts falls short. In respect of the conclusion of Psalm 137, while fully conceding that the gruesome literal meaning was the author's intention, Wolterstorff nonetheless insists on a metaphorical interpretation as what God has authorized through the text.[40] But can quite so simple a model work? Is it not nearer to the truth that even if treated metaphorically, the metaphor is itself embarrassing because of the analogy on which it draws? So to attribute the words as in any sense from God just will not do. Yet this is not to say that either this psalm or its much longer equivalent in Joshua should never have appeared in the canon in the first place for, however much we dislike the acknowledgment, it does reflect one aspect of the history of the community of which we are part, and indeed, as noted above, can continue to speak to the community of faith, in alerting it to the dangers to which the contemporary world, and indeed ourselves, remain subject.

Triggers, Criteria and Objections

The objection most commonly raised against such a developmental account of revelation is that it is in the end reductionist, in assuming endorsement of the wider social norms of the time. But this is very far from being so (unless external influence is seen as in itself reductionist), for whatever issue we take, whether it be war or women or more recent debates about homosexuality, it is still the case that Christianity is able to offer a distinctive perspective, in the type of commitment required. One might note the difference in war, for instance, in Christianity's insistence on protection of the innocent, reconciliation and the avoidance of triumphalism,[41] or again, still more obviously, in sexual relations in the avoidance of casual sex.

Even so, some will undoubtedly take exception to the fact that I am prepared to concede that the primary impetus towards change may sometimes come as a 'trigger' from well beyond the Church. Take, for instance, the equality of the sexes. If we judge by quantity of texts alone, the Bible, it seems to me, is overwhelmingly against such equality, and so no deduction towards that conclusion can be made either from the Bible as a whole or even from the New Testament on its own. Instead, the Church needed to hear new discoveries of what women were capable in order for Christ's own relative freedom in relation to women now to be applied more widely.[42] Sadly it is a point that most conservative biblical scholars still seem unwilling to concede, with the result that the relevant material is presented as though it already bore a clear message for change, and later, largely clerical, obstinacy blamed for preventing such an insight. But even the most quoted text in favour, Galatians 3:28, almost certainly means no such thing, as expositions in both Luther and Calvin well illustrate, where it is taken to mean equality of access to salvation despite difference in nature and corresponding status.[43] Thus in Romans 11 Paul leaves us in no doubt about the continued privileged position in the divine plan for Jews over against Gentiles, just as elsewhere he accepts the privileged legal status of masters over slaves.[44] The attempt to claim that the New Testament writers thought otherwise strikes me as a dangerous form of self-deception, premised on reluctance to concede that the framework of the biblical canon may not always be ultimate.

This is not to deny that the new view can be brought under some relevant overarching New Testament principle such as love requiring what is now seen as an appropriate valuing of women, nor indeed that Galatians 3:28 might not be reinterpreted to perform just such a role. But it is to object to any narrowing account that pretends that reflection need not ever have gone beyond Scripture. Rather, it is precisely because God has spoken through the natural world (in the new estimate of women's potential) that the message of the Bible can now be plausibly reinterpreted in this way.

It is precisely that complex interplay between changing empirical observations in external society and specific existing principles internal to the community that make change within any religion not only difficult but also at times traumatic. One can see the point at work in present disputes over homosexuality. It would be absurd to arbitrate the issue in a short paragraph. But what one can note is the pressures for change from both within and without. Without, there has been the discovery that homosexuality is in general not a chosen condition, while the whole notion of complementarity between the sexes is now under severe empirical attack, not least from feminist critics. Within, the community has (admittedly only relatively recently) widely retreated from the view that the sexual act should always have implicit within it a procreative function.[45] The irony is that in some ways advocates of change are their own worst enemies, since like their opponents many suppose themselves committed to the absolute authority of Scripture and so are tempted to offer what often seem highly implausible interpretations of the condemnatory passages.[46] But in the end it is not those particular passages that matter but how much wider principles are played out. Indeed, with so many of their opponents running against the clear sense of Scripture in prohibiting divorce, it is hard to comprehend why there is not more mutual comprehension about the complexities of the issue. Instead of hypothesizing that Jesus was gay, it would make more sense to reflect why his likely opposition to homosexual practice might not, even for a Christian, be allowed the last word.[47]

Such a reference to the conditioned character of Jesus' thought leads to consideration of another possible objection to this way of thinking of revelation, that it precludes any real originality for Jesus or indeed for the Bible generally. Here, it needs first to be emphasized, I am speaking of cultural conditioning, not determination. The latter would of course make any real development in thought impossible, whereas the former merely stresses how difficult it is to move very radically outside of the deep-seated assumptions of one's age. Even so, Jesus did challenge many of these, as the Sermon on the Mount clearly indicates. But that emphatically does not mean that there were no limitations even for him, such as his choosing all male disciples. In a similar way, no one prior to well on into the twentieth century could have predicted the change of attitude towards homosexuality, while on the horizon there may well be fresh surprises, some of which I will mention in my concluding observations.

One final objection that must be considered is that such a model might well seem to call into question the justice and morality of how God acts since it apparently entails that the divine allowed immoral conduct in its name to continue for centuries without any attempted rectification. Three brief responses may be offered. First, one may observe that even without revelation in one particular direction, human beings quite commonly have acted in a similar way. So, for example, Greece and Rome both opposed homosexuality except in very limited circumstances, and their conduct of war was, if anything, more violent than what was portrayed in the book of Joshua.[48] Secondly, even in the midst of the negative there were also sometimes positive features. So the Bible may have taught the subordination of women in marriage but, as I have already indicated, it did also require care and responsibility for them, and to a higher degree than was common in the ancient world more generally. Again, even the doctrine of hell had its positive side in encouraging a seriousness about ethics that might well not have existed otherwise.[49] But, finally, I come back to the positive value of accepting the conditioned character of human existence, for it means that new perceptions arise when they can be most easily understood not just as arbitrary commands but as injunctions with easily intelligible foundations.

Conclusion and Implications

If the old model for revelation was of a simple divine address, here what I am suggesting is contextual reflection under divine grace, and a more gradual process of discovering the divine will, though without any absolute guarantee of always proceeding in the right direction. It is also a dialogue that allows us to hear not only God's voice but also that of the community listening to God, and so sometimes the divine will manipulated to the community's own selfish purposes even as it believes itself piously motivated. There are two further implications that I want draw from such a model.

First, complex though the account may be, it does at least allow us to take seriously the possibility of God also interacting with other communities of faith, even those beyond the Christian fold, and them perhaps discovering insights that are as yet not as prominent in, or perhaps only incipient within, the Christian tradition. In some earlier writing I explored how Judaism, Christianity, Islam and Hinduism seemed in their traditions of revelation eventually all alike to converge on the supreme value of self-sacrifice, though through different foundational or differently told stories.[50] But it might also sometimes be possible for Christianity to learn from another tradition of revelation: for example, from Islam on the valuing of women in a way that prevents their exploitation as sex objects,[51] or from Hinduism on the status of animals. The point is that, if all revelation proceeds in the context of a conditioned community, then it is possible to envisage different communities preceding at different rates on different issues. This is not to say that such insights cannot be self-generating,[52] but it is to note that such a model encourages listening to one another. Nor need this be seen as abandoning an indispensable role for Christ since, if we follow Origen, Christ as the transcendent Logos could be seen as the primary agent within such developments outside the Christian tradition.

Secondly, there seem obvious liturgical implications. The modern conclusion to public reading in church, 'This is the word of the Lord', clearly assumes too easy an entrance to the appropriate meaning, which is why something like the more challenging, 'Hear the word of the Lord' would seem better, asking us, as it does, to reflect carefully on what we have heard and so sometimes discern God not in the surface meaning but instead hidden in deeper layers. Indeed, as we have seen, prayerful listening may lead to the discovery of the divine will not in the voice of God's official spokesman as the text apparently proclaims but in those who have suffered at that spokesman's hand.[53]

Notes

1 'God who gives life has the right to take it away': Richard Swinburne, *Revelation: From Metaphor to Analogy* (Oxford: Oxford University Press, 1992), 190n43.

2 Five models are identified in Avery Dulles's influential volume, *Models of Revelation* (Dublin: Gill and Macmillan, 1982).

3 Nicholas Wolterstorff, *Divine Discourse: Philosophical Reflections on the Claim that God Speaks* (Cambridge: Cambridge University Press, 1995). For a similar adoptionist model in a theologian, John Webster, *Holy Scripture: A Dogmatic Sketch* (Cambridge: Cambridge University Press, 2003), 27–30.

4 Phyllis Trible, *Texts of Terror: Literary-Feminist Readings of Biblical Narratives* (Philadelphia: Fortress, 1984).

5 For an attempt to draw a direct parallel with conventional approaches to the problem of evil, Kenton L. Sparks, *Sacred Word, Broken Word: Biblical Authority and the Dark Side of Scripture* (Grand Rapids: Eerdmans, 2012), 12–22, esp. 18.

6 David Brown, *The Divine Trinity* (London: Duckworth; La Salle, IL: Open Court, 1985), 69–98.

7 David Brown, *Tradition and Imagination: Revelation and Change* (Oxford: Oxford University Press, 1999), 1, 321.

8 David Brown, *Discipleship and Imagination: Christian Tradition and Truth* (Oxford: Oxford University Press, 2000), 389–405.

9 *Spiritu sancto dictante* was a phrase deployed at the Council of Trent (4th session, 8 April 1546), and repeated in the encyclical *Providentisssimus Deus* of 1893 from Pope Leo XIII.

10 The view encapsulated in Cyprian's famous phrase: *extra ecclesiam nulla salus*.

11 Augustine, *On the Psalms*, Library of Nicene and Post Nicene Fathers VIII (Grand Rapids, MI: Eerdmans, 1957), 631.

12 Gregory of Nyssa, *Life of Moses*, Classics of Western Spirituality (New York: Paulist, 1978), 75.

13 Augustine, *On Christian Doctrine*, 3.10.12; Swinburne, *Revelation*, 189–190.

14 For example, Sparks, *Sacred Word, Broken Word*; and Eric A. Seibert, *The Violence of Scripture: Overcoming the Old Testament's Troubling Legacy* (Minneapolis, MN: Fortress, 2012).

15 Contrast the rules for foreign slaves in Leviticus 25:44–46 with the compassion urged towards Israelites who fall on hard times.

16 Judges 19 seems to imply that it is acceptable to substitute a woman for a man threatened by rape.

17 E.g. Jeremiah 13:22–27; Ezekiel 16:35–42; Nahum 3:5–6.

18 E.g. Douglas S. Earl, *The Joshua Delusion? Rethinking Genocide in the Bible* (Eugene, OR: Cascade, 2010).

19 James Barr, *Biblical Faith and Natural Theology* (Oxford: Clarendon Press, 1993), 209.

20 A two-day orgy, killing Israel's now defenceless enemies, is how the book ends (9:1–16).

21 He appealed to 1 Samuel 15. See Tim Gorringe, 'Political Readings of Scripture', in *Cambridge Companion to Biblical Interpretation*, ed. John Barton (Cambridge: Cambridge University Press, 1998), 67–80, esp. 67.

22 E.g. the lectionary of the Church of England stops the reading of the story of Elijah on Mount Carmel before his slaughter of the priests of Baal: 1 Kings 18:40. Likewise in the following chapter the slaughter that follows 'the still small voice' is omitted (19:17).

23 The position of both Origen and Augustine; for the patristic and later approaches more generally, and in particular for the influence of the Septuagint version of Psalm 22, see Gérard Rossé, *The Cry of Jesus on the Cross* (New York: Paulist Press, 1987), 73–87.

24 Two of the most prominent advocates of a more traditional approach are colleagues at St Andrews, Richard Bauckham and N.T. Wright.

25 For an exploration of the history and a defence, see my *Divine Humanity: Kenosis and the Construction of a Christian Theology* (London: SCM; Waco, TX: Baylor University Press, 2011).

26 For example, his finger pricked by a thorn in Verrocchio (National Gallery, London). For a contemporary, *in utero* example, see Chris Stoffel Overvoorde's 'That Glorious Form', in Christopher R. Brewer, ed., *Art that Tells the Story* (Grand Rapids, MI: Gospel through Shared Experience, 2011), 64–65.

27 Psalm 82, 86, 97; contrast 1 Corinthians 8:4.

28 Contrast Exodus 20:5 or the story of Achan in Joshua 7, esp. 24–6 with Jeremiah 31:29 and Ezekiel 18:2.

29 Mark 9:1 is most naturally interpreted this way: see D.E. Nineham, *Saint Mark* (Harmondsworth: Penguin, 1963), 231–232. Much the same is true of Mark 13:24ff.

30 Galatians 2:11ff. is particularly telling.

31 I. Howard Marshall, *Beyond the Bible: Moving from Scripture to Theology* (Grand Rapids, MI: Baker, 2004), 66–69. For my own more cautious approach, *The Divine Trinity*, 116–119.

32 E.g. Mark 12:35–37; Matthew 19:8.

33 Alan Torrance '*Auditus fidei*: Where and how does God speak? Faith, Reason, and the Question of Criteria', in *Reason and the Reasons of Faith*, ed. Paul J. Griffiths and Reinhard Hütter (New York: T & T Clark, 2005), 27–52, esp. 33–34.

34 As in the Garden of Gethsemane or the Cry of Dereliction on the Cross.

35 I am grateful to Robert MacSwain for this observation.

36 See further my 'God and Symbolic Action', now republished in *Scripture, Metaphysics and Poetry: Austin Farrer's* The Glass of Vision *with Critical Commentary*, ed. Robert MacSwain (Farnham: Ashgate, 2013), 133–148.

37 Walter Bruggemann, *Theology of the Old Testament: Testimony, Dispute, Advocacy* (Philadelphia: Fortress, 2005).

38 Here I agree with the approach adopted by Seibert *The Violence of Scripture*, e.g. 81–87, 98–103.

39 The attacks of 7 January and 13 November 2015.

40 Wolterstorff, *Divine Discourse*, 217.

41 Note, for instance, the very early moves after the Second World War towards reconciliation between the churches in Coventry and Dresden, or the dispute between Mrs Thatcher and Archbishop Runcie over how the end of the Falklands conflict should be celebrated.

42 For a fuller discussion of this issue, see my *Discipleship and Imagination*, 11–31.

43 For Luther and Calvin on Galatians, including quotations and references, my *Discipleship and Imagination*, 14n3. See esp. Romans 11:7, and on slaves e.g. Colossians 3:22.

44 For Gentiles as a wild olive grafted on to more native stock, Romans 11:17.

45 Only with the 1930 Lambeth Conference did Anglicanism begin to move slowly in a different direction: cf. Resolution 15.

46 This is the strategy adopted by Adrian Thatcher in what is otherwise a rather good book: *The Savage Text: The Use and Abuse of the Bible* (Oxford: Wiley-Blackwell, 2008), 15–35. Contrast Robert Song's *Covenant and Calling Towards a Theology of Same-Sex Relationships* (London: SCM, 2014) which argues for change but takes seriously that at times the Bible thinks quite differently. His own view is that change can still be brought under clear biblical principles; my own that, whichever way the Church finally decides, it will need to acknowledge a deep debt to wider revelation in the experience of society as a whole.

47 I find it inconceivable that a first century Jew would have endorsed homosexual practice in whatever form.

48 Homosexuality in Greece was given limited approval when the younger partner was just coming to manhood. Otherwise, the passive role in particular was despised. See further K.J. Dover, *Greek Homosexuality* (Boston: Harvard University Press, 1978).

49 As I argue in *Discipleship and Imagination* 130–136.

50 *Tradition and Imagination*, 237–260 (seen through developments in how the story of the sacrifice of Isaac is presented in the three western monotheistic religions, and in the story of Nachiketas in Hinduism).

51 See e.g. Katherine Bullock, *Rethinking Muslim Women and the Veil: Challenging Historical and Modern Stereotypes* (Herndon, VA: International Institute of Islamic Thought, 2007). Women are freed, she argues, from being defined by sex appeal.

52 For one impressive recent attempt: David Clough, *On Animals Systematic Theology*, vol. 1 (London: T & T Clark, 2012).

53 I am grateful to the two Editors for comments on earlier drafts, and also for further helpful comments from students and staff present at its presentation at the Allen Society at Oriel College in Oxford, 9 February 2015.

6 From Past Meaning to Present Revelation

Evaluating Three Approaches

Sometimes, as with the problematic passages discussed in the previous essay, a relatively simple story can be told of how a maximal reading has duly been replaced by one that gives strong priority to certain passages over others in the Christian interpretation of Scripture. Much change is, however, far more complex than this, under which the text is now seen within the community of faith at least to have a substantially different meaning from what it once had (assuming, that is, the essential correctness of the views of the general guild of biblical scholars). For examples one need look no further that what is commonly said from the pulpit, where Trinity, incarnation and atonement are nearly always assumed to be present in fully developed form whatever the preachers may have learnt at university, and however much they may continue to endorse privately the views of their erstwhile teachers.

My own view is that this gap needs to be faced, and a story told of continuing revelation, with God present in both the original meaning and in how the text is now used. While backward looking reference is still common among both liberals and conservatives, what I want to do in this chapter is examine in turn three rather different strategies towards how the text is now read prevalent in the subject's sub-disciplines, testing their relative strengths and inadequacies. In the case of systematic theologians the most common approach is to view the text either through a christological lens or else more widely through what is sometimes called 'the great tradition', the common assumptions reached by the end of the patristic period. With analytic philosophers of religion the most common strategy might be labelled 'saving appearances', defending a meaning (sometimes historically derived, sometimes not) that allows a maximal amount of text to be seen as revelation. Then, finally, there are the biblical scholars themselves, once exclusively attached to original contextual meanings but now increasingly engaged with histories of reception, but not always very clear about the implications of such research. In the course of my examination, while critiquing all three, I hope also to suggest ways forward. I begin then with the work of the theologians.

Theological Readings of Scripture

What the possibilities are here is perhaps best indicated by considering two major series that have appeared in recent years. One might be described as essentially christological in its approach, and that is the Brazos Theological Commentary on the Bible, with R. R. Reno as general editor.[1] The other is patristic in orientation, and called Ancient Christian Commentary on Scripture, with Thomas C. Oden as overall editor. I shall first briefly consider the two approaches before going on to develop some thoughts of my own.

The basic idea behind the latter series is to make material from the first eight centuries easily available to a wide audience, particularly as a resource for preaching and reflection.[2] Oden himself stresses the present dearth of such knowledge, as well as his desire to reflect 'a consensual tradition': 'not fixating on problematic edges or controversial points but looking for those comments that would be most widely received by the whole church, East and West.'[3] While such an approach could be criticized for ignoring the complexities of history, a defence could easily be mounted on the basis that there was more common ground than difference. More worrying is an apparent reluctance to admit problematic features in the writings of the Fathers such as anti-Semitism or disdain for women,[4] as also the tendency to see the approach as a substitute for the critical method rather than its supplementation. So, significantly, the new Evangelical interest in patristic exegesis is portrayed entirely positively as a work of the Spirit without any caveats expressed about its possible use as a means of circumventing the challenges presented by biblical criticism.[5] Without considerably reducing the amount of patristic material made available, it was probably impossible to bring modern and traditional commentary within the same volume; but it would seem to me the better ideal, as indeed even now very occasionally occurs, as in Johanna Manley's extensive 1995 work on Isaiah, where in each chapter passages from conventional biblical scholars like R.E. Clements follow the patristic extracts.[6] As she observes in her Introduction, the book of Isaiah was itself constantly being rewritten until it reached its canonical shape and indeed has continued to be reinterpreted ever since, as a series of different questions has been addressed to it.[7] In her view we need to hear that range, with everything from an ancient coronation hymn to ourselves as temples of God brought to bear on how we understand a famous verse like Isaiah 7:14.[8] Certainly, that seems to me a more plausible approach than one which assumes God ceased to speak to the community of faith either when the last canonical work was written or else when the innovations of the patristic period came to an end. Not that Ancient Christian Commentary always avoids such issues. Andrew Louth, for instance, in his Introduction to *Genesis 1–11* is careful to underline the difference made by the Fathers's belief that the Septuagint was inspired and that Moses was a prophet.[9] But even so, nowhere does one perceive the range of divine activity proposed by Manley.

Quite different in orientation is the Brazos Theological Commentary, where no time constraints are set and the perspective is primarily christological. Although there are some Roman Catholic contributions (for example, Paul J. Griffiths on Song of Songs or the often entertaining Francesca A. Murphy on 1 Samuel), more typical and more consistently christological would be commentaries like Robert W. Jenson on Ezekiel or Ephraim Radner on Leviticus. Again, while most try to include some reference to the whole sweep of Christian history (or in the case of

David Lyle Jeffrey on Luke to literature and poetry as well), some have a much more modern ring, as with Stanley Hauerwas on Matthew where Barth and Bonhoeffer appear as often as Augustine, as well as contemporary topics like homosexuality and abortion that might seem to have little to do with Matthew's text or at least the history of the exegesis of that text.

Given such variety, it is hard to generalize. But at least two criticisms would seem appropriate. The first is that in general the approach is seen as an alternative to biblical criticism rather than a means of supplementing or enriching it. A conspicuous exception is Griffiths on the Song of Songs, where as much weight is given to human erotic desire (the likely original meaning) as to Christ's love for his Church. Examples of evasion of difficulties in the original, however, are all too common. Taking a case almost at random, with the hermeneutical rule established for 2 Kings 2 that Elijah should be seen as a type of John the Baptist and Elisha as one for Jesus, Elisha's treatment of the children who mock his baldness (bears are summoned to kill them, vs. 23–25) becomes a model for the power of God mediated through his prophets rather than indicative of their human limitations.[10] But, secondly, there is the whole question of what is meant by a christological criterion. Writers tend to assume an almost self-evident application. But even if we assume reference to the transcendent Christ rather than the historical Jesus, an element of wrestling with alternative possibilities is surely required. That is one reason why I find the comments of one future contributor to the series (on Ephesians) so puzzling. John Webster, endorsing Calvin, maintains that 'the human reception of the Word' should be characterized by 'submission, obedience and affection'.[11] But what is surely needed at the very least is an informed obedience, a submission that has first been able to make some sense of how God has led his people to this point. That is why in my own writing I have tried to tell some story of how past revelation (the way the text was first understood) has transmogrified into its present form.

An early attempt to do so on my part was *The Divine Trinity* in which I sought to argue that trajectories from the biblical text could be seen to justify the Nicaean doctrine of the Trinity even if that doctrine was not to be found explicitly anywhere in the New Testament.[12] What I did not say there, though I believe it to be the case, is that such an argument would also justify reading Scripture retrospectively in a trinitarian way. So, for example, the concluding formula at the end of Matthew's Gospel (28:19–20) could now legitimately be given such a sense. Similarly, even though 'Son of God' may well originally have carried no claims to unique divine status and so authorize a translation earlier in the same gospel of the centurion's words at the foot of cross as suggesting no more that 'truly this was *a* son of God', nonetheless it is entirely appropriate for the contemporary church to use the verse with the definite article as an expression of its own faith.[13] So there would be revelatory content both in the initial revelation of such verses and in the way they are commonly used today, revelatory in that both can be seen as disclosing truth about God: in the former, a temporary truth that was on its way to something more profound but also a permanent truth, that God chooses to work through such methods. The imposition of the later grid could of course be treated as a purely human exercise but that I think would be a mistake. God can surely be seen just as much in the culmination of the process by which the early community of faith came to believe in the divinity of Christ as in the intermediate stages through which such notions passed, and which provided the grounds on which such belief was justified (as, for instance, in the claims Jesus made during his life, his resurrection vindication and so on). Indeed, recent increasing scrutiny of the textual tradition of the New Testament has demonstrated that rewritings of the text itself were equally part of that story, with scribes correcting what were seen as earlier inadequacies, as for instance in the addition of 'Son of God' at the beginning of Mark's Gospel.[14] Far from being a 'corruption' of the text, it may be seen in my view as its enhancement. As with the other examples mentioned above, we may speak here of a *principle of retrospective inference*.

A related process can be most usefully explicated by exploring treatments of the nativity where later interpretations have become so deeply imbedded that most practising Christians are unaware that they are not original to how the two key texts of Matthew and Luke were once intended. As the matter is discussed in some detail in a work I wrote fifteen years after *The Divine Trinity*, I will make here some of its key points only very briefly.[15] My namesake, the distinguished Roman Catholic biblical scholar, Raymond Brown, has suggested that the two narratives originally functioned like the prologues to Greek tragedy, that is, in suggesting future rather than present action.[16] Thus in Matthew Joseph is told to call the child Jesus because 'he *will* save his people from their sins' (1:21) while in Luke Mary's song or Magnificat (1:46–55) makes most sense in the light of Christ's death and resurrection. Indeed, such an understanding continued throughout the first millennium, if we are to judge from the iconography of the period, in which the child Jesus is commonly presented as a mini-adult rather than any interest shown in the child as such.[17] But a marked difference is observable in the second millennium, in portrayals of interactions between Mary and the child and of course in the whole tradition of the crib that has been associated with both the Franciscans and the Beguines. Anyway, if anything like this history is true, then that change of attitude towards Jesus as child (as reflected in contemporary Christian beliefs) is not justified by the original narrative as such, but a hitherto unappreciated significance that the doctrine of the incarnation can provide to childhood, which could now be imposed as a grid on these narratives.

That *principle of doctrinal expansion* may also be illustrated by a more complex case, but one which like the application of the incarnation to Jesus' nativity is now a common theme in contemporary preaching on the cross, and that is God's identification with human suffering. In actual fact nowhere can Scripture be seen to make such a move. Not only do Luke and John omit the cry of dereliction, its presence in Mark and Matthew had in their eyes probably most to do with atonement theology, that is to say with the cost involved rather than any perceived desire on the part of God to identify with humanity in suffering more generally. Thus Mark 15:34 should probably be read in the light of 10:45, significantly also retained by Matthew at 20:28. Nor will it do to suggest that the idea is in Hebrews, even though on the surface this might seem so, as with verses such as 4:15: 'we have not a high priest who is unable to sympathize with our weaknesses, but one who in every respect has been tempted as we are, yet without sinning' (RSV). The point is that, as in its nearest parallel (2:18), the focus is on identification in temptation not suffering. Moreover, even where Jesus' suffering is mentioned in this epistle, Jesus is praised as human pioneer made perfect through suffering (2:10) and not as a divine being who sought in suffering to identify his suffering with our own. So it looks as though making such a move is a projection of a once unnoted aspect of the doctrine of the incarnation back onto the scriptural text rather than actually present there even in inchoate form.

Again, to illustrate a different principle, there is good reason to believe that the common modern Christmas narrative of rich kings and poor shepherds has no good foundation in these texts in the sense that the *magoi* of Matthew are clearly astrologers and not kings, while the shepherds seem to be there in Luke to argue for continuity with the house of David as shepherd-king.[18] Even so, it is possible to provide a justification for the new grid by what we might call a *principle of analogical predication*. In the case of Matthew, the astrologers were clearly intended as the pagan equivalent to his repeated mention of the fulfilment of Old Testament prophecies. In other words, the implicit argument is that, just as Jewish longings can be seen to be realized in Christ through these prophecies, so can pagan hopes in their nearest equivalent, in the searching of the stars.[19] It was a dramatic way of asserting the universality of Christ's relevance but less powerful and pertinent once Jewish converts became numerically less significant. So what emerges is a new and more effective way of making the same point analogically, the shepherds now seen primarily as poor and the wise men as kings from the three then-known continents (Europe, Asia and Africa) and themselves of three different ages (young, middle-aged, and old). In other words, through such depictions all are seen to need Christ, a truth surely no less profound than the form it once had taken in the original intentions of the two evangelists. As a matter of fact, of course, a holistic reading of Scripture also played its part in generating this change, with the desire to draw on passages that speak of worshipping kings (like Psalm 72:10–11 and Isaiah 60:3ff.). Even so, it is worth observing that of themselves such passages would scarcely have pointed to such inclusiveness and variety.

In identifying these three principles, I do not pretend to a complete list. To give another almost at random, one way of defending some allegorical readings would be to speak of a *principle of symbolic enrichment*. For example, to read Psalm 23 christologically not only allows development of the image of Christ as the Good Shepherd in John 10 but also him as guide through 'the valley of the shadow of death', a powerfully evocative image retained to this day despite its absence from the original Hebrew.[20] No doubt readers will disagree with this or that illustration or principle. But more important than such details is how the overarching christological criterion has been re-interpreted. Appeal to intuition (A. Torrance) or obedience (Webster) is quite wrong. There is no independent access to the authority of Christ except through careful sifting of how past text relates to present reality.

Philosophical Readings of Scripture

While of course more than one approach is found among philosophers, here I want to focus on the strategy adopted by two of the most influential philosophers in the analytic tradition, Richard Swinburne and Eleonore Stump, both of whom adopt what could be described as a maximizing approach, with the attempt to read every text as directly expressive of the mind of God, even if it also bears other meanings.

One criticism that can no longer be lodged against Swinburne is any complaint that he attempts to bypass the history of biblical interpretation. The first edition of his book *Revelation* (1992) has been substantially rewritten (2007) to take broad cognizance of both current biblical criticism and the history of pre-Reformation exegesis. The result is a serious attempt to make the kinds of link that, in the previous section of this chapter, I said were badly needed between historical original and the Church's later interpretation. Even so, a number of difficulties remain. Swinburne's claim is that under the providence of God in the Christian dispensation 'God ensured that every sentence of the Bible forms part of a unity which is true'.[21] This Swinburne believes can be achieved by resorting to metaphorical or allegorical interpretation wherever the apparent meaning of the text conflicts with where the Christian community eventually established itself. The final verse of Psalm 137 is clearly a worry to him as the passage is discussed twice, though no longer with any claim to a 'natural' alternative interpretation that the first edition had made.[22] However, at the same time Swinburne does accept that an earlier, temporary and fallible revelation did occur in the Old Testament disposition through the medium of the more literal sense, justified on the grounds of the need for the gradual education of the Jews. In his discussion of such texts, many of the conclusions of modern biblical scholarship are accepted, including separate units in Old Testament books from different authors and the relabelling of some books, such as Daniel and Jonah, as non-historical. Equally, while most of the events in the New Testament (including miracles) are interpreted as literally true, occasionally another view is taken as in respect of the speeches in John or the miracle at Bethesda.[23] It is into that context that what he calls 'the original revelation' in Jesus is fitted, with a defence of Jesus' divinity, teaching and resurrection as the basis for the Church's subsequent imposition of particular patterns and assumptions on the biblical text as a whole, Old as well as New.[24]

But even granted the elegance of the interconnections, a number of criticisms can be made of his position. First, there is the problem of the very lowly position accorded to the Hebrew Scriptures. It looks as though he is requiring Christianity to declare that Judaism has nothing of permanent significance to offer to Christianity.[25] But in actual practice reflection through the psalms and on the behaviour of the patriarchs, for example, can continue to instruct Christians even if no explicit reference is made to Christ. Again, the ritual and sacrifices of the Temple were not just seen as typologically relevant through anticipating a better sacrifice,[26] but also as actual guides for the Church (at least in the Catholic tradition) in its own continuing forms of worship. Secondly, apart from the implausibility of some metaphorical readings (which Swinburne himself admits[27]), insisting on such an approach can generate in turn its own problems. For a start, it is hard to see why it should have received divine authorization as a general or universal principle. In the ancient world such readings were seen as attractive because they enveloped divine speech in an aura of mystery, but in our own age we are more likely to ask why a more straightforward process was not adopted of simply jettisoning the embarrassing passages. Instead, we are left with the extraordinary claim that God somehow successfully engineered a text with a quite different literal meaning such that it could now speak 'effectively' in this (metaphorical) way.

Thirdly, the approach seems to assume that the New Testament exhibits none of the problems characteristic of the Old, but this is far from being the case. So, for example, Swinburne praises Paul for his use of typology in respect of Sarah and Hagar but what this ignores is that Paul actually inverts the clear meaning of the original passage, as indeed he does in respect of the verse he quotes from Habakkuk where justification by faithfulness is transformed into the very different notion of justification by faith.[28] My point is not that no rationale can be provided for these moves but that it is not just a matter of linguistic rules.[29] There is a real arbitrariness to the process. Nor does metaphor remove all problems since we find the Book of Revelation using its metaphors to consign the vast majority of humans to eternal suffering, or, to give a rather different example, Augustine using words from the parable of the great supper (*cogite intrare*) to justify the persecution of the Donatists.[30] But equally on matters of morals and doctrine, it is not easy to see how every sentence in the New Testament can be interpreted as true and not in conflict with some other. So, just as in the Old Testament there is disagreement over monarchy, temple and so on, likewise in the New James and Paul cannot be easily reconciled, while the Book of Revelation even implicitly includes Paul among those condemned for temporizing.[31]

Although those sorts of issue are not mentioned, a whole chapter is devoted to arguing that the New Testament already contains the resolution of some of today's most controversial issues. The claim, though, is less interesting than the form of argument. Take the issue of homosexuality. Key biblical texts are expanded to suggest that homosexuality is a 'disability' because not open to complementarity of the sexes and family life.[32] Yet in accepting contraception, Swinburne makes no mention of how the case against homosexuality is correspondingly weakened through the severing of the providential link found in all the major religions between sexual activity and leaving to God the *procreative* decision. Equally, if complementarity is so important, it is odd that Swinburne's opposition to the ordination of women is couched not in those terms (as with Balthasar) but rather with a very modern argument, as a means of severing any connection between leadership and moral worth.[33] My point lies not in the specifics of these arguments but in Swinburne's general approach. Rather than keeping to the reasoning of the first century fresh arguments are deployed, thus suggesting openness after all to alternative directions from where the New Testament seems to point.

In other words, the New Testament is a much looser document that Swinburne would like to believe, often explorative rather than necessarily always providing propositional truth. Certainly, if one looks for a single approach to suffering in the Bible, more often than not one often comes up against alternative and indeed sometimes incompatible responses.[34] It is therefore of particular interest to observe how the matter is dealt with by one of Swinburne's most esteemed colleagues in the philosophy of religion, the American Eleonore Stump, in her massive work, *Walking in Darkness*, where her account of the Book of Job's approach to suffering is a central theme.[35]

The key significance of the work is undoubtedly indicated by its sub-title, 'Narrative and the Problem of Suffering', for, while there is the usual series of careful arguments and distinctions that one has come to expect of philosophers in this tradition, a major departure is in Stump's insistence that not everything of importance can be captured by these means.[36] In particular, in considering the problem of evil, she suggests only focus on specific illuminating narratives will begin to approach anything like a helpful response. I express matters thus because Stump is insistent that she is not engaged in a theodicy or 'solution' to the problem as such but only in canvassing one possible way forward (itself uncharacteristically modest for someone writing in this tradition).

Her suggestion is that suffering is justified where it constitutes a successful means for drawing the person closer to God, in a second-person relationship of union, an approach that she finds present, though underdeveloped, in Aquinas. Her own expansion consists in detailed consideration of several key biblical narratives, including, as well as the Book of Job, the sacrifice of Isaac, the story of Samson, and Jesus' relations with Mary of Bethany. The various writers she sees as all culminating their accounts of different types of suffering in a much closer identification with God than existed at the beginning of the narrative. In then applying her conclusions more widely, she makes two key points. First, she observes that because of human freedom God may well initiate such possibilities without them all necessarily coming to fruition. Secondly, explicit religious belief need not be a prerequisite for success. So, for example, the impact of an autistic child on deepening a mother's love may be described by the mother in terms of the child itself as gift even though ultimately that gift is God's.

The extent of Stump's conversion to the irreducibility of contributions other than formal argument can scarcely be in doubt. Each chapter is now prefaced by a piece of poetry, to mark the change in her perceptions. However, the approach is premised on what often appear to be highly contentious interpretations of Scripture. Again and again, she argues against various biblical commentators that her own account of the narrative is the most appropriate and plausible.[37] This is presumably because she wishes the authority of revelation to provide backing for her own view. But that desire seems to me misplaced since it leads her to distort some of the texts. So, for example, the Book of Job must on her view be concerned to offer an account that finds Job drawing closer to God, not one in which any full solution to the problem of evil is effectively denied.

Yet historical exegesis is overwhelmingly against her, with the book almost always now seen as part of continuing debate about how innocent suffering is to be approached. Thus while the book attacks the idea that suffering always involves a divine judgment on the guilty, subsequent writers engaging with the book challenged the author's own account at a number of different levels, including his own very cursory description of a positive experience of God in the later chapters.[38] This can be contrasted with the later treatment of the same material in the Jewish *Testament of Job* or Pope Gregory the Great's commentary in his *Moralia*,[39] where the authors have already moved closer to a position like that of Stump. So the question becomes whether there is a way of seeing their responses as authoritative in a way that might also help Stump extricate herself from such artificial impositions on the biblical text. Then, we would at least avoid the odd spectacle of her, for example, insisting that the opening dialogue with Satan in the Book of Job is really about God's concern to make possible the flourishing of Satan.[40]

As with my comments on Swinburne, the best way forward would seem to me to recognize that, so far from the Bible always being a closed book, at various points it really does offer an invitation to further exploration. This, though, is far from saying that anything goes. While more open-ended than the specificity of the principle of doctrinal expansion, it is a prayerful searching for what more can be said by utilizing the full resources of what we already know of God. This is precisely what Gregory does in internalizing Job's struggle, as a means of drawing closer to God.[41] Even so, Gregory's impositions need equally to be resisted as impositions. Instead, their value lies precisely in their independent Christian reflection, to be heard only once Job's own distinctive questionings have been given voice, which is surely where most sufferers begin.

Perhaps not surprisingly, it is that same strategy of self-containment that Swinburne and Stump deploy when faced with apparent divine immorality in war as depicted in the Hebrew Scriptures.[42] Of the two, Stump's approach is the more interesting because it so obviously displays the need to go beyond the text, even as she denies that necessity.[43] So in an essay on the total destruction of the Amalekites, in an alleged attempt to remain subordinate to the authority of Scripture she argues for an interpretation of the divine reason for the command that, like her account of God's interest in Satan in the Book of Job, finds no justification in the text itself. After exploring a wide range of options, she declares that the motive was to form a people 'by showing them what will not work to cure them of what needs to be healed in them'.[44] But the actual words of Scripture point in a quite different direction: 'Thus saith the Lord of hosts, I remember that which Amalek did to Israel … Now go and smite Amalek, and utterly destroy all that they have.'[45]

In short, then, my point in respect of the two representative philosophers is that defence of a closed canon is bought at too high a price, by pretending to meanings present in the text that are not there. Instead, a ***principle of prayerful reception*** needs to be acknowledged, one in which the text is respected but allowed to carry believers further, as the rest of their understanding of God and his purposes are brought to bear on its final import.

Biblical Scholars and Reception History

While nineteenth- and early twentieth-century biblical commentaries usually sought both to follow the principles of historical criticism and to offer theological conclusions, increasingly as the twentieth century advanced this became much less common, as biblical scholars adopted for themselves the model of objective historians even where they were also committed believers. Not surprisingly, this has produced a reaction in the most frequent users of such commentaries, the much larger group of practising Christians as distinct from the relatively small academy of scholars and students. One form the revolt took was commentaries specifically directed at a church readership. Among the most impressive of these is *Interpretation: A Bible Commentary for Teaching and Preaching*.[46] But even biblical scholars themselves have begun to see the limitations inherent in the historical method: partly, there was increasing scepticism about how much anything that is truly new could now be learnt through such methods; and partly, because of postmodern challenges to any claim that there is only one single way towards the truth. Accordingly, whereas the standard nineteenth-century textbook on the history of exegesis had bemoaned its barrenness,[47] the pleas of church historians such as Henri de Lubac and David Steinmetz have now begun to fall on fertile soil.[48] An early example was the work of the Swiss biblical scholar Ulrich Luz. Although he is excellent at identifying material, there is not as much consideration of underlying reasons as might have been hoped. So, for example, although the change from wise men to kings is duly noted, no mention is made of the type of factors in changed social conditions that I mentioned earlier in this chapter, and so also no mention of possible underlying justifying reasons.[49]

To assess the impact of reception criticism more generally, or, to give it its German name, *Wirkungsgeschichte*, the best place undoubtedly to look is the Blackwell Bible Commentary series. If the most common fault among philosophers is the assumption of a single valid meaning, as biblical scholars move to less assured territory the opposite fault is the most common that one is likely to detect, and that is a total free-for-all with no attempt made to discriminate between the astonishing variety of accounts given in the subsequent history of the Church. An obvious case in point is Mark Edwards's discussion of John where the complete range of perspectives across the centuries is presented but without any real attempt to engage with any of them.[50]

So for me the more interesting commentaries are those that wrestle with possible meanings for today. One example is the joint work of Paul M. Joyce and Diana Lipton (a male Christian and a female Jew) on Lamentations, in which they opt for the term 'reception exegesis' over reception history 'because it signals that the enterprise involves not merely cataloguing cases of reception but also critical analysis'.[51] In this they see their work as offering something like the Babylonian Talmud where a community of readers across history can share the same reading room as they reflect how the book might be applied across different emerging contexts.[52] In a similar way Judith Kovacs and Christopher Rowland in their commentary on the book of Revelation also seek to address present issues but, in their eagerness to do so, one misses any sense of engagement with the moral limitations of the author.[53] Certainly, such investigations can throw up some real surprises. For example, it turns out that the letter of James was a major source of inspiration for the ex-slave Frederick Douglass in his fight against the institution,[54] while it was Ecclesiastes that produced the most impassioned attack on slavery from any of the Church Fathers.[55] While the phenomenon might be taken to illustrate the multivalent density of much of Scripture, that is its ability to generate a wide range of different meanings, it is possible to detect principles at work in both these cases. Thus with Douglass it was a case of doctrinal expansion, of him linking the injunction to care for the fatherless and widow to others similarly in need of disinterested care, while with Gregory of Nyssa's use of Ecclesiastes one can see anticipated the victims's readings discussed in my previous essay.[56]

A methodology only in its initial stages, it is hard to predict how fruitful it will eventually prove. What can, though, be said is that its success would be greatly advanced if philosophers and theologians actively engaged with the conclusions of such research, in particular posing pertinent questions about the range of factors that generated such change.

Conclusion

In this chapter I have been concerned to take seriously both the original historical setting of biblical texts and how the Church now currently interprets them. In the process, I have argued against any simple christological criterion, in favour of various other ways of bridging that gap, just as I also challenged any universally applied notion of a closed text. All of this has, I hope, provided greater intelligibility to the idea of revelation as a developing tradition in which God continues to speak to the community of faith across the centuries. On such a model I would argue the role of Christ is strengthened, not weakened, as text interacts with triggers from the wider world (itself also a locus of revelation) to discover fresh and relevant ways in which to speak to God's creation.[57]

Notes

1 Published by SCM in the United Kingdom.
2 Ending with John of Damascus in the East and Bede in the West: Thomas C. Oden and Christopher A. Hall, ed., *Mark* (Downers Grove, IL: InterVarsity, 1998), xi.
3 Ibid., xxxi.
4 Oden, 'General Introduction', in Manlio Simonetti, ed., *Matthew 1–13* (Downers Grove, IL: InterVarsity, 2001), xxv–xxvi.
5 Ibid., xix–xx.
6 Johanna Manley, ed., *Isaiah through the Ages* (Menlo Park, CA: Monastery Books, 1995).
7 Ibid., xi.
8 Ibid., xii, 112–121, 130–136.
9 Andrew Louth, ed., *Genesis 1–11* (Downers Grove, IL: InterVarsity, 2001), xl–xlvii.
10 Peter Leithart, *1 & 2 Kings* (London: SCM, 2006), 171–177, esp. 171, 176.
11 John Webster, *Holy Scripture: A Dogmatic Sketch* (Cambridge: Cambridge University Press, 2003), 78.
12 *The Divine Trinity* (London: Duckworth; La Salle, IL: Open Court, 1985).
13 The indefinite article is deployed in the New English Bible (1970) with the alternative of the definite article relegated to a footnote. In the Old Testament the term is used of angels, Adam and the king.

14 Bart D. Ehrman, *The Orthodox Corruption of Scripture* (Oxford: Oxford University Press, 1993), 72ff. David Parker's work is especially helpful in this area. A popular introduction *The Living Text of the Gospels* (Cambridge: Cambridge University Press, 1997) is supported by a number of more learned works, such as *Textual Scholarship and the Making of the New Testament* (Oxford: Oxford University Press, 2012).

15 David Brown, *Tradition and Imagination: Revelation and Change* (Oxford: Oxford University Press, 1999), 72–105.

16 R. E. Brown, *The Birth of the Messiah* (London: Geoffrey Chapman, 1993 ed.), 585–586.

17 Jesus' treatment of children (Mark 10:13–16) might seem a counter-example but in fact all the incident indicates is his interest in their simple trust.

18 Brown, *The Birth of the Messiah*, 420–424.

19 An intriguing aspect of that fact is the concomitant implication that Matthew in effect accepts here a form of natural theology since, to provide a proper parallel, prediction through the stars must be no less true than through Jewish prophecy. To the modern mind accustomed to the nonsense of contemporary astrology that may seem unlikely; but it should be remembered that even as late as the sixteenth century Christian society (and its theologians) continued to assume some sort of connection between the stars and the human condition (e.g. *King Lear*, IV, iii, 34).

20 The original speaks only of a 'dark valley', whereas the Vulgate reads: *in medio umbrae mortis*.

21 Richard Swinburne, *Revelation: From Metaphor to Analogy* 2nd ed. (Oxford: Oxford University Press, 2007), 240. A weaker view where some error is admitted is considered only to be rejected (e.g. 240, 279–280).

22 Ibid., 267, 270–271.

23 Ibid., 140–141.

24 Although admitting that 'the considerable majority of New Testament scholars hold the opposite opinion', he insists that Jesus knew he was divine (146). One appeal he makes is to the ending of Matthew, but since baptism in Acts is in Jesus' name only, this verse is surely more plausibly interpreted as a later development.

25 E.g., Ibid., 263, 280–281.

26 Swinburne's narrow view: Ibid., 258–259.

27 E.g., Ibid., 284–285.

28 Ibid., 259–260 and Galatians 4:22–6; Habakkuk 2:4, quoted in both Romans 1:17 and Galatians 3:11.

29 For my own attempt to reconcile the original Abrahamic tradition with later Christianity, see my *Tradition and Imagination*, 213–237.

30 E.g. Revelation 20:1–10; Luke 14:15–24, with 'compel them to come in' at v. 24; Augustine, *Treatise on the Correction of the Donatists*; *Retractions* II, 5; *Epistles* 48, 50.

31 Revelation 2:14–16; compare 1 Corinthians 6:12ff.

32 Swinburne, *Revelation*, 303–306.

33 Ibid., 319–322.

34 Contrast, for example Psalm 37's unqualified equation of prosperity and merit, and Psalm 73's questioning of the same thesis.

35 Eleonore Stump, *Wandering in Darkness: Narrative and the Problem of Suffering* (Oxford: Oxford University Press, 2010), 177–226. Although this is her main discussion, she repeatedly returns to Job throughout the book.

36 In Stump's stress on narrative, the influence of Martha Nussbaum is apparent.

37 Marvin Pope's Anchor Bible Commentary, 3rd ed. (New York: Doubleday, 1973), she describes using as 'my foil': 184.

38 Job 42:1–6 is most naturally read as Job's submission to mystery rather than any deep experience of union with God.

39 For my own exploration of the history of the book's exegesis, see my *Discipleship and Imagination: Christian Tradition and Truth* (Oxford: Oxford University Press, 2000), 177–225.

40 Stump, *Wandering in Darkness*, 197–199.

41 See my summary in *Discipleship and Imagination*, 208–210.

42 Both essays are in Michael Bergmann, Michael J. Murray and Michael C. Rea, ed., *Divine Evil?: The Moral Character of the God of Abraham* (Oxford: Oxford University Press, 2010).

43 Eleonore Stump, 'The Problem of Evil and the History of Peoples: Think Amalek', in *Divine Evil?*, ed. Bergmann, Murray and Rea, 179–196.

44 Ibid., 194.

45 1 Samuel 15:2–3.

46 Particularly attractive is Samuel Balentine's approach to what most readers would regard as the most difficult book in the Bible: *Leviticus* (Louisville: John Knox Press, 2002) e.g. 27–29 on sacrifice.

47 Frederic W. Farrar, *History of Interpretation* (1886; republished Grand Rapids, MI: Baker Book House, 1961).

48 Henri de Lubac, *Exégèse médiévale: Les quatre sens de l'écriture* (1959–1964; English translation from Eerdmans, 1998 ff.); David Steinmetz, *Taking the Long View: Christian Theology in Historical Perspective* (New York: Oxford University Press, 2010), esp. 3–14.

49 Ulrich Luz, *Matthew 1–7* (Edinburgh: T & T Clark, 1990), 128–141, esp. 139ff.

50 Mark Edwards, *John* (Oxford: Blackwell, 2004).

51 Paul M. Joyce and Diana Lipton, *Lamentations through the Centuries* (Oxford: Wiley-Blackwell, 2013), 18.

52 Ibid., 195.

53 Judith Kovacs and Christopher Rowland, *Revelation* (Oxford: Blackwell, 2004), 11.

54 James 1:27 and 3:17 are frequently quoted in his surviving speeches: David B. Gowler, *James through the Centuries* (Oxford: Wiley-Blackwell, 2014), 140, 224.

55 4th Homily of Gregory of Nyssa on Ecclesiastes 2:7: quoted in Eric S. Christianson, *Ecclesiastes through the Centuries* (Oxford: Wiley-Blackwell, 2012), 158–159.

56 'Solomon's arrogance' in his talk of getting slaves and slave-girls is what sets Gregory off.

57 This chapter was first delivered as an extramural lecture sponsored by the University of Edinburgh and hosted by St John's Episcopal Church, Princes St, on Saturday, 9 May 2015. I am indebted to Stephen Holmes the organiser, and to the very lively questions raised by the participants in the day conference.

Part III

Incarnation, Trinity, and Redemption

Introduction

In terms of the content of Christian doctrine, my published essays (as distinct from books), have almost always been in response to external stimuli, usually an invitation to write something. What I had not realized until deciding the content for this volume with Chris and Rob was that overwhelmingly I had focused on three areas: the Trinity, presumably as a consequence of my 1985 volume *The Divine Trinity* (four essays); St Anselm, the result of an initial decision of mine to write an essay on his view of the atonement (three essays); and heaven (four essays), in this case self-generated, the result of my conviction that contemporary Christianity has lost something important in concentrating so heavily on a resolution at the end of time. So important do I regard that issue that a separate final Part is devoted to the question.

Here, however, in considering the significance of Christ's life, the Trinity, and Anselm did not seem quite adequate by themselves, and so that is why two additional essays are included, to offer a more balanced perspective of my views. The first of these, which opens the Part, consists of a short piece on the incarnation (drawn from a recent book of mine[1]). Two reasons motivated its inclusion here at the beginning of the Part. First, incarnation is epistemologically a more fundamental Christian doctrine than Trinity, inasmuch as it is revelation that draws us into asserting that more complex reality to the divine. But, secondly, how the incarnation has been understood has changed dramatically over the centuries and not least because of changes in our understanding of revelation, itself one of the themes of the previous Part, and so forming a natural transition.

For almost all its history Christianity has operated with a very simple (not to say simplistic) model of how God acted through Christ, with the divine nature entirely directing the human. The result has been that, although Apollinarius (or Apollinaris) of Laodicea was condemned as a heretic at the Council of Constantinople in 381, in effect his views (Apollinarianism) were in fact what triumphed.[2] The danger now is that, as our understanding of revelation becomes more complex, the other extreme is resorted to, and Christ is spoken of as only in some metaphorical sense God (Nestorianism).[3] Kenosis, the self-emptying of God in the incarnation, not only offers an alternative approach but also one that can be seen to fully accord with the nature of Scripture as outlined in earlier essays. God can be seen as consistently addressing humanity through a self-effacing enticement rather than in any sense one of an overwhelming and overweening authority. Indeed, the proposed analysis of revelation and of incarnation can thus be seen as mutually reinforcing one another rather than being in any way in tension.

The particular analogy suggested for the incarnation is new, whereas in the essay that follows on the Trinity, I pursue defence of a model that is sometimes treated as highly contentious, the social analogy of a community of persons. Here my position has been sometimes misunderstood, and indeed sometimes caricatured. If in earlier writings the image was developed in strong opposition to a psychological analogy of a single mind with three faculties of the type found in Augustine,[4] later writings sought to elaborate a more nuanced perspective, and it is one of these that is included here, in which self-consciousness is confined to the Trinity as a whole with consciousness alone being present in the persons as distinct entities.[5] What I was trying to get at in that suggestion was the notion of a social understanding quite different from what customarily prevails in modern western societies.

In effect I had conceded that, pulled out of such careful elaborations, the model could be just as potentially misleading as the psychological analogy. It was an insight that was carried further when I turned my attention to how artists had treated the Trinity.[6] Instead of picking out one particular type of image as the best guide to truth, I urged careful consideration of each in context. 'The tragedy of much of the history of Christian attitudes ... is that simple verbal tests had been mindlessly applied to works of the visual imagination',[7] whereas they can in fact be used to enrich and complement one another. Analogies, whether verbal or visual, do not after all necessarily carry the same implications that their literal counterparts would entail.

It is that same stress on attention to context that runs through my consideration of the doctrine of the atonement here. What had initially attracted me to Anselm was the clarity of his argument in defence of the conviction that atonement theory necessitated the incarnation.[8] However, the more I pursued the details of his claims, the more convinced I became of the inadequacy of his argument as a whole. However, I was equally irritated by theologians who summarily dismissed his approach as though failure in such argument revealed a deeper flaw, in an entirely culture-bound account of what Christ had been trying to achieve. Instead, it seemed to me that a sympathetic reading was required that allowed his wider concerns to come to the forefront of consideration. This I attempted to do in two later articles, one of which is included here.[9]

Such struggles to reflect his position more faithfully had the merit of forcing me to the realization that neither philosophical nor theological analysis can of itself achieve the whole truth. Exclusive philosophical focus on the arguments of *Cur Deus Homo* ignored the subtle theological appeals of the *Meditation on Human Redemption*, while exclusive attention on the latter ignored that Anselm had sought to integrate his theology into wider philosophical concerns. But there was an implicit deeper warning to both philosopher and theologian alike, and that is the need to look more broadly to the New Testament witness as a whole. Sadly, Anselm as both philosopher and theologian exhibits a fault that is common to both disciplines as they seek to approach the question of atonement, and that is the desire for a simple, single answer. Instead, the new essay offered here, 'Images of Atonement: Metaphor and the Dangers of Doctrine', suggests that there is a richness to Scripture that defies both disciplines's attempts to codify the question into a single pat answer. Although less comprehensive than the topic would properly justify, I hope that it demonstrates how analogy and metaphor can enrich and complement one another without always forcing a definitive choice in one direction.

Notes

1 David Brown, *Divine Humanity: Kenosis and the Construction of a Christian Theology* (London: SCM; Waco: Baylor University Press, 2011), originally published in France as *La tradition kénotique: dans la théologie britannique* (Mame-Desclée, 2010).
2 In order to guarantee a single person in Christ, Apollinarius suggested that the Logos took the place of the human mind. Although the cost was admitted to be too high, later theologians acknowledged a human mind without giving it any real freedom of action.
3 Nestorius was condemned at the following ecumenical council, Ephesus in 431. Although he talked of God and Jesus having the same *prosopon*, he played on the ambiguity inherent in the Greek, which can mean both presentation ('face') and ontological personhood.
4 David Brown, *The Divine Trinity* (London: Duckworth; La Salle, IL: Open Court, 1985); David Brown, 'Wittgenstein against the "Wittgensteinians"', *Modern Theology* 2 (1986), 257–276.
5 David Brown, 'Trinitarian Personhood and Individuality', in *Trinity, Incarnation and Atonement: Philosophical and Theological Essays*, ed. Ronald J. Feenstra and Cornelius Plantinga (Notre Dame: University of Notre Dame Press, 1989); included in this volume. More briefly developed in 'Trinity', in *A Companion to the Philosophy of Religion*, ed. Philip L. Quinn and Charles Taliafero (Oxford: Blackwell, 1997), 525–531.
6 David Brown, 'The Trinity in Art', in *The Trinity: An Interdisciplinary Symposium on the Trinity*, ed. Stephen T. Davis, Daniel Kendall and Gerald O'Collins (Oxford: Oxford University Press, 1999), 329–356.
7 Ibid., 351.
8 David Brown, '"Necessary" and "Fitting" Reasons in Christian Theology', in *The Rationality of Religious Belief: Essays in Honour of Basil Mitchel*, ed. William J. Abraham and Steven W. Holtzer (Oxford: Clarendon Press, 1987), 211–230.
9 David Brown, 'Anselm on Atonement', in *The Cambridge Companion to Anselm*, ed. Brian Davies and Brian Leftow (Cambridge: Cambridge University Press, 2004), 279–302. The most recent is 'Anselm, Knowledge and Beauty', in *The Oxford Handbook of the Epistemology of Theology*, ed. William J. Abraham and Frederick D. Aquino (Oxford: Oxford University Press, forthcoming).

7 Incarnational Models Revisited

In effect, from the nineteenth century onwards theological understanding of the incarnation has been subject to what might be seen as little short of a revolution. At least three factors were at work. First, historical research forced on the Church a radically different conception of the nature of Scripture and consequently of how revelation works. No longer seen as an external imposition from without, it was now viewed, like all other thought, as subject to the contingencies of history, and so a gradualism was acknowledged in what was perceived to be true. And incarnation and revelation reinforced one another in that perception, inasmuch as with the almost universal acceptance of the priority of Mark, a gradualism was also detected in both the growth of Jesus' own perception and in how the early Church came to see him, with John's later reflections projected back into that life.[1] Then there was the new interest in psychology, and the recognition that the traditional presentation of Jesus' divine consciousness failed to guarantee an adequate humanity. In effect, the unity of the person had been achieved through denying any significant contribution from the human nature. Finally, thanks largely to Hegel, there was recognition that Christianity need not be bound by the classical, essentially Greek, view of God that had been adopted without question for most of its history. Timelessness and impassibility, for instance, need no longer be seen as attributes that could not be abandoned, even temporarily, without God ceasing to be God.

The result has been changes in approach even among more conservative philosophers and theologians. Gone almost universally, for example, is the conviction found in Aquinas that Christ's human nature was infused with all divine knowledge from conception.[2] But with such an admission has also come increasing strain for the traditional understanding of the two natures model that was inherited from the compromise reached at the Council of Chalcedon in 451. In effect, a looser relationship between the two natures has had to be postulated, and that in turn has made problematic the question of whether there is really one person there in Christ after all. So, for example, in one influential modern philosophical discussion the author talks of 'two minds' while in another it is of 'a divided mind'.[3] Some, of whom Wolfhart Pannenberg is the best known, have gone instead for a single human mind that is retrospectively adopted into the divine identity,[4] while yet others have argued that some kind of category mistake is involved in supposing that divinity could ever be put alongside the human and so both classical and modern formulations are wrong.[5]

In earlier writing I did defend the two natures model, suggesting that we think of the maximum interchange possible between the two identities,[6] while at the same time refusing to be bound by that one particular model, insisting that Chalcedon was essentially concerned to defend the view that Christ was both human and divine: how exactly this was achieved was then seen as an essentially secondary matter.[7] Throughout most of the nineteenth century and well into the twentieth, some sort of kenotic alternative was in fact pursued, under which various degrees of change in the divine nature were accepted. Although in more recent years that approach has become less fashionable, in other ways it would be true to say that the whole notion has come to dominate theology, at least in the sense that such Kenoticism is now almost universally applied to the life of the Trinity itself in the relation between the three persons, with a kenotic incarnation then treated as concomitant of that life.[8] What such a concession leaves unresolved, though, is how best to understand the incarnation as such. So what I would like to do here is examine whether anything new can be said on the matter. My suggestion is that one of the three kenotic models that were canvassed in the nineteenth century can be injected with new life when understood against the backdrop of an analogy drawn from the world of the theatre. But first something needs to be said about the other two models which are still sometimes proposed.

Competing Models for Kenosis

In classical nineteenth-century discussions of kenosis three models vied with one another, two from the German theologians Gottfried Thomasius and Wolgang Friedrich Gess, and the third from the Danish bishop, Hans Lassen Martensen.[9] While over the course of the next century or so all three were to influence British theology, today advocates tend to favour one or other of the first two. As will emerge in due course, my own preference is for Martensen but let me first note the strengths and the limitations of the other two models.

One major consequence of contemporary theology's diffidence before metaphysics is that Thomasius and Gess have largely ceased to be discussed by theologians. Instead, they have become almost exclusively the preserve of philosophers, in particular American writers inspired by the analytic tradition. Although Gess's simple model of God the Son literally becoming a human being found few followers within Britain, it is important to acknowledge that he was not quite as naïve as he has been so often portrayed.[10] His exclusive biblical focus did at least make two things crystal clear: that the incarnate Christ should have a single consciousness and that this should be fully human. It was good to see the requirement stated so baldly, for those were ideas endorsed in all versions of Kenoticism, even including advocates who firmly resisted offering any corresponding metaphysical explanation. Thus, just as John Austin Baker declares that 'when God chooses to exist within the terms of our environment a man is what he becomes', so Hans Urs von Balthasar observes: 'There is nothing whatever in his life … that is not an expression and manifestation of God in the language of created being.'[11] The objection that such a description sounds altogether too mythological to be acceptable met suitable responses in the discussion of Oliver Quick and Vincent Taylor. They observed that such language is in any case unavoidable in theology, and so runs through much of Scripture and the creeds.[12] More serious was the challenge Gess presented to an essentialist view of divine attributes, an issue to which I shall return in a moment when considering Thomasius. But in the meantime we may observe that his acceptance of change in God hardly stands in isolation in the way it once did in his own day. More recently, fresh analogies have been canvassed, among them the notion of an infinite series of progressive self-emptyings.[13] There has also been acceptance of the fact that, in order to make complete sense of the process, a strong social doctrine of the Trinity is required.[14]

Where Gess in fact fell down was not on a conceptual impossibility or the evidence as such. Rather, in his desire to avoid too much complexity he had in effect turned God into something else, not merely a depotentiated divinity but humanity pure and simple. The result was merely a temporary divine gift to the world, since at the Ascension the only option was reversal of the change, and so humanity disappearing as full divinity was once more restored. In my own earlier writing, I had thought the latter issue unimportant.[15] I am now convinced that I was wrong.[16] So the difficulty remains.

Most contemporary American advocates in fact follow Thomasius, and so avoid that particular problem, since on his view, while the divinity of God the Son is reduced to the level of human consciousness, there remains also a purely human element. Stephen Davis, Stephen Evans, and Ronald Feenstra have done the most work in exploring how one might most appropriately speak of the temporary abandonment of attributes customarily deemed essential to divinity. There is no need to rehearse all the details of their philosophical analysis here. Even Richard Swinburne, the best-known English advocate of the more traditional approach to the concept of God, was forced to concede, on the basis of the so-called paradox of the stone, that divine omnipotence must include the ability to limit its own omnipotence.[17] Davis's later formulation (following a suggestion of Morris) seems not too far removed: 'being omnipotent or omniscient-unless-freely-and-temporarily-choosing-to-be-otherwise'.[18] Morris's 'Anselmian' intuitions eventually led him to reject kenotic theories.[19] Yet the question must surely be posed, why philosophical understandings should be supposed necessarily to take precedence over what Scripture appears to reveal. Swinburne's primary grounds for rejection are somewhat different, more on grounds of divine simplicity than of perfection.[20] Yet such a criterion would seem to tell equally against the doctrine of the Trinity. Tertullian is surely wiser when he insists that it would be foolish to rule out a priori even incarnation into an animal, since God's standards are not ours.[21] What we can at least say is that thanks to Thomasius and those who followed him the belief is now all but universal that the need for fresh thinking about the incarnation makes no less imperative new ways of thinking about the nature of divinity itself. The result is virtual unanimity within modern theology in also applying kenosis to the life of the Trinity.

The other main area of difficulty for Thomasius's approach parallels an issue we already noted in respect of Gess. It is usually quoted in the form of William Temple's challenge: 'What was happening to the rest of the universe during the period of our Lord's earthly life?'[22] Re-arrangement of the work of the three persons still tends to be the most common answer.[23] Mackintosh's suggestion, however, seems preferable, that the world is upheld by God, not by a constituent or part of God.[24] Yet even so it is hard to get away from the idea that the proposal amounts to radical disruption in the life of God. Not of course that God would be unwilling to go that far on behalf of humanity, but it does sound too much like an ad hoc solution, an unexpected adjustment to circumstances rather than something that an omniscient being had foreseen from all eternity. Admittedly, much the same objection might be raised against any version of the incarnation that takes the Fall as its starting point, but that is precisely why some theologians have always resisted that particular kind of sequence, and instead insisted that the incarnation would still have occurred, even if there had been no Fall. Among Anglicans B.F. Westcott is a notable example.[25] Rather than desperate ad hoc remedies, what would seem much better is some account that portrays the incarnation as the deliberate culmination of a plan for relating divine and human personality that has been progressing throughout history.

It is not, therefore, surprising that the great majority of British kenoticists went for some version of Martensen, with two parallel strands to the life of God the Son, one permanently part of the heavenly divine life, the other fully kenotic in the incarnation and thereafter: each thus directed to different but overlapping eternal goals in fulfilment of divine life and all human life. In English theology the notion can be traced all the way through from Charles Gore to Brian Hebblethwaite, sometimes with accompanying analogies and sometimes not.[26] For the latter type of theologian, resort to mystery was usually taken as sufficient, while for the former an even more basic appeal is commonly included, as in Forsyth's observation: 'if the infinite God was so constituted that he could not live also as a finite man then he was not infinite'.[27] But to my mind something is missing imaginatively, if some sort of analogy is not forthcoming. So I would like to offer here one of my own, but first it needs to be set within a wider framework.

Divine Projection and Enticement

Given contemporary theological accounts of the nature of the trinitarian reality that is God, the incarnation can now be seen as the culmination of a pattern already inherent in the divine life, of yielding space to the other. The kenotic pattern is then repeated in creation and incarnation, but with each projection significantly different from the other. If I may put it like this, the incarnation lies midway between the projection of another self within the divine life of the Trinity and projection of the world as wholly other in creation. That is because the incarnation is, as with the Trinity, a matter of projection of the divine self, but also, as with creation, this time into the wholly other. Yet, put that starkly, the contrast is surely overdrawn, since even the created order is not 'wholly other'. What the phrase is intended to denote is the absence of any ontological identity in creation. Even so, connections need to be acknowledged since, as Scripture reminds us, humanity was made in the divine image. Again, in respect of the rest of creation, the willingness of Augustine and many others to speak of nature as 'the second book of revelation' pinpoints a key role for a divine self-expression that discloses signs of God's creativity and love.[28] But the nature of that projection must not be misunderstood. What both contemporary science and biblical scholarship indicate is the need for a model closer to enticement than to imposition.

While there continues to be much of value in Augustine's account, the conclusions of modern science were not of course available to him. Where these make a difference is in arguing for a stronger kenotic version of God's relation to the world than would have been thought plausible by previous centuries. It is not that God grants a relatively independent existence to the world qualified by everything still being very firmly set within the pre-determined aims set by an overall, divine plan. The more radical conclusion suggested by the now known complex history of the universe is of a world not closely ordered to a set pattern at all, but with the novel and unexpected now also playing an integral part in the story, as the Holy Spirit works alongside what has been created to allow each thing to realize its own specific potential. Evolution is thus a matter of God allowing things to develop at their own particular pace and potential. So, although there are undoubtedly some ultimate goods in view, we need not think of each and every thing shaped in advance by a specific programme, but rather God enjoying and valuing each stage as it emerges. Now extinct species, therefore, should not be seen as mere instruments on the way towards some higher evolution, but themselves also valued for what they were potentially, and could, and indeed sometimes did, become. Pre-historical 'monsters' thus turn out to be a misnomer. We should not think immediately of the hideous and frightening, as the English word now suggests, but of the term in its original Latin sense – a divine marvel.[29] The Spirit cared for the flourishing of the dinosaur no less than for that of the dog. Indeed, the lesson is already there in the way the Book of Job slides easily between God's delight on the one hand in hippopotamus and crocodile, and on the other in Behemoth and Leviathan.[30]

It is against that wider backdrop that God's relationship with human beings in general, then, should be understood. As I have sought to argue elsewhere, in any such relationship, true love and creativity will be demonstrated not by directive control from above (even where it is for the individual's 'benefit') but in the fostering of innate potential where difference is respected and engagement sought in enticement towards self-understanding and self-motivation. Despite the historical predominance of other models, this has always been one way in which biblical revelation has been understood. Gradualism in the educative process was maintained as a suitable model as early as the Cappadocian Fathers.[31] The rise of historical consciousness, and with it biblical criticism, has now made development and dialogue natural categories with which to approach Scripture. So, for example, it is not just that there happen to be no references to the Trinity in the Old Testament but rather that there could not be. First, Israel had to be brought gradually to an awareness of a single creator God, and only then could a more complex account of that God be given. Similarly, limits to revenge had first to be learnt before a gospel of forgiveness could be preached.[32] Again, it is only with the resurrection that the disciples understood retrospectively who Jesus really was. John's words for Jesus to Mary Magdalene, 'Stop clinging to me, for I am not yet ascended', thus beautifully express the way in which it was only with Christ's departure that his greater reality and availability could become apparent.[33] And so on. Vulnerability is thus inherent to any such dialogue. God dialogues with his people and moves at their pace, and not necessarily the one he himself might wish.

Yet, even today many still find it easier to speak of the Bible as though it were entirely the product of a God determined to communicate directly and not through dependence on fallible human beings. Of course, one root of such inclinations can be difficulties in appreciating an alternative. So it is perhaps not altogether surprising, therefore, that similar models of compulsion have dominated accounts of the incarnation, with Christ's human nature merely passive under the direction of the divine will. However useful the language of nature may be for approaching the philosophical issues, it has done great damage in suggesting quite different static realities set in opposition to one other. The readiness of Sergius Bulgakov and Hans Urs von Balthasar to use alternative language is, therefore, most welcome.[34] Even so, the new terminology will similarly founder unless a way can be articulated of indicating why such parallel activities amount to more than the way divine grace operates in any other human being.

The Analogy of Method Acting

That is why an appropriate analogy is so important. Where the numerous suggestions in earlier forms of modern kenosis failed was, I suggest, in focusing in the wrong place, in what was abandoned rather than in what had been assumed. Of course, the story invariably went on to describe the latter. Even so, the net result was to turn the entire process into a picture of divine wrestling with what seemed the impossible task of trying to get rid of its own inherent identity. However, that need not be so. Consideration of parallels in human creativity may represent a possible way forward. Not that all creativity is of essentially the same kind, as may be seen by contrasting on the one hand creativity in the visual arts and in novel and play writing, and on the other how performers (the actors) customarily exercise the same potential. The difference can be significant. The former, though, seems better suited to describing God's relationship with the created order in general rather than the kind of identity God took in the incarnation. Finely sketched by William Vanstone, I have sought to develop his position in terms of a creativity that involves artists in a genuine valuing of the materials themselves that make such creativity possible.[35] Here, however, we need an analogy that suggests rather more than respect or empathy, in total identification with the human condition. Fortunately, just such an analogy is available in one particular approach to acting that dominated much of the twentieth century in theatre and film. Although it has its limitations, it is upon this approach that I want to draw for a suitable analogy. Known as method acting, it was based on the theories of the Russian theatre director Konstantin Stanislavsky (1863–1938) and taught from 1947 onwards at the Actors's Studio in New York, where Elia Kazan and Lee Strasberg were leading lights.

The basic idea was that realistic portrayal was most likely to be achieved through total absorption in the character's identity: seeing the world through the particular character's eyes such that, while the film or drama is being produced, the actor actually lives the part both on and off stage. While a central directive was that 'what needs to burn is your imagination', also relevant were close observation of others and drawing on what was already known from personal experience.[36] There is no doubt that the method did help produce some of the most memorable screen performances of the twentieth century, including Marlon Brando's roles in *A Streetcar Named Desire* (1951) and *On the Waterfront* (1954), and James Dean's in *East of Eden* (1955).[37] Other powerful exponents included Dustin Hoffman, apparently notoriously difficult to work with because of his absolute determination to think himself completely into the part. When commissioned to play the young Vito Corleone in *The Godfather Part II* (1974), another exponent, Robert De Niro, insisted on spending some time in Sicily to familiarize himself with the local dialect, while for *Raging Bull* (1980), he worked out each day in the gym to parallel the practice of the boxer whom he aimed to represent, and then put on sixty pounds to age for the later events of that same life.[38] Admittedly, the extremes actors sometimes went to in order to identify with their characters perhaps say more about their commitment than any acting success achievable through such bizarre means. For example, Marlon Brando spent several weeks in bed to weaken his legs before playing a handicapped war veteran in *The Men* (1950), while Sean Penn stubbed a cigarette out on his hand to get into the character of a teenage dropout he played in *Fast Times at Ridgemont High* (1982).

Some of these latter examples might suggest exaggerated performances in role, but this was very far from the intention. Performances were often low-key, and sometimes with pauses and hesitations that suggested real struggles to communicate. The aim was, by one means or another, so to infuse one's own self with the thoughts, emotions, and personality of the character that one actually became, at least for the duration of the film, that character. Of course, there has been no shortage of critics. On stage quite the opposite strategy is sometimes advocated. Lack of realism, it is sometimes suggested, can be more effective in encouraging audiences to reflect, precisely because of the dissonance between how the events are portrayed and how they might be envisaged.[39] Again, even as early as Diderot (d. 1784) the appropriate imaginative exercise for the actor was being set in opposition to such deep emotional involvement on the grounds that the latter inevitably distracts both audience and actor.[40] But Stanislavsky believed that real communion with the character was possible. Even details lacking in the script could easily be supplied, so deeply had the character entered the actor's sub-conscious.[41]

It is the nature of all analogy to prove inadequate at some point. That is what makes it a comparative exercise, and not just another example of the same class of thing. So, while some loss of awareness of his own identity is inevitable for the actor, in the divine case there will be no corresponding general loss of awareness, since such occlusion is confined to the incarnation itself. The divine trinitarian life thus remains as intense as it ever was. It is only within the projected divine life of the Son in Christ that new experiences arise through the deliberate merging of the projected divine consciousness with a particular human history. Again, in the case of the incarnation there is the major difference that the identification is with more than a fictitious character: it is with the actual humanity conceived of Mary. Finally, it should be noted that in some accounts of method acting rather too much stress is placed on behaviour and not enough on entering into the other's mental and spiritual identity; so here too the analogy might prove less than adequate.[42] This is not the place to explore all possible objections that might be raised. Some, I suppose, might object to such limited occlusion in the divine consciousness as in principle impossible, but, if so, I quite fail to see why. Human beings can partially achieve such a result, so why not divinity in full? Others might take exception to the merging of two natures into a single consciousness. Here my response would be twofold. There is no reason to think ontological boundaries quite as fixed as this objection implies. Secondly, given the changed modern understanding of the nature of the biblical evidence it is the very rigidity of the traditional two-natures christology that has resulted in the present implausibility of the very idea of incarnation: two natures now so minimally interacting that the notion of there being a single person involved makes no real sense.

So, despite the analogy's obvious limitations, I still find it profoundly illuminating, not least because its starting point is not taken to be the necessity of loss but rather the acquisition of an added dimension through total, absorbed commitment to the other. 'Communion' is such that there is a real merging into a single consciousness, even if its contents are derived, strictly speaking, from two quite different sources and so technically remain 'two'. The divine 'nature' becomes the subject of the specific humanity derived from Mary that also sets it within a specific social and cultural context. Even so, it would be wrong to envisage the divine nature wholly in control, since the point of the identification is to allow every aspect of the human reality to affect its being. What occurs is thus significantly different from empathy. The latter is a matter of trying to enter into another's experience while fully aware that it is not one's own. Usually it is not long before severe limitations are experienced, as with attempts to enter the world of animals, even much-loved pets. Indeed in a well-known article the philosopher Thomas Nagel argued that in some cases the attempt is doomed from the start. So different, for example, is the sonar perception of bats from how human beings perceive the world that the imaginative exercise 'tells me only what it would be like for *me* to behave as a bat behaves. But that is not the question. I want to know what it is like for a *bat* to be a bat.'[43] Here, however, we have something quite different, so focused that the strain of contrast is deliberately excluded, and, of course, Christian doctrine asserts that the projection is not into the wholly other, since human beings have been formed (however conceived) in the divine image.

There is no shortage of reasons why God might wish to accomplish such a projection. Elsewhere I have devoted quite a number of pages to the issue.[44] Suffice it to say here that it is the easiest way of making sense of the images in Paul and John of salvation as incorporation into Christ, but it also allows total identification of God with humanity in actual divine experience of what it is to be human. Even so, some may object that the type of awareness acquired could in God's case be secured by other means. While it is true that omniscience guarantees that God will know all that it is possible to know, this still precludes the type of experiential knowledge that only comes from the inside of an experience, as it were. That is to say, omniscience will still lack any sense of the totality of the experience, since one of its main sources in uncertainty of outcome is inevitably removed, as also any of the accompanying bodily sensations that can sometimes accompany even mental pain.[45] So, to generalise, fully to enter into human experience must involve entry from the inside, as it were, which is precisely where this analogy is so helpful. The image is of an actor getting so beneath the skin of a particular character that it becomes appropriate to talk of total identification. Of course, it remains only an analogy, but even so it shows clear signs of approximating to what a kenotic incarnation would involve: a total commitment to humanity such that every thought and action now takes human form. If I may dare to put it like this, it is not so much God with a human skin as *God under our very skin*.

One further objection that might be raised is that the problematic division between two minds noted in earlier proposals is simply repeated but in a new place, between the kenotic and non-kenotic aspects of the life of God the Son. However, while it is true that differences in consciousness must be maintained if there is to be a real kenosis in such drawing alongside of humanity, it is also possible to identify at least two respects in which such differences will be to a significant degree transcended. First, there will be, if not exactly the same life in both, at the very least an important paralleling of form. Admittedly, earlier kenoticists who spoke of some subliminal awareness of divinity probably pushed the point too far, at least in terms of the available evidence. Yet it was a wise intuition, for, if not exactly the same consciousness as the divine unkenotic aspect of its divine nature, there will be a parallel kind of consciousness, as indeed a number of writers have noted. As Austin Farrer succinctly expressed matters:

> What was expressed in human terms was not bare deity; it was divine sonship. God cannot live an identical godlike life in eternity and in a human story. But the divine Son can make an identical response to his Father, whether in the love of the blessed Trinity or in the fulfilment of an earthly ministry …. Above, the appropriate response is a co-operation in sovereignty and an interchange of eternal joys …. Below, in the incarnate life, the appropriate response is an obedience in inspiration, a waiting for direction, an acceptance of suffering, a rectitude of choice, a resistance to temptation, a willingness to die.[46]

What of course makes all this possible is that, as in method acting, the projection did not proceed like a complete *tabula rasa*, but at times also drew on Christ's subliminal awareness of, if not exactly who he was, at least some inkling of the kind of relationship his non-kenotic self continued to enjoy.

So very much more holds the two sides of the divine nature together than just the intention of the unkenotic divine that this projection should occur, and the eventual full awareness granted to the kenotic aspect of precisely whose underlying life he has been living. There is a parallel form of Trinitarian life experienced both within the life of the Godhead itself and as it might be experienced under the conditions of human existence. Nor is such a pattern uniquely relevant to the Christ of the incarnation since Scripture promises that it will one day be the lot of us all, as Christ comes to live fully in us, with ourselves now part of his own larger body.[47]

But there is also a second feature that needs noting. Precisely because the kenotic divine and the human consciousness interpenetrate one another so deeply, it becomes possible to talk of a mutual flow not only between the two natures in the kenotic Christ but also beyond into the Godhead itself. Thus, the incarnation is not just a matter of the penetration of our own human nature by the divine but also, and uniquely in this case, of the penetration of the divine by human experience as the flow passes beyond the particular temporal and spatial situation. So many others have written movingly of Christ's entry into suffering and estrangement, doubt and uncertainty, that there is no need to repeat such ideas here. But it does need to be stressed that the garnering of human experience would be a daily reality and not just one confined towards the end of Christ's life. As Bulgakov observes:

> The authenticity of the human nature ... demands authenticity of feat, of struggle and temptations, and the God-man's entire earthly life was filled with them. He had to struggle *unceasingly* against the inertia of the infirm flesh ... and against the hostility of the sinful world with its temptations.[48]

So 'the union of the natures in the God-man ... does not signify their serene and harmonious co-existence and interpermeation but the intense and unceasing struggle in which this harmony is accomplished'.[49] In insisting on an element in the temptations that was distinctive to Christ's unique vocation, Forsyth was after all right.[50] Such identification did raise the struggles onto quite a new level. At the same time it is important that these be set within divine acceptance of social conditioning. Increasing awareness of the difficulty of doing the right thing under such circumstances added to the magnitude of the task. Sadly, when it came to considering the extent of the changes necessary to older positions, even Bulgakov's instincts go askew at this point. He makes the astonishing claim that as perfect man Christ must have been without sexual temptation, thereby effectively depriving humanity of divine identification with one of its most basic challenges.[51]

That is why I am unpersuaded by the once common Christian objection against such acting analogies: that acting is in effect a form of deceit, pretending to be what one is not. On the contrary, the fault has more commonly lain within Christian theology itself, with qualifications introduced that effectively prevented any real involvement with the human condition, perhaps not as blatant as in this comment from Bulgakov but no less pernicious. The rhetoric of the sermon thus came to exist in standing contradiction to preachers's more qualified reflections in their study. Indeed, one of great ironies of the history of Christianity is that in the first iconoclastic controversy icons were defended on the grounds that God had in effect painted himself in the incarnation, whereas instead of the static image a better analogy could have come from the world of the theatre, had not the Church already connived at its disappearance.[52]

Equally, in adopting method acting as my analogy, I do not wish to suggest that other approaches to acting might not also be illuminating. Indeed, precisely because it is analogy, there is no reason in principle why insights from different approaches might not be complementary rather than conflicting. I have surveyed some of the main approaches elsewhere.[53] Given that the 'script' was being written as the drama unfolded, in relation to a very specific set of social and historical circumstances, the notion of 'improvisation' that has become quite popular in recent theology can also still find its place.[54] So too can even Brecht's notion of 'disruption' or 'estrange-ment', with not only us now as readers finding the story subverting our expecta-tions but, as the gospels themselves indicate, even at times those of Christ himself, as, for example, his encounter with Peter over his growing sense of his mission may suggest, as also possibly the encounter with the Syro-Phoenician woman in respect of a divine purpose for the Gentiles.[55]

Implications for Human Salvation

Bulgakov rightly speaks of the entire incarnate life as a life of sacrifice: 'it is a sac-rificial offering from the very beginning, the winter grotto in the humble crèche, to the very end, the crucifixion on Golgotha'.[56] That sentiment I heartily endorse, but a false note is introduced when he goes on to equate such a life with 'con-stant suffering'. This is to distort the precise nature of the shock that Christ's life presented, as indeed also the one to which God calls us. 'Sacrifice' literally means something set apart, something made sacred in dedication to God. So, just as there were included in the world's various sacrificial systems, as well as bloody rites, joy-ful offerings of harvest, so Christ's feasting joyfully with sinners must be seen as no less a sacrificial offering to his Father than the way in which his life ended.[57] Any service of another is sacrifice, whenever what is offered at once to God and to the other is placed before self-interest. Nor need such self-giving be always seen or experienced as a burden.

Indeed, the positive character of self-sacrifice is surely precisely where responses to feminist critiques of sacrifice need to focus. The encouragement of passivity in women on the basis of Christ's example in death was of course wrong.[58] But sacrificial service of others should in any case never have been presented as always necessarily a passive, joyless activity. Instead, it will characteristically bring its own positive fulfilment in the joy of seeing others flourish.[59] So it is not just in total identification with humanity in a single being that Christ's life finds its meaning for us. Equally important is the kind of life that he led, not just in the pain of sacrificial self-offering but also in the joy it can bring.

Finally, with exaltation to heaven any uncertainties or occlusions will of course disappear. Not only can there be considerably more interaction between Christ's adopted persona and his divine alter ego, but also a much wider span of action becomes possible in relation to other human beings, both living and departed. Even so, there will not be total absorption, since through the incarnation a quite different and unique history and self-understanding have in effect been created, and so a distinctive human identity will remain. That fact is important as it is precisely that identity which constitutes the medium for drawing the rest of humanity into the same life, an interpenetrated consciousness which continues to be active in this world in all experience of the grace of Christ, as human minds and bodies are gradually conformed to Christ's own pattern of self-offering and so made part of that larger entity that is now the body of Christ. Indeed, precisely because this latter body is more than a single human being, there is a sense in which even the purely human Christ has become more than simply human.

Yet, even as this happens, kenosis does not cease. Christian theology has long expressed the work of the Holy Spirit in kenotic terms: its activity usually unacknowledged and pointing, as it does, to others, in particular to Christ and his Father. Indeed, even the unfortunate convention of using the neuter pronoun helps to underline the degree of such kenosis. What needs also to be accepted, however, is a similar continuing kenotic role for the Son, even as the veil is lifted. Although no longer through total immersion in a human life lived here on earth, there is still a functional kenosis, in the desire to persuade rather than compel. Certainly, biblical revelation, more fully understood than in the past, continually reminds us of a radically different kind of power at work: God as the great enticer, as it were, rather than with power that simply overwhelms in its majesty and awesomeness.[60]

Notes

1 Wrongly so in terms of historical accuracy, but rightly so in terms of Jesus' ultimate significance. I defended that view in *The Divine Trinity* (London: Duckworth; La Salle, IL: Open Court, 1985), 101–158.

2 Aquinas, *Summa Theologiae* 3a. q.7, a.4 responsio; cf. 3a. q.10, a.2 responsio.

3 For the former, Thomas V. Morris, *The Logic of God Incarnate* (Ithaca: Cornell University Press, 1986), 103–107, 149–162, 182–186; for the latter, Richard Swinburne, *The Christian God* (Oxford: Clarendon Press, 1994), 201–211.

4 Wolfhart Pannenberg, *Jesus—God and Man* (London: SCM, 1968). He was anticipated by Isaak Dorner in the nineteenth century. A similar notion in the form of progressive realization is also now found in Sarah Coakley's essay, 'Does Kenosis Rest on a Mistake?', in *Exploring Kenotic Christology*, ed. C. Stephen Evans (Oxford: Oxford University Press, 2006).

5 E.g. Kathyrn Tanner, 'David Brown's *Divine Humanity*', *Scottish Journal of Theology* 68 (2015), 106–113, esp. 112.

6 Brown, *The Divine Trinity*, 245–271.

7 Now defended at rather more length in my *Divine Humanity: Kenosis and the Construction of a Christian Theology* (London: SCM; Waco, TX: Baylor University Press, 2011), 14–25.

8 Discussed in Brown, *Divine Humanity*, 220–242.

9 G. Thomasius, *Beiträge zur kirchlichen Theologie* (1845); H.L. Martensen, *Den Christelige Dogmatik* (1849); W.F. Gess, *Christi Person und Werk* (1856). Discussed in detail in Brown, *Divine Humanity*, 36–75.

10   Accepted by, among others, Mackintosh and Taylor: H.R. Mackintosh, *The Doctrine of the Person of Jesus Christ*, 3rd ed. (Edinburgh: T & T Clark, 1914); Vincent Taylor, *The Person of Christ in New Testament Teaching* (London: MacMillan, 1958).

11   John Austin Baker, *The Foolishness of God* (London: Collins, 1970), 319; Hans Urs von Balthasar, *The Word Made Flesh* (San Francisco: Ignatius, 1989), 21.

12   Oliver C. Quick, *Doctrines of the Creeds* (London: Nisbet, 1938), 136; Taylor, *The Person of Christ*, 266–267.

13   P. Forrest, 'The Incarnation: A Philosophical Case for Kenosis', in *Oxford Readings in Philosophical Theology, vol. 1: Trinity, Incarnation, Atonement*, ed. Michael Rea (Oxford: Oxford University Press, 2009) 225–238, esp. 235.

14   Thomas R. Thompson and Cornelius Plantinga, Jr, 'Trinity and Kenosis', in *Exploring Kenotic Christology: The Self-Emptying of God*, ed. Evans, 165–189. My own approach in Brown, *The Divine Trinity* is supported, 179n18. Earlier in the book Thompson ends his historical survey by explicitly supporting Gess (Thomas R. Thompson, 'Nineteenth-Century Kenotic Christology: The Waxing, Waning, and Weighing of a Quest for a Coherent Orthodoxy', in *Exploring Kenotic Christology*, ed. Evans, 111.

15   Brown, *The Divine Trinity*, 234.

16   For some counter-arguments from a kenoticist, Ronald J. Feenstra, 'Reconsidering Kenotic Christology', in *Trinity, Incarnation, and Atonement: Philosophical and Theological Essays*, ed. Ronald J. Feenstra and Cornelius Plantinga (Notre Dame: University of Notre Dame Press, 1989), 128–152, esp. 144–149.

17   Richard Swinburne, *The Coherence of Theism* (Oxford: Oxford University Press, 1994), 157–158. The paradox concerns whether an omnipotent being has the power to create a stone too heavy for such a being to lift.

18   Stephen T. Davis, *Christian Philosophical Theology* (Oxford: Oxford University Press, 2006), 177. His earlier position can be found in *Logic and the Nature of God* (London: Macmillan, 1983), 118–131.

19   'Anselmian' is Morris's term for reflection on what attributes are necessary to divine perfection.

20   Swinburne, *The Christian God*, 232.

21   *De carne Christi*, 4.

22   William Temple, *Christus Veritas* (London: Macmillan, 1924), 142.

23   C. Stephen Evans, 'The Self-Emptying of Love: Some Thoughts on Kenotic Christology', in *The Incarnation*, ed. Stephen T. Davis, Daniel Kendall and Gerald O'Collins (Oxford: Oxford University Press, 2002), 246–272, esp. 259. Two new analogies for kenosis are offered, in a brain operation and in Platonic forgetting of knowledge acquired in previous lives: 262–263.

24   Mackintosh, *The Doctrine of the Person of Jesus Christ*, 485.

25   B.F. Westcott, 'The Gospel of Creation', in *The Epistles of John* (London: Macmillan, 1883), 273–315.

26   Gore's two key works on this matter are *The Incarnation of the Son of God* (1891) and *Dissertations* (1907), both of which are discussed in my *Divine Humanity*, 133–144. For Hebblethwaite, *The Incarnation* (Cambridge: Cambridge University Press, 1987), esp. 68.

27   P.T. Forsyth, *The Person and Place of Jesus Christ*, 8th ed. (London: Independent Press, 1955), 315.

28   Genesis 1:26; Augustine, *De civitate Dei*, XVI.

29   Though even in the Latin *monstrum* the negative sense of an unwelcome prodigy soon dominated.

30   The writer intended to allude to the latter, but uses the former to shape his description, in the process thereby indicating that all four seem equally valued by God: Job 40:15–41:26.

31   E.g. in Gregory of Nazianzus's *Fifth Theological Oration*: Oration 31, 25. For examples in Judaism and Christianity (from Origen to Lessing), Stephen D. Benin, *The Footprints of*

God: Divine Accommodation in Jewish and Christian Thought* (Albany, NY: SUNY, 1993), esp. 13, 111, 203.

32 It is often forgotten that the (to us harsh) *lex talionis* ('an eye for an eye, a tooth for a tooth') puts an end to the normal pattern of blood feuds, characterized as they are by escalation.

33 John 20:17. The usual Latin translation, *Noli me tangere* ('Touch me not') does not quite capture the force of the Greek.

34 Both use 'nature' terminology but also draw attention to its limitations, and so are found also speaking in terms of parallel activities.

35 W.H.Vanstone, *Love's Endeavour, Love's Expense: The Response of Being to the Love of God* (London: Darton, Longman & Todd, 1977); Brown, *Divine Humanity*, 193–200.

36 Constantin Stanislavski, *An Actor Prepares* (London: Methuen, 1980), for quotation, 43; for close observation of others, 91, for drawing on personal, and sometimes painful, experience, 24. The translator adopts a minority practice in the transliteration of Stanislavksy's name.

37 All directed by Elia Kazan.

38 Other followers of the Method include Montgomery Clift, Julie Harris, Al Pacino, and Rod Steiger.

39 For a helpful survey, including Brecht's notion of *Verfremdung* (estrangement), Daniel Meyer-Dinkgräfe, *Approaches to Acting Past and Present* (London: Continuum, 2001).

40 Denis Diderot, *The Paradox of Acting* (New York: Hill and Wang, 1955).

41 Stanislavski, *An Actor Prepares*, for communion, 193–222; for the subconscious, 281–313.

42 Such accounts reflected the popularity of reductive behaviourism in the United States at that time.

43 Thomas Nagel, 'What is it Like to be a Bat?', in Thomas Nagel, *Mortal Questions* (Cambridge: Cambridge University Press, 1979), 165–180, esp. 169; author's italics.

44 Brown, *Divine Humanity*, 172–219.

45 Surprisingly Stanislavsky seems to have neglected the more physical side until his later years: Vasily Osipovich Toporkov, *Stanislavksy in Rehearsal: The Final Years* (New York: Routledge, 1998), 154.

46 Austin Farrer, 'Incarnation', in *The Brink of Mystery*, ed. Charles Conti (London: SPCK, 1976), 20.

47 Not only in Body of Christ language, but also in Paul's frequent allusion to Christ living in the believer, and the believer living in Christ, for example 2 Corinthians 5:17, Galatians 2:20.

48 Sergius Bulgakov, *Lamb of God*, trans. Boris Jakim (Grand Rapids, MI: Eerdmans, 2008), 295; italics author's own.

49 Ibid., 243.

50 Forsyth, *Person and Place of Jesus Christ*, 52, 301–303.

51 Bulgakov, *Lamb of God*, 299.

52 For such arguments on icons, John of Damascus, *Orations on the Holy Icons*, esp. I.15; II, 5; III, 8; III, 26. Although the stage was banned, liturgy almost unknowingly took on a not dissimilar role.

53 David Brown, *God and Mystery in Words: Experience through Metaphor and Drama* (Oxford: Oxford University Press, 2008), 173–185.

54 For example in Samuel Wells, *Improvisation: The Drama of Christian Ethics* (Grand Rapids, MI: Brazos, 2004); Kevin J. Vanhoozer, *The Drama of Doctrine: A Canonical-Linguistic Approach to Christian Theology* (Louisville: Westminster John Knox Press, 2005). For a detailed study of the approach within the theatre, Anthony Frost and Ralph Yarrow, *Improvisation in Drama*, 2nd ed. (Basingstoke: Palgrave Macmillan, 2007).

55 Mark 7:24–30.

56 Bulgakov, *Lamb of God*, 336–337.

57 Matthew 11:19; Luke 7:34.

58 Though its misuse in application to men, as with Charles de Foucauld, should also not be forgotten: see Fergus Fleming, *The Sword and the Cross: Two Men and an Empire of Sand* (London: Faber and Faber, 2003), e.g. 127, 152.

59 For a more developed response to the attack of Valerie Saiving and others on sacrifice and kenosis, see the article by Ruth Groenhout, 'Kenosis and Feminist Theory', in *Exploring Kenotic Christology*, ed. Evans, 313–321.

60 The above has been largely adapted from my *Divine Humanity*, 250–259, an idea that was first inspired by a request from the German theologian, Benjamin Dahlke, to publish a translation in German. See his 'Der wahre Gott als wahrer Mensch: Zum Aktualität der kenotischen Christologie', *Catholica* 67 (2013), 72–80. The extract reproduced here is by kind permission of the book's publishers, SCM in Britain and Baylor University Press in North America.

8 Trinitarian Personhood and Individuality

The most common objection raised against defenders of the social model for the Trinity like me[1] is that it must inevitably lead to tritheism, given its understanding of Father, Son, and Holy Spirit as three distinct persons. Sometimes the objection is simply that the analogy must necessarily fail, since we know that we ourselves as persons are in no more fundamental sense one entity with other persons, while from those with a better knowledge of history the argument is rather that this is not what was intended by 'person' in the original context of the formulation of the doctrine, and then Augustine is quoted with what is thought to be good effect: 'The answer "three persons" is given, not that something should be said, but so as not to remain wholly silent.'[2] So, for example, we find Barth commenting that 'it is somewhat of a relief to find that a man of Augustine's standing declared openly (*De trin.* V 9, VII 4) that to call the thing "Person" was a matter of *necessitas* or *consuetudo loquendi*',[3] and Rahner too finds it no more than 'a manner of speaking'.

That the term has greatly changed its meaning over the centuries cannot be denied, and so theologians like Barth and Rahner are certainly right that questions of consciousness were not originally in play. But what is worrying is their failure to offer any analysis of what the various relevant terms might mean. Thus Rahner, in the course of three short pages, ranges across 'three individuals', 'several spiritual centers of activity', 'several subjectivities', and 'three consciousnesses', apparently assuming that all must imply tritheism, while Donald Baillie, summarizing Barth, can in the space of a single sentence move between 'the attribute of self-consciousness', 'three distinct centers of consciousness', 'three self-conscious personal beings', and 'tritheism'.[4] In fact, it will be the argument of this chapter that, so far from defenders of the social model being firmly trapped by modern understandings of the person, it is their detractors who are trapped – so singularly have they failed to appreciate that there is more than one way of understanding what it is to be a person, depending on the meaning we attach to these very terms that they use so casually.

To begin, one important question to consider is whether the social model must be taxed with proposing three *individuals* in God. Here Stephen Lukes is helpful in drawing a fascinating contrast between the use of *individualisme* in France and *Individualität* in Germany in the early nineteenth century. For while the former term was apparently coined by conservative thinkers to label Enlightenment notions of the autonomy of the individual which they so despised, in Germany the notion of *Individualität* was being developed in a way which suggested that individual realization was possible only in relation to a social whole.[5] The corresponding terms in English of 'individualism' and 'individuality' have no such precision, but for clarity of exposition I shall assume these meanings, and reserve a third term, 'individuation', for the logical property of being an individual or particular. That said, to ascribe individuation to the Trinity is surely uncontentious, at least for anyone who wishes to subscribe to the orthodox doctrine of the immanent Trinity that there are three distinct elements in the Godhead. For all one is claiming is that there is some way of counting three, even if as with Aquinas's reference to an '*individuum vagum*'[6] one has some uncertainty about how best to characterize these three particulars. Again, equally clearly, individualism cannot be ascribed to God without tritheism because the autonomy concerned would be so strong as to be tantamount to three gods. But individuality is quite a different matter. The question that arises for the social model is therefore whether sense can be made of the logical individual being so related to the social whole that the latter can appropriately be seen as assuming primacy.

In order to answer this question we shall of course have to consider what we should understand by 'person', but, as I shall look at the history of attitudes to its use in some detail, no more need be said at this point, except to note that very different conceptions of the person are going to emerge, depending on whether its use is aligned with individualism or individuality. The same applies to the question of self-consciousness. The word is sometimes used simply to mean awareness of oneself as a distinct entity. Here the sense corresponds to the notion of individuation and though, as we shall see, not all societies seem to generate the concept,[7] it seems sufficiently uncontentious for me to speak simply of 'consciousness' when I have that in mind.

The more problematic aspect of the concept can best be illustrated by again drawing a contrast, this time between English and German usage. In English when we speak of someone as 'self-conscious' we tend to imply that he is at his most reflective, at his most turned-in-upon-himself, often with the added implication of anxiety or embarrassment about how these reflections are being viewed by others. Such stress on self-reflection would seem to connect naturally with notions of autonomy and individualism. By contrast the German *selbstbewusst* indicates a positive sense of one's own worth; and since not only is any essential reference to self-reflection excluded, but also since many German philosophers, including Hegel,[8] have argued that such feelings of self-worth can originate only socially, it would seem not too fanciful to connect this sense of self-consciousness with individuality. With this contrast we are now enabled to express the issue for the social model, as I see it, in another way, namely whether the self-reflective account of the person can be challenged and a more social understanding of self-consciousness put in its place. Of course there are many different ways of an individual relating to a social whole, and some will be more adequate in defending a social analogy than others. In fact, part of my argument will be that there comes a point at which the self is most appropriately identified with the social whole.

But enough has probably been said by way of preliminaries. My argument proceeds by three stages. In the first section I shall argue that, though the ancient view of the person was very different from that dominant in the modern world, so far was this from being a disadvantage to the social model, it made its advocacy in that world entirely natural. If the first stage of my argument involves the concession that self-consciousness was not an issue for the ancient world, my second challenges the essentially modern, post-Cartesian view that such reflectiveness is necessarily a good. Instead I shall argue that its good is essentially derivative on something bad, a disordered society. Finally I shall argue that in any properly ordered society self-consciousness is most appropriately seen as residing in the society as a whole rather than in particular members of it, and so the social analogy should strictly speaking be interpreted as claiming that self-consciousness resides in the Godhead as a whole and only consciousness in the particular persons.

Premodern Concepts of the Person

Clearly, before assessing its implications, we must first ascertain what the ancient view of the person was. The Greek word for person, *prosōpon*, began life with the meaning of 'face', and then came to refer to the mask held up before the face of Greek actors, there being no attempt through the use of make-up or facial expression to represent as in modern plays. These masks seem often to have been exaggerated characterizations or caricatures, and so – perhaps hardly surprisingly – the word then developed into meaning the sort of character portrayed, and from that came the final development: *prosōpon* began to refer to the bearer of that character, the particular individual concerned. All these meanings survive throughout the patristic period, and indeed the ambiguity between 'character' and 'bearer of a character' is essential to understanding the christological heresy of Nestorianism. Nestorius played on the claim that because God and Jesus displayed the same character, they must therefore be the same bearer of that character, an ambiguity which is, of course, not so easy to detect if one is accustomed to using the same word in both cases.[9]

Meanwhile, a similar development was taking place with the Latin word *persona*, though with the difference that the word actually begins its history by meaning a mask, apparently having been borrowed from the Etruscan. However, its most frequent use came to be as bearer of a particular character, and this is how the word came to play a major part in Roman law. For those before the courts were viewed under whichever social role was relevant, for example father, husband, or landowner. Though occasionally it is to be found simply with the meaning 'human being' even as early as the late first century, this incidence is sufficiently rare not to be taken as significant.[10]

Given, then, such an intimate connection in both words between individual personhood and external projection in character, it would not be surprising if we found in general in classical society an understanding of personhood in terms of external relations rather than internal reflection, and that is what we do discover. Indeed if we go back to the time of Homer we find that there is even a dispute among classical scholars as to whether the idea of a mind or unitary self is present at all. Thus Bruno Snell has entitled one of his books *The Discovery of the Mind*. In it he argues that Homer has a unitary view of neither the human body nor the human mind. Instead, Homer concentrates on the distinct role of the different limbs, and models his three mental elements of *thymos*, *psychē*, and *noos* on them, with the result that 'there is in Homer no genuine reflection, no dialogue of the soul with itself'.[11] Instead, external forces in the form of the actions of the gods are seen as the pressures that arbitrate between the conflicting impulses coming from these elements.

But such a denial of consciousness has not gone unchallenged. Thus Hugh Lloyd-Jones in *The Justice of Zeus* argues that if we take seriously the idea of double responsibility, of a god and human at one and the same time being responsible for one and the same action, much of the plausibility of the case collapses.[12] This is obviously not the place to enter into the details of such a dispute. What one can say with confidence is that even once the mind was discovered, whether sooner or later, it was still a mind whose reflection was turned outwards, not inwards.

One must therefore be on guard against misinterpreting apparently introspective claims. Thus an obvious counter-instance would seem to be the Delphic Oracle's famous injunction to 'know yourself'. Certainly, in the later history of philosophy, as in Abelard and Hegel, it was to acquire a very different application. But, so far as the original meaning is concerned, Martin Nilsson identifies an important contrast:

> For us it signifies the need for self-knowledge, for its own time it meant 'know that you are human and nothing more'. That saying is the kernel of the doctrine concerning man's relation to the gods on which Apollo insisted. Mankind is to be conscious of its own impotence and the power of the gods, and submit to them.[13]

As for how such an understanding was applied to the Trinity, particularly enlightening is Irenaeus's talk of the *prosōpa* of the four gospels.[14] For what he clearly has in mind are their individuating characteristics, and in fact this seems to have been the most basic use of the word in this connection. Thus, whether person, hypostasis, or substance was used was initially not regarded as important. Rather, what was regarded as important was that thereby a logical individual was identified with individuating characteristics. So, for example, Tertullian argues that because Father and Son are subjects productive of different speeches, they must therefore be different persons.[15] However, one must be very careful not to read too much into such usage, something that is unfortunately very easily done if one takes the comments of patristic scholars out of context. For example, Grillmeier can write that 'Tertullian had no difficulty in transferring to the Godhead the designation for human individuality',[16] while Wolfson says of both the Latin and Greek term that it had 'by that time already the meaning of "individual"'.[17] But that still leaves the matter ambiguous as among the three senses of individual that I distinguished earlier. From my reading of the texts I conclude that only the logical notion of individuation was initially in play. Nor is it hard to see why *persona* and *prosōpon* should be used to put it in play. The very grounds for drawing the distinction were based on personal features like speech.

But that was by no means the only or most significant meaning that the Fathers attached to the word 'person'. For the history of its usage continued to have effect. That being so, 'person' could not but have suggested, as well as this concept of individuation, the notion of individuality, of the self in social relation. We have already noted the way in which for classical culture self-identity was sought not internally, but externally: to be a person meant to be the bearer of a certain character, a certain external projection. Moreover, the conclusion that one was indeed the bearer of such a character (i.e., of this 'person' and not another) required social confirmation. In such a context to speak of a plurality of persons in the Godhead cannot have been seen as a source of special difficulty, since the very idea of a person would require others in relation to make the notion intelligible to the ancient mind. The reason we fail to appreciate this point immediately is that for us any adequate notion of God must be personal, whereas in classical thought when God is thought of as unique, pre-eminently perhaps in Neoplatonism, personhood is also denied.

Perhaps the most dramatic illustration of the ancient insistence on the impossibility of personhood except in social relation to others comes from Roman law with its famous tag: *Servus non habet personam* (A slave has no personhood).[18] At a stroke, it is estimated, roughly 200,000 human beings, a fifth of the population of imperial Rome, were thereby deprived of personhood, simply in virtue of the fact that they were incapable of entering into social relationships that were in any way distinguishable from their masters's. As a result they existed only as *res* (things), entirely outside the law and totally at the whim of their masters, a position that had originally applied in Roman law also to children under the age of maturity, with fathers having the right to put to death their own children – again on the grounds that there was no distinct social identity in play.

Prosōpon does not appear to have been used in the same way in Greek law, but this should not mislead us into thinking that there are essential differences in attitude in those pre-eminent advocates of the social analogy, the Cappadocian Fathers. One possible source of misunderstanding is our modern tendency to equate character with individual idiosyncrasies: to suppose that this is what distinguishes the three persons of the Trinity is clearly problematic. But it is important to recall that for the ancient world character and role were not as distinct as they are for us, ancient historians and biographers, for example, being more interested in types of character than unique features.[19] A good illustration of difference in attitudes is on the question of portraiture. For even as late as the end of the first Christian millennium one can find a scribe producing a 'portrait' of the new emperor by the simple expedient of writing his name above an engraving of his predecessor![20]

It is against this conception of character as role that the Cappadocian discussion becomes most readily intelligible. For it helps explain their choice of analogies on the one hand and the attention they devote to discussing the trinitarian relations themselves on the other. Thus, just to take two of their analogies, that of the family and an army,[21] a family is not a family without the social relationships of father, mother, and child, while an army is not an army without the chain of command

and the specific roles of each of the combatants mutually reinforcing one another. Again, though undoubtedly part of the rationale of discussing the trinitarian relations is to search for a basis of their unity, to take this as central would be not only to ignore what it meant to be a person in the ancient world but also seriously to distort where in fact they *do* find the real source of the Trinity's unity.

This has been correctly identified by Cornelius Plantinga,[22] among others, and that is in their Platonism, with its priority of the universal over the particular. Gregory of Nyssa can write that 'saying they are "many men" is a customary abuse of language',[23] and it was a Platonic defence of the unity of the Trinity that is to be found even as late as Anselm: 'If someone does not understand how several men are in species but a single man, how can he understand that ... several persons can be one God, yet each a perfect God?'[24] Although such Platonism is no longer an option for us today, it does illustrate how natural the social model would have been for the Cappadocians. For the classical understanding of the person would have demanded plurality of persons within the Godhead, if there were to be persons at all, while Platonism could provide the ultimate rationale of why they must nonetheless be one.

But it is not just the abandonment of Platonism that makes the social analogy more difficult for us today; equally, we must face a different understanding of what it is to be a person. The extent of the difference is well illustrated by the fact that later advocates of the social analogy have had to state explicitly the premise that personhood does not mean individualism. So the poet John Donne, who was a near contemporary of Descartes, has to state that 'no man is an island, entire of itself', just as he has to state that 'God himself would admit a figure of society'.[25] But even in the Middle Ages such an understanding of the person could no longer be assumed. Thus the best-known exponent of the social analogy in that period, Richard of St Victor, has to argue that a person is incomplete unless he has an object of comparable worth to love,[26] while the following quotation from Aquinas may be used to illustrate the way in which 'person' has lost any essential social reference:

> Although angels and souls of the blessed are always with God, nevertheless it would follow that God was alone or solitary if there were not several divine persons. For the company of something of quite a different nature does not end solitude.[27]

No doubt a major influence on Aquinas's changed usage was his adoption of Boethius's definition of a person as an 'individual substance of a rational nature'.[28] But since the causes go deeper than that, I turn now to the second section of my essay, to analyse both how the alternative conception of the person was generated and what is wrong with it.

Modern Concepts of the Person

If the argument of the previous section of this chapter was that the ancient view of the person can be explicated without any reference to self-consciousness and in a way that makes a social analogy for the Trinity a natural outcome, my argument here in considering the development of the modern view of the person is to challenge whether self-consciousness in the sense of self-reflection is quite the ideal it has traditionally been supposed to be.

In considering the origins of modern intellectual views, an obvious starting point, here as elsewhere, would seem to be Descartes. For if one asks in what activities Descartes would have identified the individual human being as at his most personal, there can be no doubt about the response. We are at our most personal when we are at our most self-conscious, at our most self-reflective: *Cogito, ergo sum*. In Descartes's case this of course also went with a dualistic conception of the mind–body relationship and a foundationalist view of knowledge. But even with both jettisoned, it is still possible to be essentially Cartesian in one's view of the person, that is, to think that it is only when we are at our most reflective that we can truly claim to be fully human, fully personal.

What the alternative might be in a post-Cartesian world I shall explore in due course. For the moment note simply how hard it becomes in terms of this model of humanity as self-conscious or self-reflective ego to think of the transcending of that ego into some higher unity as anything more than a mere metaphor, because the ego remains necessarily self-referential. The problem is made even more acute when one observes a further development of this Cartesian position in Kant. For Descartes had at least exempted the moral life from this highly reflective view of thinking, whereas with Kant there is now added a moral philosophy of a will which is only truly rational, truly moral and personal, when it is self-reflective, when it consciously tests its acts by conformity or otherwise to the categorical imperative. In other words, for anyone who takes Descartes or Kant as their guide to what it means to be a person, this must necessarily mean being turned in upon oneself as a reflective being in a way that makes any external relation at most secondary and perhaps even peripheral.

But, remarkably, when one looks for antecedents of this view one finds them, not of course in any advocate of the social analogy but in the writings of St Augustine, the very theologian most responsible for moving the Church in an alternative direction and the one who is in fact the first to call into question the legitimacy of using the term 'person' at all in this context.

Nor am I by any means alone in thinking this. Marcel Mauss, in his famous 1938 essay on the concept of a person, accepts that a social understanding was the first to emerge and notes that even the earliest notion of what it was to acquire a name may well have been in terms of acquiring a social role, some clans apparently even fixing the number of names available to correspond with the numbers required for each social role.[29] Though Mauss attributes some of the impetus towards the subsequent internalization of the concept to Stoicism, he follows Schlossmann in assigning the major role to Christianity,[30] and a recent discussion of Mauss's views by a group of sociologists, philosophers, and historians endorses this suggestion of his. For instance, the historian Momigliano concedes that despite some Greek foreshadowing it is really Augustine who can be credited with the first authentic 'inner-life' biography,[31] while the French scholar Louis Dumont, though stressing the gradual character of the development within Christianity, also detects a decisive role for Augustine in his stress on the will.[32]

If we turn now to the situation today, whether we take major figures in continental or Anglo-Saxon philosophy, it is often thought that they represent a decisive break with the Cartesian past. Certainly this is true in one very obvious sense: in both contemporary traditions one finds challenges to the unity of the self.

Thus within the analytic tradition one thinks immediately of Derek Parfit's major and influential 1984 work, *Reason and Persons*.[33] But he is by no means alone. For example, in a collection of essays on *The Multiple Self* David Pears and Donald Davidson both infer from such phenomena as self-deception the need to admit 'the idea that there can be boundaries between parts of the mind' such that 'the agent cannot survey the whole without erasing the boundaries',[34] and that such 'sub-systems' do 'compromise the unity of the person'.[35] Another contributor urges us to take the Buddhist position seriously and view 'the person as a set of simple elements which has no reality in itself but only in the mind of the observer'.[36] Parfit, though acknowledging overlap between his own account and that of Buddhism, does not wish to go this far. But he does claim that personal identity is a relative notion and that there is only identity insofar as we can perceive a reason in our present consciousness for being interested in the future state of this particular organism – through, for example, a common concern. That is to say, in contrast to the traditional position, which explains unity of consciousness in terms of the ownership of the different experiences by a continuing underlying ego, for Parfit there is no more to personal identity than psychological continuity and connectedness. Accordingly, one is even justified in treating different temporal segments of what has traditionally thought to have been the same person, including oneself, as in fact different persons. For his argument is that no reason can be given in the absence of psychological connectedness for taking any more interest in a temporally remote segment of this body's existence than in the existence of any other, different person. In fact, one may well have more reason to be interested in the fate of some nearer, other person.

Again, numerous French philosophers assert the disappearance of the individual, among them Lévi-Strauss, Foucault, Derrida, and Lacan. The extent of French pessimism on the subject is perhaps best illustrated by the work of Giles Deleuze, who, while accepting Lacan's structuralist position that the individual is no more than the effect of social, anthropological, and psychoanalytic laws, finds little more to recommend in response than a sort of active schizophrenia, which 'deliberately scrambles all codes'.[37] The schizophrenic is seen as alone able to resist the pressures to conform to current social determination of one's identity, though he can do this only by celebrating the 'desiring machines' that make up parts of his identity. That is to say, he has no power to resist the social pressures to conform in such a way as to fashion an overall coherent personal unity of himself. He can only resist the pressure by shattering himself into parts.

Yet, though both these developments are on the surface very different from Cartesianism and combine in rejecting an underlying ego, it does seem to me that the Cartesian heritage has remained fundamental to both traditions. For, whether one takes Deleuze from the continental tradition or Parfit from the analytic, both can be seen as continuing the Cartesian perception of when it is that we are at our most personal, namely, when we are at our most self-conscious and self-reflective. Thus Deleuze insists that it is only when we are self-consciously asserting ourselves over against our society that we are at our most free, while Parfit in his account of personal identity only acknowledges its existence in proportion to our awareness of it. Equally in his ethics, Parfit demonstrates a conception of the ethical, and so too of the personal (in his sense), as maximally reflective. For his proposed revision of ethics is essentially atomistic in its strident utilitarianism; and its insistence on self-reflective acts follows Kant in extending the Cartesian model of humanity to moral theory.

If one then asks why, despite the abandonment of so much in the Cartesian tradition, self-reflection nonetheless continues to be seen as the heart of what it is to be a person, the reason is not hard to find: we are considered as then most characteristically exercising our free will, our personal responsibility. We are thought of as standing back from our intellectual and moral commitments and pondering whether to endorse them or not. In other words, the model depicts disengaged, atomistic reflection. All our intellectual knowledge is required to be reflectively endorsed, as it is built up once more from its foundations, while at the practical level we have essentially a morality of individual acts, whether one takes a Kantian position at the one extreme or utilitarianism at the other. In the Kantian case one is required to reflect on the maxim under which the proposed action seems to fall, in the utilitarian on the consequences that will ensue from the performance of this particular action.

Now contrast this analysis of human morality with pre-Enlightenment attitudes, as they are portrayed, for example, in Alasdair MacIntyre's *After Virtue*.[38] The ambiguity in his title is of course deliberate. He sees us as living in a post-virtue world, in which individual acts are stressed rather than, as in the past, character formation, that is, the acquiring of certain virtues (powers or habits) of behaving in a certain kind of way. But he also intends 'after virtue' to mean *in pursuit of virtue* because it is his wish to advocate a return to virtue-oriented ethics. In this he is not alone. In moral philosophy one thinks of defenders of the naturalist tradition like Elizabeth Anscombe and Philippa Foot, and in Christian ethics one notes not merely continuing interest in this type of approach among Roman Catholic moral theologians, but also a revival of interest within Protestantism, most notably, perhaps, in the writings of Stanley Hauerwas.[39]

Even so, none of these writers properly recognizes that this different view of morality also carries with it a different view of human self-consciousness and thus a different view of the person. For according to the virtues account of morality the truly moral act is not the most self-reflective act, but the least, that is, the one that occurs most spontaneously because it is most deeply rooted in personal disposition. Accordingly, it is not the individual resolve to act charitably in a particular case that is taken as the norm, but the natural or spontaneous outflow of love towards others – the sort of love, for example, that does not need to reflect whether to give money to charity, or whether to jump into a river to save a drowning person, but simply does so.

Now, of course, we would not be prepared to endorse completely an individual's morality, however good the particular acts falling under it, unless he had at some stage engaged in self-reflection and personally endorsed that kind of morality, rather than simply acting out of a habit acquired, for example, in childhood. So my point is not that self-reflection can be entirely eliminated on this model in our present society. Harry Frankfurt, who makes self-reflection definitional of personhood, is therefore right to that extent.[40] But it remains only a very limited extent. For my point is that it is only once such reflection is transcended that we should be prepared to endorse fully that particular person's character and morality. Self-reflection is thus a necessary but merely preliminary and transitional stage to true personhood. Indeed, we can go further than this. For from a dispositional perspective the need to reflect on each occasion of action must seem evidence of an essentially disordered personality, an unwillingness to make the kind of commitments that will generate virtuous habits.

Especially from a Protestant perspective, with its stress on personal decision and notions like justification by faith, it is very easy to suppose that Christianity must necessarily endorse the self-reflective model of personhood. In fact, it largely failed to do so prior to the twelfth century. This can be well illustrated by taking only two issues, penance and atonement, and noting the way in which Abelard can be seen as symptomatic of transformed attitudes. Thus the earlier system of penance was entirely external, operating in terms of the severity of the offense committed, not the degree of guilt involved, and this contrasts markedly with Abelard's stress on intention. Indeed we can make the contrast starker by noting his use of *Scito Te Ipsum* as the actual title of the work which we now more commonly know as his *Ethics*. For here 'know yourself' clearly means something quite different from its Delphic use – no longer knowing one's place in the scheme of things but examining the nature of one's intentions.

Again, Abelard produces a new atonement theory that is sometimes labelled 'subjective' simply because of the close connection it makes with the individual's subjective response. In this it is certainly at a great distance from the earlier dominant *Christus Victor* approach where, as Colin Morris notes, the nature of society was such that 'writers did not discuss the question of how the victory of Christ was relevant to the individual, for it would not have presented itself to them as a problem'.[41] The contrast finds dramatic confirmation in the changed character of crucifixes at this time, with Christ in majesty on the Cross replaced by a suffering Jesus, the earliest example of the latter appearing just before the end of the first millennium in the Gero Cross from Cologne Cathedral.[42] An older world saw Christ's social role as secure, whereas for a society in the process of transformation it was necessary to relate Jesus' life on a personal level to the particular circumstances of the individual, including his identification with that individual's suffering.

Personhood and the Trinity

In the first section of this chapter we discovered how natural a social model for the Trinity was for those who possessed a classical understanding of the person as inherently a social being, even if God, on this model, had to be unified by appeal to a Platonic theory of universals. Now that the immediately preceding section has called into question the modern self-reflective understanding of the person, I want in this final section to suggest possible substitutes for that appeal to Platonism and thus to complete the outline of my defence of a social analogy.

In his review of my book on the Trinity in the *Times*,[43] Nicholas Lash thought that the social model could be parodied and reduced to absurdity by suggesting that I had modelled it on the Oriel College Common Room. Rather than being shamed into silence by the comparison, let me use it here by way of illustration. For in a small, closely integrated Oxford college like Oriel, there are numerous things that a person does without thinking: in these cases social reality is mediated through a person, but not self-consciously. So, for example, a Fellow of Oriel does not generally reflect on or consider whether or not to attend Governing Body, whether or not to give tutorials, whether or not to attend a college feast, whether or not to be present in chapel for the installation of a new fellow, whether or not to take pride in Oriel's success on the river, even whether or not to take an interest in Newman (a former fellow). Of course, it is sometimes right to challenge the values embodied in a particular society, but my former colleagues believed that Oriel still retained a social identity that was fast vanishing in many Oxbridge colleges, and that this was worth retaining. Acts done in the College's name were thus often done consciously, that is with awareness, but not self-consciously, that is not reflectively.

Even if one considers society in general, even a society as pluralist as our own, one still finds many areas of life where we would think it odd that prior reflection be required. Think for example of such basic social gestures as a handshake. In England it is expected less frequently than in France or Germany, and of course in other parts of the world it can be replaced by rubbing noses or even by sticking out one's tongue. But the point is that, once a particular form is established for a society, it would be strange to require that this always be a self-reflective gesture. Rather, simply in virtue of being a member of that society, we produce such gestures naturally, without prior thought. Now this is, of course, a trivial example. But the point can easily be generalized. For any society whose citizens have to reflect, for instance, whether or not to vote, or whether or not to pay their taxes, or even whether to take pride in their nation's achievements, is surely only nominally a society. That is to say, there is something morally corrupt in its individual members or in the social fabric as a whole.

Nor is it hard to see why we must say this: the reason is as old as Plotinus. Several times in his writings Plotinus notes the inverse relationship that normally applies between self-consciousness and commitment to the activity concerned. So, for example, he remarks that 'it would seem that consciousness tends to thwart the activities upon which it is exercised, and that in the degree to which these pass unnoticed they are purer and have more effect'; or again he gives the following examples: 'A reader will often be quite unconscious when he is most intent: in a feat of courage there can be no sense either of the brave action or of the fact that all that is done conforms to the rules of courage.'[44] In other words, what is wrong with the self-reflective model for the person is that it fails to take account of the fact that we are at our most deeply committed when we are at our most absorbed but least reflective. Moreover, it fails to account for the fact that the nature of such commitment is often essentially social – the social being mediated through us rather than we directly reflecting ourselves.

But it may be objected that the examples I have given of the individual mediating the social apply only over a very limited range of cases. This is true, but there is no difficulty in finding cases where the individual's entire life seems to be a mediation of the social. Rom Harré in his book *Personal Being* provides just such an example. In Eskimo culture the language is apparently minimally indexical, with only I and non-I suffixes available (-ik and -tok respectively), but with the 'I' suffix being used not to stress personal identity, but simply location (Eskimo-here, not there). The net result is that 'in Eskimo persons are rendered as qualifications … of substantialised qualities and relations' and they 'do not use a concept of "inner" unity comparable to ours', and the consequence of this linguistic conditioning of perception is 'the extraordinary degree to which Eskimos seem to be influenced by their fellows. When one weeps, they all weep, when one laughs, they all laugh'.[45]

Despite such examples, dissatisfaction may linger, because it is felt that such societies are too primitive to be significant – indeed, that it is precisely self-reflection that makes for civilization. Whether we are entitled to be so easily dismissive of Eskimo society is questionable, since such strong social identity presumably plays a key role in ensuring survival in a harsh climate. Such dismissals aside, it is still possible to point to various ways in which things characteristically valued in modern civilization such as creativity, innovation, and variety may be as much the product of social mediation as of individual self-reflection.

Thus, in respect of creativity, think of the construction of a medieval Gothic cathedral. Architect, builder, and workers have all helped to produce this great work of art, but there is no need to think of any of them making their contributions self-consciously or of there being any process whereby they came to an agreement on principles. For Gothic architecture was produced within a tradition shared by architect, builder, and workers alike, a tradition expressed, for instance, in the skeletal structure of the building and the use of light. Thus, insofar as Gothic architectural expression is self-conscious, it lies in its participants' social identity as a whole, namely in their sense of this tradition being formed in self-conscious opposition to the earlier Romanesque style.

I mention these points to dispel any lingering impressions that 'transcendent' societies must necessarily be inferior to ones constituted by self-reflective individuals, not because I think any of these characterizations must apply in the case of God. For in that case we are postulating a perfect society, and that must make a difference. In *Self-Consciousness and Self-Determination*, the German analytic philosopher, Ernst Tugendhat, has done much to try to marry the tradition of the self-reflective person with the fact that we are social beings, particularly thanks to the influence of Wittgenstein and Mead. But in the savage critique of Hegel with which his book ends, even Tugendhat fails to take seriously the difference that a perfect society might make. For even allowing that Hegel is discussing a wholly 'rational' state, Tugendhat still refuses to concede that this would reduce in any way the requirement on us for self-reflection.[46] But that seems to be precisely Hegel's point, namely, that in such a society the social self would be so mediated through the individual self that conflict would be impossible: the relation between the two selves would be closer even than trust, without any need for reflection before choosing.[47]

No such earthly society seems to me possible. Political philosophers have no doubt been wiser to draw instead on Hegel's more famous remarks about self-consciousness being forged through conflict.[48] But that does not lessen the applicability of Hegel's other remarks to God conceived of as perfect divine society. For Hegel's line of thought suggests that we place self-consciousness in the divine society as a whole and only consciousness in the three persons, that is, awareness of themselves as logically distinct individuals.

The explanation for this is that neither of the two most obvious reasons for identifying a continuing element of self-reflection in any conceivable human society can be made to apply in the case of God. For clearly, in the first place, none of the three persons can have reason to doubt the essential rightness of the social consciousness being mediated through them. So certainly it cannot be right to call them three centres of self-consciousness. But equally absent is the second obvious reason for speaking of self-consciousness in our own case, the fact of our finite abilities and capacities producing particularized commitments to friends, families, and so forth. For clearly in God's case one divine person has no reason to distinguish himself from another in terms, say, of having a dispositional commitment to Bloggs and not me. For all are equally committed to each other's actions.

To this it may be objected that we must surely at least say that the second person of the Trinity was self-conscious of himself as incarnate. But it seems to me that the matter can be better put by saying that he is conscious of the fact that one of the persons became incarnate and that that person was himself. But because self-consciousness belongs to the Trinity as a whole, that act is not thereby ascribed a significance that sets him over against the other two persons, as though they were somehow less committed to the act of incarnation.

Prestige ends *God in Patristic Thought* with the comment that Greek theology can be encapsulated 'in the formula that in God there are three divine organs of God-consciousness, but one centre of divine self-consciousness. As seen and thought, he is three, as seeing and thinking, he is one.'[49] Despite similarities of language, my position is very different from Prestige's. He exhibits little sympathy for the social analogy and his starting point is always the unity of God, whereas for me the richness of the Christian concept of God lies precisely in its notion of personhood transcended. That too is why it seems to me vitally important to retain the idea of the persons as centres of consciousness. For only if an individual is aware of himself as an agent, as the distinct cause of a particular action, does it make sense to speak of him as a person at all. So on the one hand we need consciousness to affirm personhood of the three individuals, while self-consciousness as something social is equally needed to explain how such individuality is transcended in the affirmation of one God, a transcending to which we are also called as we are shaped after the pattern of Christ.

Though I have not explored the issue here, one reason for being tempted towards such a social analogy is the way in which it can help to make much better sense of the Bible's concentration on social images – the community of Israel in the Old Testament and metaphors like the Body of Christ and the vine and its branches in the New. However remotely, the intention was for our social relationships to be modelled after the pattern of the divine reality. But rather than embark on such a substantial new question now, let me end by attempting to counter what are perhaps the two most obvious means of resistance to my account.[50] For the claim might be made either that the persons of the Trinity without self-consciousness are no persons at all or that the Godhead as a whole so obviously becomes a person on my account that I am left with a quarternity instead of a Trinity.

On the first point let me confess at once a failing in the chapter. For I have not yet defined what I mean by self-consciousness. Instead I have sought to characterize it, partly through distinction from consciousness, which I defined as 'awareness of oneself as a distinct entity', and partly through a historical investigation of the various ways in which self-consciousness has come to be linked with a certain form of self-reflectiveness. The reason why in this case as with 'person' I offered no definition was that it was precisely the contention of this chapter that the meaning of terms like 'person', 'self-consciousness', and 'reflection' must vary depending on the sort of society that is being envisaged. But note that we would normally[51] regard consciousness as I have defined it as sufficient to identify a person; so there can be no question but that the three entities in the Trinity should be described as persons. Thus it was never my intention to deny that they would be aware of being distinct from one another just as even in the most 'unreflective' society the individuals would still be aware that it was their body that did such-and-such an action and not someone else's.

If it then be objected that the analogy is uncomplimentary to the Trinity in that it suggests that the persons are 'unreflective', my response would be that this once again demonstrates the difficulty (or at any rate my difficulty!) of producing accurate terminology in an area in which all the words in dispute can be used in a wide range of very different senses. Thus in our society 'reflective' tends to imply conclusions that the individual has reached independently for himself, and so 'unreflective' implies not self-reflective. But, as I shall suggest below, there are other ways of being reflective than this. First let me caution against a possible misreading. I certainly do not intend to suggest that either 'reflective' or 'unreflective' should immediately connote either approval or disapproval. In fact in some societies it would seem to me better if there were much more reflection going on, in others less, and exactly the same applies to us as individuals. So, for instance, I would certainly be a better person if I could do some things without thinking (e.g., deciding to vote), while with others I would be a better person if I did a great deal more thinking about it (e.g., deciding how to vote). So it is certainly no part of my argument to make general moral claims about self-reflection in ordinary human society. Both its presence and its absence can be signs of maturity and immaturity, of good and evil.

In God's case there is of course the basic difference that a wholly good, omniscient being does not need to reflect, in the sense that there is no process of reasoning that has to be gone through. But this does not mean that the notion of reflection cannot be made to apply to God. That would be so only if we allowed ourselves to be bewitched by one particular model for self-reflection. Rather, what we need to consider is the sort of reflection that characterizes a strongly integrated society with shared values. For it is not that individuals in such a society have ceased to think or reflect but that their reflection is mediated through the social. So, to revert to an earlier example, the point of Gothic architecture could be given reasoned, intelligible expression by any particular individual within medieval society, but all would give it the same point because their reflective awareness derives from a shared social vision of reality. The individual has, as it were, absorbed the reflectivity of his society rather than having to think independently for himself. Such reflectivity is thus more like reasoned awareness (the ability to give a reasoned account if asked) than an awareness that has had to be reached through a process of reasoning. Intriguingly, in this it approaches what one might in any case think more appropriate to ascribe to a divine being. In the human case, reflectivity is embedded in the corporate wisdom of the society, with the individual showing reasoned awareness of it, while in the divine case there is the same reasoned awareness in the persons of a social vision and purposes that belong equally to them all and so to none in particular.

Though reflectivity and self-consciousness are not exactly the same thing, still I think that the more one is prepared to ascribe the former to the social, the more ought one to ascribe the latter also. This is in fact what I have done in my account. But then a very different sort of objection emerges. For, if the first objection challenged whether I could properly speak of persons if I attributed only consciousness to them, the question now arises whether in attributing so much, including self-consciousness, to the social being of God I have not postulated a fourth person (the Godhead) in addition to the other three. Certainly if a society is self-conscious it will also be conscious, that is, aware of itself as a distinct entity over against other actual or possible societies.

But even so, the implication that such a society is therefore a person does not seem to me to follow. To see why, we need once more to consider with care the slippery meaning of the term at the heart of the dispute, this time 'self-consciousness'. The word has at least three senses, depending on the nature of the society envisaged: self-independent consciousness, self-in-relation consciousness, and self-in-me consciousness. The first is characteristic of the modern world, while the second is best exemplified among my earlier examples by classical civilization, and the last by Eskimo culture. That is, it is possible to conceive of one's identity over a wide range of alternative scenarios, varying from, at the one end, the existentialist idea of one's selfhood as a personal creation, through the Greek idea of it being given by one's social role, to, at the other end, the Hegelian idea of the perfectly rational society in which the individual amounts simply to one of several modifications of the social whole. God, on my view, is clearly nearer the latter than the former end of the spectrum. But it seems to me that even if we take the most extreme version of the Hegelian self-in-me consciousness, it would still not follow that we should speak of the Godhead as a person over and above the normal three, any more than we should speak of the perfect human Hegelian society as itself a person.

This is because though such self-consciousness is not the creation of any particular individual in that society, nonetheless it exists only as mediated through and expressed in those particular individuals. Thus, though in some ways such a society functions just like a person, there remains the most important respect in which it is not a person, namely, that it has no existence in itself but only through what are already indisputably persons. Thus even self-in-me consciousness remains in-me consciousness and never becomes simply self-consciousness. In other words, self-consciousness is always a disguised, incomplete function of the form self-in-X consciousness where X, though it can stand for any individual in the society, must nonetheless be filled by some specific person before one has a complete concept capable of instantiation.[52] However, if the reader insists that, even so, the language of persons is appropriate, I do not think that much necessarily turns on the issue, provided of course that such a society is admitted to be a person in a very different sense of the word. Indeed the way in which many ordinary believers as well as some philosophers[53] are prepared to describe God *tout court* as a person perhaps already lends some legitimacy to the usage.

In short, then, though all analogies fall short in some way or other, ascribing consciousness to the persons and self-consciousness to the Godhead does seem a helpful way forward for the social model both in undercutting any suggestion of tritheism and also, one hopes, in contributing to the greater intelligibility of trinitarian doctrine.[54]

Notes

1 See David Brown, *The Divine Trinity* (London: Duckworth, 1985; La Salle, IL: Open Court, 1985), esp. chapter 7.

2 *De Trinitate.* 5.9.10 (my translation); cf. 7.4.9.

3 Karl Barth, *Church Dogmatics*, I/1, trans. G.T. Thomson (Edinburgh: T & T Clark, 1936), 408.

4 Karl Rahner, *The Trinity*, trans. Joseph Donceel (London and New York: Burns and Oates, 1970), 104–107; Donald Baillie, *God Was In Christ: An Essay on Incarnation and Atonement* (London: Faber and Faber, 1956), 135.

5 Steven Lukes, *Individualism* (Oxford: Basil Blackwell, 1973), 3–26.

6 *Summa theologiae* (ST) Ia q. 30, a. 4.

7 See the discussion of Homer at the beginning of the section below.

8 See, most obviously, G.W.F. Hegel, *Phenomenology of Spirit*, trans. A.V. Miller, with Analysis of the Text and Foreword by J.N. Findlay (Oxford: Oxford University Press, 1977), B. IV. A.

9 It is hard not to regard sentences like the following as instances of deliberate ambiguity: 'To have the *prosōpon* of God is to will what God wills, whose *prosōpon* he has'; 'This is the likeness of God, to have neither purpose nor will of its own but that of him whose *prosōpon* and likeness it has'. Nestorius, *The Bazaar of Heracleides*, trans. and ed. Godfrey Rolles Driver and Leonard Hodgson (Oxford: Clarendon Press, 1925), 59, 62.

10 Cf. the comment in Charlton Thomas Lewis and Charles Short's *Latin Dictionary*, s.v. *persona*: 'post-Augustan and rare'. The development of usage is best situated by following the examples given in the standard dictionaries: *The Oxford Latin Dictionary* (the successor to Lewis and Short), ed. P.G.W. Glare (Oxford: Clarendon Press, 1983); *Greek-English Lexicon*, ed. Henry George Liddel and Robert Scott, 9th ed. (London: Oxford University Press, 1940); *A Patristic Greek Lexicon*, ed. Geoffrey Lampe (Oxford: Oxford University Press, 1961). Maurice Nédoncelle's article '*Prosopon* et *persona* dans l'antiquité classique', *Revue des Sciences Religieuses* 23 (1949), 277–299, while helpful in many ways, is not sufficiently careful in distinguishing the logical sense of individualism from other possible meanings of individual.

11 Bruno Snell, *The Discovery of the Mind* (New York: Dover Publications, 1982), 19.

12 Hugh Lloyd-Jones, *The Justice of Zeus* (Berkley: CA: University of California Press, 1971), esp. 9–10.

13 Martin P. Nilsson, *Greek Piety* (New York: W.W. Norton, 1969), 47–48.

14 *Adversus Haereses*, 3.2.9.

15 *Adversus Praxean*, 23.4. C.F. 7.9: '*Quaecumque ergo substantia sermonis fuit, illam dico personam*'.

16 Alois Grillmeier, *Christ in Christian Tradition*, 2nd ed. (Oxford: Mowbrays, 1975), 126. In his discussion of the Cappadocians (372–373) Grillmeier makes it much clearer that logical individuation was the basic issue.

17 Harry Austryn Wolfson, *The Philosophy of the Church Fathers*, 3rd ed., vol. 1: *Faith, Trinity, Incarnation* (Cambridge, MA: Harvard University Press, 1970), 325.

18 Gaius, *Institutes* 2.15. My estimate of numbers of slaves is from W. Warde Fowler, *Social Life at Rome* (London: Macmillan, 1963), 222–230.

19 Cf. Georg Misch, *A History of Autobiography in Antiquity* (London: Routledge and Kegan Paul, 1950).

20 The transference was made between Otto III (983–1002) and his successor Henry II. See Percy E. Schramm, *Die Deutsche Kaiser und Könige in Bildern ihrer Zeit* (Leipzig: B.G. Teubner, 1928), 194, and Abbild (illustration) 73.

21 Gregory of Nazianzus, *Oration* 31.11; Gregory of Nyssa, *Tres Dei*.

22 Cornelius Plantinga, Jr, 'Gregory of Nyssa and the Social Analogy of the Trinity', *The Thomist* 50 (1986), 325–352, esp. 346–348.

23 'On "Not Three Gods"', in his *Select Writings and Letters*, trans. William Moore and Henry Austin Williams, A Select Library of Nicene and Post-Nicene Fathers of the Christian Church, vol. 5 (Grand Rapids, MI: Wm. B. Eerdmans, 1976), 332.

24 *Epistola de Incarnatione Verbi* 1, ed. Franciscus S. Schmitt (Bonn: Peter Hanstein, 1931), 10.

25 *Meditation* 17. Donne develops a social analogy in *Devotions upon Emergent Occasions* (Ann Arbor, MI: University of Michigan Press, 1959), 30–31. For the political use of analogy cf. David Nicholls, 'Divine Analogy: The Theological Politics of John Donne', *Political Studies* 32 (1984), 570–580, esp. 574 ff.

26 *De Trin.* 3.2.10, 11.

27 *ST* Ia q. 31, a. 3, ad 1, trans. Ceslaud Velecky, Blackfriar's edition, vol. 6 (London: Eyre and Spottiswoode, 1965).

28 Aquinas adopts Boethius's definition at the beginning of q. 29.

29 Marcel Mauss, 'A Category of the Human Mind: The Notion of a Person; The Notion of Self', in *The Category of the Person: Anthropology, Philosophy, History*, ed. Michael Carrithers, Steven Collins and Steven Lukes (New York: Cambridge University Press, 1985), 1–25, esp. 4ff.

30 Ibid., 19. Cf. Siegmund Schlossmann, *Persona und Prosopon, im Recht und im Christlichen Dogma* (Kiel and Leipzig: Lipsius and Tischer, 1906).

31 A. Momigliano, 'Marcel Mauss and the Quest for the Person in Greek Biography and Autobiography', in *Category*, ed. Carrithers et al., 83–92, esp. 84.

32 Louis Dumont, 'The Modified View of Our Origins: The Christian Beginnings of Modern Individualism', in *Category*, ed. Carrithers et al., 93–122, esp. 115.

33 Derek Parfit, *Reasons and Persons* (Oxford: Oxford University Press, 1984).

34 Donald Davidson, 'Deception and Division', in *The Multiple Self*, ed. Jon Elster (Cambridge: Cambridge University Press, 1986), 91, 92.

35 David Pears, 'The Goals and Strategies of Self-Deception', in *The Multiple Self*, ed. Elster, 72.

36 Serge-Christophe Kolm, 'The Buddhist Theory of "No Self"', in *The Multiple Self*, ed. Elster, 254.

37 Giles Deleuze and Felix Guattari, *Anti-Oedipus: Capitalism and Schizophrenia* (London: Athlone Press, 1984), 15.

38 Alasdair MacIntyre, *After Virtue* (London: Duckworth, 1981).

39 Gertrude Elizabeth Margaret Anscombe, 'Modern Moral Philosophy', *Philosophy* 30 (1958), 1–19; Philippa Foot, *'Virtues and Vices' and Other Essays in Moral Philosophy* (Oxford: Basil Blackwell, 1978); Stanley Hauerwas, *The Peaceable Kingdom* (London: SCM, 1983), chapters. 2, 3.

40 Harry G. Frankfurt, 'Freedom of the Will and the Concept of a Person', *Journal of Philosophy* 68 (1971), 5–20. Frankfurt's position is criticized by Daniel C. Dennett, *Brainstorms* (Brighton: Harvester, 1981), Paper 14, esp. 283ff.

41 Colin Morris, *The Discovery of the Individual, 1050–1200* (London: SPCK, 1972), 24.

42 Ibid., 140.

43 *The Times* (London), November 21, 1985, 13.

44 *Enneads*, 1.4.10. For the way this leads Plotinus to deny consciousness to God, see John M. Rist, *Plotinus: The Road to Reality* (Cambridge: Cambridge University Press, 1967), chapter 4.

45 Rom Harré, *Personal Being* (Oxford: Basil Blackwell, 1983), 85–89.

46 Ernst Tugenhat, *Self-Consciousness and Self-Determination* (Cambridge, MA: MIT Press, 1986), 319–320. The claim that Hegel's remarks are intended only to refer to an ideal state is usually based on *The Philosophy of Right*, §258.

47 The claim that the relation will be even closer than trust is to be found in *The Philosophy of Right*, §147, and that there will be no further need for reflection in the *Encyclopedia*, §514.

48 As in the famous 'lordship and bondage' passage in *Phenomenology of Spirit*, B.IV.A.

49 George Leonard Prestige, *God in Patristic Thought*, 2nd ed. (London: SPCK, 1952), 301.

50 The first half of what follows is my response to some written comments from Ronald J. Feenstra and Cornelius Plantinga, Jr., while the latter part is an attempt to reply to the comments of Professor George Mavrodes, my respondent at the Marquette Conference where this chapter was first delivered as a paper. I am most grateful for the courtesy and care they have shown to views with which they have not always agreed.

51 My remarks here are intended to allude only to the ordinary, intuitive use of the word. Formally specifying the necessary and sufficient conditions for personhood is, of course, a much more complex problem; indeed, even the criterion in the text must face some difficult cases such as multiple personality.

52 I have borrowed the notion of an incomplete function from Frege, though I remain uncertain of the degree to which further development along these lines might represent the best way forward.

53 C.f., e.g., the opening lines of Richard Swinburne's *The Coherence of Theism* (Oxford: Oxford University Press, 1977): 'By a theist I understand a man who believes in God. By a "God" he understands something like a person' (1).

54 This chapter has benefitted greatly from critical comments on previous drafts read to the Theological Society at the University of Cambridge and to the Philosophical Society at Liverpool University. I am grateful to these critics as well as to the organizers of the Marquette Conference and its participants. It was a privilege to be at Marquette and to witness the standard of dialogue between philosophers and theologians. Originally published in Ronald J. Feenstra and Cornelius Plantinga, Jr, ed., *Trinity, Incarnation and Atonement: Philosophical and Theological Essays* (Notre Dame, IN: University of Notre Dame Press, 1989), 48–78, it is reproduced here in abridged form with permission of the publishers.

9 Anselm on Atonement

Although among philosophers and in the wider world generally Anselm is undoubtedly best known for his ontological argument, this is not where he has exercised most influence. Rather, it is in the field of Christian doctrine, and particularly in his account of the Christian doctrine of atonement or redemption. This influence has been displayed in both positive and negative forms: positive in the way ideas of his were taken up and developed by some later theologians, negative in the way yet others sought to put their own views at as great a distance as possible from those of Anselm. The result is that, though he is sometimes praised, he has more often been savagely criticized, particularly in the modern period. Not all of those criticisms are fair. The problem is that historical context is either ignored or, if acknowledged, explored at an insufficiently deep level. In what follows, therefore, I want to present his position as clearly as possible, noting where misunderstandings have arisen and where potential developments have occurred, or could occur.

Atonement means simply at-one-ment, and so is concerned with the issue of how in general, despite fault on one side, reconciliation is achievable between the two or more parties involved. The word can thus be used with a purely secular meaning as in the title of a recent work by the British novelist, Ian McEwan.[1] More commonly, though, and by origin, the word has an explicitly religious connotation and then the question focuses on how, despite the presence of sin, human beings can be reconciled to God. The sacrificial system in the Old Testament, and indeed in the ancient world more generally, indicates one way in which this might be conceived, the transformation of the ritual of the Day of Atonement in the Temple at Jerusalem into modern Jewish practice of a special day of penitence (Yom Kippur) another. However, so central is Christ to Christian self-understanding that Christianity has almost invariably insisted that no such reconciliation with God is possible except through the mediation of Christ.

That mediation has been expounded in a number of different ways: ransom, victory, example, penal substitution, sacrifice, and so forth. Theologians have often described these various approaches as rival theories or 'models' but it is not clear that this is always how such talk was intended. Thus, although it is easy to identify particular verses in the New Testament that seem to support one approach or other (for example, 2 Corinthians 5:21 might be used for penal substitution),[2] there is little in the evangelists or even Paul that suggests the development of a systematic account. Rather, the often-incidental way in which the images are introduced hints at something rather different: the ransacking of a treasure-trove of potential metaphors, employed to highlight, now in one way, now in another, what the authors saw as the indispensable role of Christ in human salvation. Because the Old Testament was seen as fulfilled in Christ, whatever images of reconciliation and new life were available were applied to this new perception of faith and used to complement one another. Nor did this change much in the early history of the Church. Its preoccupation during the first millennium with how the incarnation was to be understood (Christ as simultaneously God and man) meant that no attempts were made at formal definition in this area, so only one of the two principal creeds of the Christian church insists that Christ acted 'for us', and even then offers no guidance as to how exactly this was so.[3]

All this helps to explain why Anselm's late work *Cur Deus Homo* (written between 1094 and 1098) constitutes such a major landmark in the history of Christian thought. For what is incontestably now offered is a fully developed and carefully articulated theory of how atonement is achievable only through the work of Christ. In brief, only someone who is both God and man can save us because, while it is human beings who owe recompense to God for sin, it is only God who has the power and ability to make such recompense. Anselm elaborates that basic structure into what turns out to be quite a complex, multi-staged argument.[4] A brief analysis of its form is provided in my first section below. More important in my view, though, is appreciation of Anselm's underlying strategy and terminology. Rather, therefore, than using the initial analysis as a basis for the discussion which follows, I have chosen to examine issues under a number of alternative headings: Anselm on the relation between reason and revelation; the key terms and their appropriate translation; and finally, subsequent developments and responses by others to Anselm's position.

The Argument

As I mentioned above, I do not wish to lay much stress on the analysis that now follows, but it will give the reader some indication of how much more complicated Anselm's position is than it is commonly characterized to be.

(1) All human beings have sinned: *passim*.
(2) Eternal salvation and reconciliation with God is not possible without freedom from the effects of sin.
(3) These effects cannot be eliminated by an act of divine forgiveness: 1.11 (cf. also 1.15; 1.24; 2.5).
(4) So either punishment must follow, or else compensation/satisfaction be paid: 1.13.
(5) But God does wish some human beings to be saved: 1.16–18.
(6) So compensation must sometimes be the chosen alternative.
(7) But 'to sin is nothing other than not to render God his due': 1.11.[5]
(8) So, compensation must consist in giving to God what is not his due: 1.11.

(9) But, 'if in justice I owe to God myself and all my powers even when I do not sin, I have nothing left to render to him for my sin': 1.20.

(10) Therefore, compensation must be paid by an act, not owed to God, performed by a person other than one of whom (9) is true.

(11) But, given what we owe to God, any sin is of infinite extent: 1.21.

(12) So compensation 'cannot be achieved, except the compensation paid to God for human sin be something greater than all that is beside God …. Therefore, none but God can make this satisfaction': 2.6.

(13) But it is necessary that the person paying the compensation be also a man: 2.8 ('Otherwise, neither Adam nor his race would make satisfaction for themselves').

(14) 'If, as is certain, it is therefore necessary that the heavenly community be made up of human beings and this cannot be effected unless the aforesaid satisfaction be made, which none but God can make and none but a human being ought to make, it is necessary for a God-man to make it': 2.6.

(15) But it is not fitting for the Father or the Holy Spirit to be incarnated: 2.9.

(16) Therefore, the requisite compensation must be achieved by the incarnation of God the Son, and, from (8), such compensation will involve that 'he somehow gives up himself, or something of his, to the honour of God, which he does not owe as a debtor': 2.11.

(17) But 'every reasonable being owes his obedience to God': 2.11, cf. (9).

(18) 'Therefore, it must be in some other way that he give himself, or something belonging to him, to God': 2.11.

(19) But mortality is not an essential attribute of human nature 'since, had man never sinned, and had his immortality been unchangeably confirmed, he would have been as really man' 2.11.

(20) 'Therefore, one who wishes to make atonement/satisfaction for human sin should be such a one who can die if he chooses': 2.11.

(21) So compensation/satisfaction/atonement will be made by the innocent death of God the Son.

Reason and Revelation

Anselm opens by saying that his intention is to offer an argument for nonbelievers that makes no assumptions initially regarding the historical Christ. For some theologians this has been enough to mean that Anselm sets off on quite the wrong track, a suspicion that only intensified by Anselm's own choice of words in his preface, 'removing Christ from view' (*remoto Christo*). Christ, it is said, can only be properly known through revelation, so distortion must be the inevitable result of any such approach. As one recent commentator observes, 'the attempt to "prove" the necessity and possibility of redemption without any reference to the gospel story strikes us as perverse'.[6] Although Karl Barth goes too far in his defence of Anselm when he asserts that Anselm's premises were all in any case implicitly derived from revelation,[7] there are a number of more limited observations that may be made by way of response. First, though Anselm largely obeys his own ordinance, Scripture is in fact often seen lying just beneath the surface, and sometimes explicit quotations do actually emerge.[8] More importantly, Anselm is insistent that nothing he asserts should be inconsistent with Scripture, which continues to be given supreme authority: 'I am certain that if I say anything which indubitably contradicts sacred Scripture, it is false; and I do not wish to hold it, if I should become aware of this'.[9] So it is not as though he ever subscribes to the view that the Bible could be made in theory to yield to the discoveries of reason, a distinctly modern notion. Nor is it ever the case that other texts are quoted in place of Scripture, for, in marked contrast to the theology of the time, all appeal to authority in fact disappears, a feature of Anselm's writing which deeply troubled his former teacher and predecessor as Archbishop of Canterbury, Lanfranc.[10]

Anselm seems to have been motivated in part by apologetic reasons. As we have seen, he opens by specifying 'nonbelievers' (*infideles*) by which he probably meant not atheists but Jews and Muslims. Both faiths believe that atonement is possible without an incarnation, and it may well be the case that Anselm had met intellectually plausible representatives of both groups. His biographer, Eadmer, tells us that while at Capua (where he completed the work) Anselm gained the respect of Muslims for his kind treatment of them, while his fellow Benedictine, Gilbert Crispin, had drawn his attention to the challenge presented by Jews.[11] Nonetheless, close attention to Anselm's text actually reveals a much more deeply seated concern to explicate belief more clearly for the Christian believer as such. So, for instance, he makes Boso, his conversation partner, reaffirm what Anselm himself had already asserted a couple of sentences earlier: 'it seems to me an act of negligence if, after we have been confirmed in the faith, we do not strive to understand what we believe'.[12] Mystery, he concedes, will at some stage take over as the divine recedes from our limited human capacity to comprehend,[13] but before that happens it makes sense to ask what is entailed by assuming that God does all things appropriately and well, and for that assumption he could well have quoted the authority of Scripture.[14]

Already in the preface, Anselm had announced his intention to proceed by 'necessary reasons'. 'What is inferred to be true by a necessary reason', he tells us, 'ought not to be called into doubt, even if the reason why it is true is not understood'.[15] That insistence on the limits of human understanding matches well with his repeated insistence throughout this work that in offering 'necessary' reasons he does not mean to imply any constraint on God. It is not a case of reason somehow imposing limits on God, rather, it is a matter of human beings coming to comprehend what follows from the fact that God remains consistent with his nature or else, putting it another way, is self-consistent.[16] So in the absence of any external 'compulsion' or 'constraint', we should not think of God as governed by 'necessity' but rather by his own 'eternal constancy'.[17]

One example of this is how divine mercy is understood: Anselm insists that it must be explicated in a way that is made consistent with justice, for God is both merciful and just. Simply to forgive without recompense would result in a 'God inconsistent with himself' (1.24), something external to God which he can choose, now to apply, now to reject; He is after all Justice itself (1.13). So it is not that

Anselm is committed to a narrow theory of retribution, what some have called 'rationalized vengeance',[18] but that for Anselm God cannot be portrayed as acting now in one way, now in another: punishing, according to the Bible, fallen angels and human beings who are irredeemably wicked, yet allowing others (the forgiven) apparently to escape all consequences of their sins. For 'no unfitness, however small, is possible with God' (1.20). That may sound like an unyielding God, requiring either punishment or compensation where wrong has been done, but for Anselm the issue as much concerns human attitudes; for we need to admit that we already owe everything to God. There would thus be an 'unfitness' in us accepting forgiveness without compensation being paid, no less than in God offering such forgiveness unconditionally (1.21). The result would be an 'unseemliness that violated beauty of arrangement'.[19]

That last reference illustrates a feature of Anselm's argument that is often found rather strange in our contemporary context, and that is the extent to which Anselm appeals not only to requirements of logical consistency but also to what might now be more naturally termed aesthetic considerations: what is fitting or appropriate (*conveniens/decens*). Here we need to think ourselves back into a world in which God was identified not only with Justice, Truth, and Goodness but also with Beauty. Although the inclusion of beauty has been revived in the voluminous writings of the Swiss theologian, Hans Urs von Balthasar (d. 1988), it is not an idea that comes naturally to the modern mind. It was mediated to the Western tradition particularly through the thought of St Augustine, who finds measure and form intrinsic to goodness and argues that the search for balance can help to explain the presence of evil in the world, much as a beautiful poem is set off by its antitheses.[20] Building on an emphasis found as early as in Irenaeus, Anselm speaks of 'the indescribable beauty' in the arrangement whereby salvation comes through a woman (Mary) and a cross, for the fall was through another woman (Eve) and wood's source – a tree, in the Garden of Eden.[21] But he also uses the notion much more widely. It would not be fitting, for example, he suggests, for the number of humans saved simply to substitute for the number of lost angels, for then any human being saved would have grounds to rejoice over an angel's fall, and that would not be 'appropriate' (1.18). To the modern reader that may sound like a rather weak moral consideration, but for Anselm it is decisive. In that chapter as a whole, morality merges naturally into aesthetics, as attention is given to such topics as perfect numbers and an appropriate balance between the two natures (angelic and human). Again, it would be unseemly for there to be two sons in the Trinity, which is what would happen if any other than God the Son became incarnate (2.9). Indeed, so far as God's actions are concerned, 'not fitting' is taken to imply our entitlement to draw the conclusion 'necessarily not the case' (1.10; 1.19). For would not God create a beautifully ordered world?

Although it is possible to argue that the notion of beauty is central to both Testaments with their many references to the divine 'glory' or 'splendour', it is clear that the idea of beauty in balance and proportion which Anselm employs here is more strongly part of Christianity's inheritance from Platonism, though the Bible is not without its own examples. Paul is surely arguing in similar vein when he declares that 'as by one man's disobedience many were made sinners, so by one man's obedience many will be made righteous' (Romans 5:19, JB). The aesthetic delight in the careful Greek phrasing suggests that more than just a parallel is being drawn. Estimating the relative weight of such influences, however, is not always an easy matter. This becomes particularly difficult and controversial in respect of another key element in Anselm's strategy, the question of how one man's actions, even those of a God–man, are supposed inevitably to have an impact for the whole of humanity. On first reflection, somebody else paying the penalty or offering compensation seems a poor substitute for the guilty individual's own action.

The next section, which is devoted to consideration of Anselm's terminology, is the best place to examine one commonly proposed explanation, namely that in terms of Anselm's reliance on feudal imagery. As we shall see, such a grounding is much less plausible than is usually claimed. Here, though, I want to look at two other possible sources, in the Bible and in Platonism. The methodology of *Cur Deus Homo* precludes explicit reference to either, so we must argue more indirectly and tentatively.

On the Bible, it should not be forgotten that Anselm was a Benedictine monk, so his reading would have been first and foremost the Scriptures. In the Old Testament, law and prophets address the people primarily not as individuals but as a corporate entity (Israel), and interdependence for both good and bad is a frequently reiterated notion. Although occasionally challenged, the Second Commandment's 'visiting the iniquity of the fathers upon the children unto the third and fourth generation' might be used to illustrate the interconnection in one direction, the high priest's action on the Day of Atonement the presumed connection in the other.[22] Although stress on individual responsibility is more marked in the New Testament, much of its imagery and theology continues to be corporate. For Paul we are all potentially 'in Christ' just as we were once 'in Adam', and in his letters two competing but related images of the Church as 'the body of Christ' are developed, by which something rather more than just metaphor is surely intended. The Evangelist John, too, offers a not dissimilar notion in his picture of Christ as the vine and ourselves as its branches.[23]

Although *Cur Deus Homo* avoids any supporting biblical quotation of the above sort, more than once Anselm insists that Christ had to be 'of the same kind' (*genus*) as ourselves (e.g. 2.8). Not only would an angel not do, Christ's atonement can have no impact for good on fallen angels, precisely because they are not the same kind of thing (2.21). In the second passage, if not in the first, it is clear that 'race' is the better translation, inasmuch as Anselm claims that it would not even have been enough for Christ to have had the same 'nature': there must also have been a genetic connection. But while such a connection can be used to help to explain transmission of Adam's tendency toward sin ('original sin') to successive generations, it is rather harder to see how this helps in the case of Christ's action. Yet Anselm does use positive corporate language elsewhere in his writings, especially in his devotional works. So, for instance, in a eucharistic prayer he asks of Christ that he may be 'worthy to be incorporated into your body which is the Church, so that I may be your member and you my head'.[24] One notes too his own strong sense of acting in a corporate role, both on behalf of his monastery and at Canterbury on behalf of the particular saints with whom the see was identified. Thus for him Augustine of Canterbury was anything but a distant historical figure, merely the first to hold the see. He was a living presence, whose mantle he had now in some sense adopted, and whose rights he was required to defend.[25] As one pope of the time put it, 'we behold in you the venerable persona of St Augustine'.[26]

Sadly, this whole notion of 'corporate personality' is one to which little philosophical attention has been devoted in modern times. In part the worry seems to be that, if taken seriously,[27] clear and valuable distinctions will thereby be undermined. Platonism, however, would seem to offer the possibility of a different view, and that is no doubt one reason why until fairly recently almost all commentators have assumed a Platonic background to the argument of *Cur Deus Homo*.[28] So, for instance, Sir Richard Southern observes of Anselm that 'there can be no doubt that his essential philosophical ideas are Platonic' and that 'his general tendency is to think of the species as more real than its individual components'.[29] Once again, though, there is no direct quotation, and indeed it is only Aristotle who is mentioned (once) in the course of Anselm's text.[30] So we must rely on indirect evidence. Chalcidius's version of Plato's *Timaeus* did become increasingly available throughout the eleventh century; so it is just possible that Anselm knew directly one of Plato's works.[31] More certain is that he was well acquainted with Platonism as mediated through the writings of St Augustine, for Lanfranc's stocking of the monastic library is on record.[32] We also know that in contemporary discussion of approaches to what modern philosophers call the theory of universals Platonist versions were being canvassed, and indeed according to one reading of the evidence Anselm was forced to defend himself against the charge of veering altogether too strongly in that particular direction.[33] There are even occasional passages in Anselm's works which taken on their own can sound alarmingly Platonic.[34] So, for example in the opening chapter of his rather technical work *On the Incarnation of the Word* he observes that 'anyone who does not understand how many men are one man in species cannot understand how … several person … can be one God'.

Platonism has had a long and complex history, so all I can do here is briefly indicate how such a philosophical background might have provided further underpinning to ideas already current in Anselm's mind from Scripture. In trying to resolve the question of universals, the issue of what it is that justifies the application of common or universal names as descriptions shared across unique, particular objects, Plato responds that the particulars only have intelligibility or reality insofar as they 'imitate' or 'participate in' the perfect exemplar of their kind.[35] The point is easily appreciated if we consider the term 'circle'. No matter how careful we are with our compass, any circle we draw on a piece of paper will only ever approximate to the perfect one that unqualifiedly fulfils the definition of a circle – as a figure, all points on the circumference of which are equidistant from the centre. The most real circle, as it were, lies elsewhere, so other circles are only struggling approximations. Equally, then, with Plato's own examples of knives and beds: particular knives will only be to varying degrees successful at their function of cutting well, beds to varying degrees successful at aiding a good night's sleep, and so on, and it is the ideal or 'form' that remains the appropriate standard by which to measure the goodness of the particular.

While it is true that Anselm could not have read that particular discussion of Plato's, there is much that is similar in Augustine.[36] If the ideal 'form' has moved into the mind of God, there is the same notion of degrees of participation, with lesser goods only good by participation in higher, unchangeable goods,[37] and Anselm seems to repeat that pattern of thinking in his *Monologion* (36). So far as atonement itself is concerned, the thought would then be that this is secured through us 'participating' in the perfect exemplar or 'universal' human nature that Christ came to offer. It was partly to defend that possibility that Cyril of Alexandria not long before the Council of Chalcedon (451) insisted that in the incarnation God assumed an impersonal human nature, not the characteristics that would make him a distinct human personality. Known technically as the doctrine of *anhypostasia* and much attacked in the twentieth century, it is found reflected even as late as the nineteenth in Newman's declaration of Christ that 'though Man, he is not, strictly speaking, *a* Man'.[38] To my mind this means that translating the title of Anselm's work is not as simple as it may initially appear. If 'Why God Became Humanity' is altogether too strong, 'Why God Became a Human Being' is also not without its difficulties.[39] Such problems are not unknown in the Church of our own day. In contemporary Anglican translations of the Nicene Creed 'men' is now excluded as unnecessarily sexist from the clause 'for us *men* and for our salvation', whereas 'man' has been retained in 'he became man' despite that problem, because it is thought that otherwise something important could be lost.[40] Neither Plato nor Paul nor Anselm thought that identifying the ideal or corporate reality told the whole story, but all three presupposed a strong connection which to modern minds is not so immediately apparent, so modern readers need to be made aware of how differently Anselm's text would have been heard in his own day.

If I am anywhere near right about the biblical and Platonic background to the thought-world of Anselm and at least some of his contemporaries, then his arguments might well have carried greater weight than they do in our day. Because connections were assumed, Anselm felt no need to go on in *Cur Deus Homo* to consider how a particular individual might appropriate Christ's act: in a sense, it was already his own. Even so, the need for grace is mentioned, and the force of Christ's example is stressed.[41] The latter is especially worth noting, not least because Anselm is so often sharply contrasted with his younger contemporary Abelard (d. 1142), who is often portrayed as the great exponent of an exemplarist theory, the view that salvation is secured through following Christ's moral example. In fact they are less far apart than is commonly supposed. Not only does Abelard take up some of Anselm's themes,[42] Anselm himself in a later work of 1099, his short *Meditation on Human Redemption*, uses powerful imagery to ram home the need for deep meditation on the extent of divine love shown in Christ's act. Concluding with a prayer that Christ's love should seize his whole being, he twice urges his readers to 'feed', 'chew', 'suck', and 'swallow' not only in the eucharist but whenever and wherever the story of Christ's love is retold.[43] In his influential *History of Dogma* Adolf von Harnack complained of the 'unevangelical character' of Anselm's theory,[44] but if one turns to Anselm's devotional writings, one finds a stress on dependence on Christ as powerful as anyone might desire: 'Sweet name! Name full of delights! Name to comfort sinners and bring them blessed hope. For what is Jesus if not saviour?'[45] Even tender, 'feminist' imagery finds its place, as in his familiar description of Jesus as a mother, like a hen gathering her chicks under its wings.[46] I mention this not to turn Anselm into a modern thinker, but rather as a way of insisting that his position must be seen as a rounded whole. He was no cold rationalist imposing purely external criteria on God but a devout monk concerned to explore his faith in a God, the internal logic of whose nature, he believed, entailed his never failing to act beautifully and well.

The Key Terms

Hitherto I have largely avoided the term 'satisfaction', so often presented as the core of Anselm's theory. Instead in the introduction I used the more neutral 'recompense', for, despite the centrality of the term, the dangers of misrepresentation in this word are considerable, as also in Anselm's use of the related notions of 'debt' and 'honour'. None are concepts that contemporary Christians customarily employ to describe their relationship with God, and that very strangeness is intensified by the decision of so many commentators to find an explanation for this way of speaking in the feudal system of the time, within which Anselm was of course firmly ensconced as Archbishop of Canterbury. Medieval society was a system of reciprocal rights and obligations and very strictly hierarchical within that framework. One owed certain obligations to one's lord and in return he provided protection. Violate those obligations, and some recompense was required to the lord's offended honour, either from oneself or from one's family, before normal relations could be restored. 'Satisfaction' was the usual term used to indicate such recompense. For an application nearer our own times one might think of what used to happen in sword or pistol duels. The offended party might even utter 'I demand satisfaction', as he issued his challenge to recover his own offended honour (or that of his king or lady). Still nearer to our own times would be prosecution in the civil courts for 'damages' for honour or character besmirched through libel or slander. I offer these examples not because I think Anselm would have approved, but partly to indicate that even today we sometimes think in such terms and partly (and more importantly) to indicate some of the reasons why, however expressed, such an approach might not have particularly appealed to Anselm. The analogy simply fails to take sin with sufficient seriousness (after all criminal courts and not civil deal with the greater crimes) and, as we know from his prayers, Anselm was acutely conscious of his own sinfulness, never mind that of humanity in general. Yet it can scarcely be denied that Anselm must have been influenced to some degree by this way of thinking, given how deep such notions ran in the world about him. But, recalling my earlier insistence on his desire to avoid any external restraint on God, it would not seem likely that Anselm would ever have allowed such an obviously artificial and external pattern to become central to what he had to say. That is why we need to treat with extreme caution Harnack and the many others who venture down this track. For him 'the worst thing in Anselm's theory' is its 'mythological conception of God as the mighty private man who is incensed at the injury done to his honor and does not forego his wrath till he has received an at least adequately great equivalent'.[47] Put that bluntly, and it becomes clear that Anselm could never have thought of matters in such crude terms. Recall that for Anselm God is 'that than which nothing greater can be conceived', the source of all that is and not in any sense a reflection of our own petty acts.

With so many readers relying on the English alone, it is all too easy for them to be unaware of how translations can manipulate us into particular ways of perceiving Anselm's position. To illustrate, let me offer two contrasting translations of the same sentence, the first more literal, but the second equally loyal to the meaning.[48] (1) 'Everyone who sins ought to pay back the honour of which he has robbed God; and this is the satisfaction which every sinner owes to God'. (2) 'Anyone who sins should return to God the respect and worship that he has denied him; in doing this he makes up for the sin'. Contemporary Christians are unlikely to take exception to the second version, whereas many may well recoil from the first, as it sounds like an excessively formal and external relationship. That Anselm in fact intended something quite different I want now to demonstrate by considering carefully each of the three key terms.

Take first the word 'debt'. 'To sin is nothing other than not to render God his due' (1.11), writes Anselm, and that may seem to confirm a very formal view of sin that could easily legitimate some sort of crude payback system. But the reader needs to recall that exactly this definition of sin is given at the very heart of Christianity in the Lord's Prayer. For modern versions that speak of 'forgive us our sins' or 'forgive us our trespasses' stem from the more literal 'forgive us our debts' (AV), or, more literal still, 'forgive us what is owed'. Exactly the same word is used in the Latin Bible as Anselm uses here.[49] So Anselm is picking up on notions that run deep within the New Testament itself. For him, as for the New Testament, everything in the world should be seen in essentially teleological terms, as created with a divine purpose to be fulfilled, and it is really into this context that so much of his vocabulary of 'debt' and of what is 'owed' should be set. It is not, then, that God has laid down some rules which inferiors have violated and so needs satisfaction for such infringements, but rather that human beings have been so made that they can only be fulfilled, only realize their capacity for happiness, if they fulfil or satisfy what is owed to God because of how he has made their natures. God made human beings for eternal bliss through their loving God for his own sake, which means that it is only when their natures are ordered aright in this way that salvation becomes possible for them.

It thus will not do to object that our obligation to God is limited, and so it is not impossible to pay back whatever is missing. This is a tactic that is sometimes tried, through drawing a parallel with our limited debts to our parents, which are clearly finite in extent, despite their gift of life. Such a parallel will not work because for Anselm the point is not about externally acquired duties but about the direction in which our natures are already ordered internally. But if that allows a general context for Anselm's talk of 'debt' and 'what is owed' which does not require the specifics of his own society, it also explains why he is not as far distant from justification by faith as Protestant commentators so commonly assume. For what this internal teleological ordering suggests is that there is nothing that human beings can now do that can make up to God for the wrong they have done, for any good that they might achieve is itself a matter of divine grace, of fulfilling the way in which their natures have already been teleologically ordered by God.[50] As Anselm observes, 'whatever you give you have not of yourself but from him to Whom you give'.[51]

That is why for Anselm even the God-man Christ is in no sense compensating for human misconduct in the perfect life he leads. He is merely fulfilling the destiny of human nature, which God made possible in creating it that way. Compensation or recompense, Anselm contends, must therefore lie elsewhere, and this he believes he has found in Christ's death. According to traditional Christian teaching, human nature is intended for eternal life and human beings die only because of the Fall. Therefore a life voluntarily surrendered to death has nothing to do with the tele- ology of human nature. It is something returned to God that is not owed, a purely gratuitous act, and, because it is the life of a human being who is also God, an offer- ing of infinite worth.[52]

That may seem to return us to feudal notions once more, for, as was noted earlier, feudal law did allow another, such as a parent or relative, under appropri- ate circumstances to make satisfaction on behalf of the person who had actually done the wrong. But, if that were really the point, the exception would now have become the norm, and that seems unlikely. Earlier I drew attention to an alterna- tive explanation, to how biblical and Platonist assumptions could be used to help to make this notion of one acting on behalf of all more readily intelligible. In denying any alleged major role to the feudal analogy, added to this should now be the various other ways in which Anselm seeks to distance what is happening from standard feudal practice. The act is entirely voluntary: it is not part of an established pattern where such conduct is expected, and where satisfaction is in one form or other simply assumed. Again, there is no gain on the part of the person receiving the satisfaction. God, Anselm insists, cannot be benefited in any way because divine impassibility means that God cannot have been hurt or harmed in the first place by human sin, the majesty of God requiring that nothing be outside his power (1.14–15). To suggest otherwise would be for Anselm to impugn the very mean- ing of the word 'God'. Finally, human beings as the recipients of the benefit can- not receive it purely passively as in the feudal situation without any further action required on their part because salvation only becomes activated, as it were, by their actively pleading Christ's act in their own cause, as we saw with Anselm's injunction to his readers to absorb Christ's story by 'chewing', and so forth.

But all this has still not yet really brought us to the heart of the issue of termi- nology, which is the question whether the language of 'honour' and 'satisfaction' can, like 'debt', be liberated from its medieval context. One reason for thinking that this might indeed be so is because, despite the eminence of his position in society, Anselm does not seem to have committed himself deeply to the formal structures of the time. This period marked the beginnings of the investiture controversy during which Pope Gregory VII (d. 1085) and his successors sought to wrest some of the powers of the monarchy over the Church back into their own hands. Anselm was an uncompromising opponent of the two kings under whom he served (William II and Henry I), but the surprise from the available historical evidence is that he was not at all interested in investiture issues as such, and only really acted because he believed himself bound by an oath of obedience to proceed in the way he did.[53] This surely suggests that his focus in *Cur Deus Homo* may also have been elsewhere than in the details of medieval legalism. Anselm saw himself primarily as a monk rather than as a feudal lord.

The suspicion that feudalism does not provide the key to his meaning is confirmed when we turn to Scripture. Although many, if asked, might well declare 'honour' not to be a biblical word, this misleading impression is created only because so often its use is yoked with others, especially 'glory'. So, significantly, God is repeatedly offered 'glory and honour' in the worship of heaven, and that is also seen as an appropriate ascription to God here on earth.[54] More puzzlingly, it is not inconceivable that Paul may have thought 'honour' a legitimate human aspiration also.[55] Whether so or not, more relevant to note here is the implication of all of this, that Anselm would have already found a context for 'honour' in his daily reading of Scripture as a monk. That surely radically changes the nature of his question: the issue was not how to pacify God, like some offended potentate, but rather how to show proper respect and worship toward the Being to whom one owes everything but whom one has nonetheless let down. If of the three key terms it is 'satisfaction' which remains the most difficult to extricate from its medieval context, even here one should note that its root meaning would have been consciously at the forefront of Anselm's mind in a way that is no longer so even for the classicists of our day. It was a matter of when one had 'done enough', a question that remains independent of the specifics of any particular penitential or feudal system. Indeed, it may have been that basic sense of 'making up enough' that initially set Anselm on the track of realizing that there could never be 'enough' (*satis*) on our part, so that is why the act of the God-man was required.

Later Developments

In dispensing with any inescapable dependence on feudal ways of thinking, however, all problems are scarcely at an end for Anselm's approach. One obvious difficulty that remains is that few of us now read the story of the Fall as literally as Anselm clearly did. To him death was a consequence of sin, so a perfect life would necessarily be exempt from death, and that is what made Christ's offering so gratuitous. But evolution suggests that humanity is naturally destined to die, whatever may happen to us thereafter. If that is so, then simply in virtue of taking on human nature, the God-man must have committed his humanity to die, whether or not he led a perfect life. That is a characteristically modern objection. So too would be the complaint that his Christ is too unlike us to make any meaningful identification possible, for Anselm insists on a Christ who was never without full and perfect knowledge even as a child; so Luke's comment about the young boy growing in 'wisdom and stature, and favour with God and man' needed reinterpretation.[56]

That, however, is not where his immediate successors found difficulty, so it will be as well to look first at earlier objections before seeing how his theory might be defended today.

It was only gradually that his approach gained wide acceptance, but by the century following his death we find that Aquinas, for example, 'comes very close to Anselm's position'.[57] The major difference is in the former's insistence that there are a number of other ways that God could have acted to achieve the same end, for 'nothing is impossible with God'.[58] It is worth noting that where Anselm and Aquinas differ is in their understanding of the divine nature. For, as we have seen, Anselm agrees that there can be no external restraints on God, but his view is that there is nonetheless an internal constraint on the divine nature (something owed to himself) which means that God not only always acts consistently but also 'fittingly'. Even Anselm, though, has problems with this kind of approach when it comes to identifying the sense in which Christ 'owed' or 'ought' to have done what he did: he was bound by what he wished, Anselm suggests, not by the fact of the debt (2.18). A little later Duns Scotus (d. 1308), while retaining the language of satisfaction, is much more radical in his critique.[59] He wants to sweep away all talk of *infinite* debt and satisfaction which Aquinas had retained, and in its place put a system of merit supervening even in the case of ordinary human beings. The principal way of gaining merit, though, remains for him also in identification with the death of Christ.

Although Calvin rejected any talk of merit on our part, what comes as a surprise to many is the extent to which his views were continuous with those of Anselm, even to the extent of frequently using the language of 'satisfaction'. Admittedly, Calvin prefers to talk of 'a heavenly decree' rather than any 'absolute necessity'; nonetheless, it requires a 'God-man' 'to present our flesh as the price of satisfaction to Gods righteous judgment'.[60] Although a life of obedience is also now part of that price, there is little doubt that for Calvin the death remains the main focus, but with its gruesome character stressed in a way that would have been quite foreign to Anselm. For Anselm it was enough that Christ had given up what he did not owe (his life), whereas for Calvin the satisfaction borne is the punishment that might otherwise have been imposed on us. 'Making up enough' can thus for Calvin no longer be compensatory and so potentially different in kind, instead, it must be exactly the same sort of thing: punishment exactly matched by punishment. The effect is particularly conspicuous in the treatment he accords the reference to Christ's descent into hell in the Apostles' Creed. For, rejecting the traditional interpretation, which found in the phrase an allusion to the liberating effect of Christ's death on those who died before him, he transformed the meaning of 'hell' from 'the place of departed spirits' to a hell of suffering that Christ had endured on humanity's behalf in order 'to bear and suffer all the punishments that they ought to have sustained'.[61] That is why Calvin can be seen as in some ways more truly medieval than Anselm. For, despite the accusation that is sometimes made that it is Anselm who sets the trend for the medieval literary and artistic obsession with the horrors of Christ's death,[62] nowhere does Anselm dwell on such details or characterize them as a divinely imposed punishment.

The most commonly raised objection against Calvin is the difficulty of comprehending the justice of an innocent man paying the price for the guilty in complete violation of any plausible theory of retributive justice. Although I earlier rejected the analogy, it is certainly very much easier to understand how 'damages' might be paid by another, and indeed modern states sometimes do just that, for example in cases of negligence in hospitals where the hospital board pays on behalf of the offending doctor. In speaking of crime rather than debt it is thus far from clear that Calvin has improved the argument. Of course, where he thought he scored was in underlining the seriousness of sin. Anselm, though, as we have seen, never denied the seriousness, only that further punishment was the remedy. Yet the way in which Calvin tries to extricate himself from the retributivist objection can perhaps be allowed to provide an indication of how Anselm's own position could be adapted for continuing use.

Calvin frequently reminds us that, though 'we shall behold the person of a sinner and evildoer represented in Christ, yet from his shining innocence it will at the same time be obvious that he was burdened with another's sin rather than his own'.[63] Taking up such hints, modern followers such as Barth in effect transform Calvin's theory into a way of seeing ourselves.[64] The punishment is not something required of Christ or of us by God, but rather how we need to see ourselves (as totally undeserving of God's love) before change can begin to be effected in us. Anselm could also be read with a similar transformation. The important point is our identification with a life of making amends, of seeing ourselves at one with that life and death. Anselm of course thought that only death fulfilled this role because it was the giving up of something that was not due, but one could question his argument by observing at this point that God the Son's taking up of a human life was also a gratuitous act. For it is far from clear that, simply in virtue of being a human life, all he did was owed to the Father, since it was not a human life that emerged as part of the natural course of things but rather one by special divine decision and action. Indeed, even Anselm himself on occasion seems to come close to identifying the life as well as part of the atonement.[65] But, whether part of his historical position or not, it would certainly make greater sense in our modern context.

Moreover, the model would have one obvious advantage over Calvin, in that it would not just look to the negative effects of sin but also direct attention to what happens thereafter, the pursuance of a particular style of living, one that continued that pattern of making amends. The requirement that Christ be both God and man would also still be preserved. Christ must be human because only in that way can we identify with his offering as our own; but equally he must also be God because only in that way is it an offering that is in no sense required: God the Son only became human in virtue of becoming incarnate and was not unconditionally and by definition human as we are. Yet, though deeply embedded in so much of Christian theology, some may still recoil from the denial to humanity in general of any positive contribution of their own. I noted earlier one possible response from Anselm to the objection that God cannot claim to have granted us life as a gift if he insists on all the credit subsequently as well. But there is also another way of reacting, that to speak at all of 'a credit balance' in the individual case is already to invite the temptation of pride and a lack of a proper sense of dependence on divine generosity and grace.[66] Even as modern a philosopher as Kant thought it folly to pretend that we had ever done enough.[67] In insisting therefore that only one person has ever performed that enough (*satis*-faction), Anselm ensures a particular way of looking at ourselves. Intriguingly, atonement figures in novels are almost invariably themselves flawed figures. Think, for instance, of Prince Myshkin in Dostoevsky's *The Idiot*, of Sydney Carton in Dickens's *A Tale of Two Cities*, or, more recently, of the whiskey priest in Graham Greene's *The Power and the Glory* or the brawling McMurphy in Ken Kesey's *One Flew over the Cuckoo's Nest*. Anselm preserves the recognition of that flaw in his claim that only a God-man could offer an unqualified 'enough'.[68]

Notes

1 Ian McEwan, *Atonement* (London: Jonathan Cape, 2001). There is no final resolution within this novel. For an exploration of some implicitly Christian examples, see F. W. Dillistone, *The Novelist and the Passion Story* (London: Nelson, 1960).

2 'He made him to be sin for us, who knew no sin' (AV). Similarly, possibilities for ransom would include Mark 10:45; also, for example, John 3:16, for victory over the Devil, Luke 10:18; for sacrifice, Hebrews 9:26, and so on.

3 The Apostles' Creed merely recites the outline of Christ's life, while the Nicene at least talks of that life being 'for us and for our salvation' and 'for our sake'.

4 For discussion of the stages listed below, see my '"Necessary" and "Fitting" Reasons in Christian Theology', in *The Rationality of Religious Belief: Essays in Honour of Basil Mitchell*, ed. William J. Abraham and Steven W. Holtzer (Oxford: Clarendon Press, 1987), 211–230, esp. 212–214.

5 All the translations that follow are my own (from the Schmidt edition).

6 Timothy Gorringe, *God's Just Vengeance: Crime, Violence and the Rhetoric of Salvation* (Cambridge: Cambridge University Press, 1996), 85–103, esp. 100.

7 Karl Barth, *Anselm: Fides Quaerens Intellectum* (New York: Meridian, 1962), 55–57.

8 E.g., several times in 1.9. In 1.18 he actually considers rival textual versions of Deuteronomy 32:8 ('sons of Israel' versus 'angels of God').

9 *Cur Deus Homo*, 1.18.

10 Epistle 72 describes how Anselm sent the *Monologion* to Lanfranc for approval, only for Lanfranc to complain of his failure to appeal to appropriate authorities.

11 For Muslims, see Eadmer, *Life of St. Anselm*, ed. Richard W. Southern (Oxford: Clarendon Press, 1962), 111–112 (xxxiii); for Jews, Richard W. Southern, *Saint Anselm: A Portrait in a Landscape* (Cambridge: Cambridge University Press, 1990), 198–202.

12 1.1.

13 1.1; cf. *Proslogion* 16.

14 'Shall not the Judge of all the earth do right?' (Genesis 18:25; AV). The sentiment catches Anselm's thinking well, even if the Vulgate translates the passage quite differently.

15 1.25. A similar point is made in *Monologion* 44.

16 For some helpful comments in this direction, see E. Fairweather, '*Iustitia Dei* as the *Ratio* of the Incarnation', in *Spicilegium Beccense*, ed. P. Grammont (Paris: Librairie Philosophique J. Vrin, 1959), 327–336.

17 2.10; cf. 2.5; 2.17.

18 Cf. Gorringe, *God's Just Vengeance*, 199–200.

19 1.15: The Latin words are *deformitas* and *ordinis pulchritudo*.

20 For the former point, *On the Nature of the Good*, 3; for the latter, *City of God*, 11.18.

21 1.3; 2.8. Cf. Irenaeus, *Against Heresies*, v, 19.

22 Exodus 20:5 (AV); Leviticus 16, esp. vv. 18ff. For a challenge to corporate thinking, Ezekiel 18:20.

23 1 Corinthians 12:12–30; Colossians 1:15–20; in the later Paul Christ is treated as the head rather than identified with the whole body. See also John 15:1–11.

24 *Anselmi Opera Omnia*, ed. F. S. Schmitt (Edinburgh: Nelson and Sons, 1946–1961), III: 10; English available in *The Prayers and Meditations of Saint Anselm*, trans. Benedicta Ward (London: Penguin, 1973), 100–101, esp. 101.

25 Cf. Southern, *Portrait*, 330–347, esp. 332, 346.

26 Epistle 452. His contemporary Pope Gregory VII (d. 1085) exhibits similar attitudes: cf. M. Maccarone, 'I fondamenti petrini del primato romano in Gregorio VII', *Studi Gregoriani* 13 (1989), 55–128, esp. 96ff.

27 For a counter-example, see Rom Harré, *Personal Being* (Oxford: Blackwell, 1983), 75–140, esp. 85–89.

28 Although challenging Platonist influence, Iwakuma Yukio concedes that this has been the dominant view: 'The Realism of Anselm and His Contemporaries', in *Anselm: Aosta, Bec, and Canterbury*, ed. D.E. Luscombe and G.R. Evans (Sheffield: Sheffield Academic Press, 1996), 120–135, esp. 120n3.

29 Richard W. Southern, *Anselm and His Biographer* (Cambridge: Cambridge University Press, 1963), 62; Southern, *Portrait*, 214.

30 2.17 (424B): on the necessity of the future.

31 For statistics, C. Stephen Jaeger, *The Envy of Angels: Cathedral Schools and Social Ideas in Medieval Europe, 950–1200* (Philadelphia, PA: University of Pennsylvania Press, 1994), 174.

32 Cf. Southern, *Portrait*, 57.

33 In responding to Roscelin: Southern, *Portrait*, 174–181.

34 'Alarming' because it would seem to commit him to the view that God is an entity distinct from the three persons of the Trinity in much the same way as the Platonic Man is from men.

35 Plato used his example of 'bed' to argue that the work of artists is at a lower level than that of artisans, since what they create is only an imitation of an imitation: *Republic* 595–602.

36 *The Republic* was not available at this time.

37 Cf., e.g., *De Trinitate* 8.3.5.

38 For exposition and some discussion, see D.M. Baillie, *God Was in Christ* (London: Faber and Faber, 1956), 15–20, 85–93.

39 This is to express disagreement with Jasper Hopkins in his *A Companion to the Study of St. Anselm* (Minneapolis, MN: University of Minnesota Press, 1972), 198–202, esp. 201.

40 First introduced in the American *Book of Common Prayer* (1979) and then followed by the Church of England in its *Common Worship* (2000).

41 For references to grace, 1.20; 2.5; for example, 2.11, 2.18. Grace as aiding his critical acumen is also mentioned in 1.1.

42 It is altogether too simplistic to reduce Abelard to an exemplarist and nothing more, since elsewhere in his *Commentary on Romans* he speaks of both cross and the mass in terms of satisfaction and sacrifice. Anselm's concern with beauty means that comparisons with Bernard can also be given a certain plausibility: M.B. Pranger, 'The Mirror of Dialectics', in *Anselm: Aosta, Bec, and Canterbury*, ed. Luscombe and Evans, 136–147.

43 This *Meditation* is available in *Prayers*, 230–237.

44 Adolf von Harnack, *History of Dogma*, vol. 6 (London: Williams and Norgate, 1899), 54–78, esp. 68.

45 S III: 76–79; toward the end of the First Meditation in *Prayers*, 221–224.

46 Part of his Prayer to St Paul: *Prayers*, 153–154 (lines 397–415). He is developing Matthew 23:37.

47 Harnack, *Dogma*, 76. Contrast John McIntyre's view that the concepts 'undergo transformation in the new contexts in which he set them': *St. Anselm and His Critics: A Re-interpretation of the* Cur Deus Homo (Edinburgh and London: Oliver and Boyd, 1954), 203.

48 From the end of 1.11 (377A).

49 Matthew 6:12. The only difference is that the Gospel uses the plural *debita* and Anselm here the singular *debitum*.

50 For a commentator taking such teleology seriously, see R. Campbell, 'The Conceptual Roots of Anselm's Soteriology', in *Anselm: Aosta, Bec, and Canterbury*, ed. Luscombe and Evans, 256–263.

51 1.20 (392c).

52 For death not required of the sinless, 1.9; for the infinite value of the offering, 2.6 and 2.14.

53 Southern, *Portrait*, 228–307, esp. 234, 280–284, 305.

54 For heaven, Revelation 4:9, 11; 5:12; 7:12. For ascriptions, e.g. 1 Timothy 1:17; 6:16. Christ receives 'honour and glory' from the Father in 2 Peter 1:17.

55 Romans 2:7. For disputed interpretations, see C.E.B. Cranfield, *The Epistle to the Romans*, vol. 1 (Edinburgh: T & T Clark, 1980), 147.

56 1.9; 2.13; cf. Luke 2:52 (AV).

57 Brian Davies, *The Thought of Thomas Aquinas* (Oxford: Clarendon Press, 1992), 324–332, esp. 327.

58 *Summa Theologiae* 3a, 46, 2.

59 For an exposition of similarities and differences, see Richard Cross, *Duns Scotus* (Oxford: Oxford University Press, 1999), 129–132.

60 John Calvin, *Institutes of the Christian Religion*, vol. 1, ed. John T. McNeil (Philadelphia: Westminster Press, 1960), 464–467, esp. 464, 466 (Bk. II, 12.1–3).

61 Calvin, *Institutes*, vol. 1, 512–520, esp. 516 (Bk. II, 16.8–12). The Latin *infera / inferna* literally means 'below' or 'the depths', though the associations of the latter, less used variant might well be taken to hint at what Calvin wanted to imply.

62 Gorringe, *God's Just Vengeance*, 103.

63 Calvin, *Institutes*, vol. 1, 509 (Bk. II, 16.5).

64 For Barth briefly, *Dogmatics in Outline* (London: SCM Press, 1949), 101–107, 114–120.

65 As when Boso sums up his position at the beginning of 2.18.

66 The phrase is adopted by Richard Swinburne in his own account of atonement in *Responsibility and Atonement* (Oxford: Clarendon Press, 1989), 81–92, 148–162, esp. 81.

67 Immanuel Kant, *Religion Within the Limits of Reason Alone*, trans. T.M. Greene and J.R. Silber (New York: Harper and Row, 1960), 60–72, esp. 65–66.

68 I am grateful to Brian Davies and Ann Loades for commenting on earlier drafts. This chapter first appeared in Brian Davies and Brian Leftow, ed., *The Cambridge Companion to Anselm* (Cambridge: Cambridge University Press, 2004), 279–302, and is reproduced here with permission of the publishers.

10 Images of Atonement
Metaphor and the Dangers of Doctrine

In reflecting on the significance of the death of Jesus and its possible relevance to our own lives, Christian theologians have sometimes developed what have been called theories of atonement, logical or semi-logical structures that attempt to explain why that death was necessary for human salvation.[1] The most detailed was the theory of satisfaction elaborated by Saint Anselm at the end of the eleventh century (in 1098) but best known today is undoubtedly the idea of penal substitution, the notion that someone had to pay the price of sin and so Jesus took our place. Indeed, so central has such an idea become in the minds of some Christians that it is for them in effect an article of faith. Yet, the idea only first came to prominence at the Reformation in the theology of John Calvin. Although ever since appeal has been made to various biblical texts, what I want to suggest in the reflections that follow is that much has been lost in adopting single approaches like those of Anselm and Calvin.

Such argumentative structures may have an appealing simplicity but what in effect they do is narrow down possibilities rather than allow us to enter fully into the wonderful richness offered by the New Testament and later Christian discussion, where an impressive range of complementary metaphors are deployed not only to illumine Jesus' death but also enable us to engage with its relevance to our own lives. But in order for readers fully to appropriate such complementarity, it is necessary for me to remind them of one very basic feature of metaphor, and that is how it differs from literal truth. Take some of the basic metaphors that we use to talk about God: for example, King and Shepherd, Judge and Saviour, Rock and Living Water, Light and Shade. To state the obvious, something cannot literally be both light and shade, or again cannot literally be both a rock and a king. Yet God can be all of these things, precisely because in using such terms metaphorically we intend that only aspects of the literal truth apply, not every element in the word's usage. So, for instance, God is strong and durable like a rock,[2] but in claiming God such we certainly do not mean that God is physical, still less that if we tried to kick him we would end up with a sore foot! So, similarly, that is why God can be simultaneously both light and shade – light if we are thinking about how our minds might be illumined by him, shade if we are thinking of ourselves overwhelmed by the oppressive heat of the world and in need of some relief.[3] Similarly, then, with metaphors for Christ's death, not every aspect of the literal meaning need be carried through. Redemption, for instance, literally means to buy someone back from slavery, but as a metaphor all it need entail is delivery from something like enslavement, not that there was anyone in particular to whom the ransom had to be paid. So, equally as with light and shade, apparently conflicting images about atonement, about how Jesus made us once more at-one with God, need not be read as of necessity in some form of deep conflict. However, rather than explore that aspect further here, what I want to do instead is consider three of those metaphors that have been most subject to criticism in modern times, and explore how far the fault lies not in them as such but rather in their hardening into dogmas or something similar. The three are considered roughly in the historical order in which they have come to prominence.

Sacrifice

The oldest image of all is that of Christ's death as sacrifice: oldest if only because it draws on an already rich tradition within the Hebrew Scriptures of the term applied literally to ritual practice and in its reapplication through metaphor. Sadly, however, despite that length of usage, today sacrifice is one of the most contested concepts in contemporary culture, and indeed has been so ever since at least the time of the First World War. The reason lies in the way it has been seen, at any rate retrospectively, to have been used to justify some of the most horrific of human actions in war. A hundred years ago at the outbreak of that war conscription proved unnecessary, so enthusiastic were young men to volunteer to fight on behalf of king and country and, if necessary, to die in their service. British youth, no less than German, were persuaded, indeed duped, by the propaganda of the time. And it is that fact against which Wilfred Owen protests in his poem 'The Parable of the Old Man and the Young', loosely based on the story of Abraham's sacrifice of Isaac, 'the old man' of the poem being leaders in government and military who failed to see beyond their own pride to the possibility of a more peaceful solution to the problems that the conflict was supposed to resolve. Hence those chilling lines with which the poem ends with the angel urging the offering of 'the Ram of Pride' instead but 'the old man' refusing and slaying not only his own son but 'half the seed of Europe, one by one'.

So powerful a critique did the poem offer of misguided notions of sacrifice in war that it was this same poem that the composer Benjamin Britten used in his *War Requiem*, commissioned to celebrate the opening of a rebuilt Coventry Cathedral.[4] There Wilfred Owen's words are set against the traditional Kyries of the liturgy, and strongly dissonant tritones repeatedly used to emphasize the terrible tension that exists between appeals for sacrifice in war on the one hand and the ideals of the Christian faith on the other.

But, if appeal to sacrifice in war is one reason why the metaphor proves so difficult to use in the contemporary world, another is its misapplication to women, with the long dominant ideology promulgated by men that had seen the role of women to serve and sacrifice in the home. Indeed, the tone of such objections had been set as early as 1879 in a famous, controversial play by the Norwegian playwright,

Henrik Ibsen, who had taken such questions as the major theme of *A Doll's House*. Therein he depicts a wife reduced by her husband to a mere puppet doll, and the wife's gradual awakening and self-discovery. Much of the wife's change of perspective is set against appeals by the husband to traditional Christian notions of female self-sacrifice. In the end the wife leaves husband and children, protesting that it is an altogether too one-sided perspective: of the wife's readiness to offer herself for her husband but no comparable willingness in the opposite direction. Indeed, perhaps the most devastating lines in the text are when the husband defends himself by saying, 'but nobody sacrifices his honour for the one he loves', only for his wife to reply: 'Hundreds and thousands of women have.'[5]

All this may suggest that sacrifice is too problematic a term in the modern context for any insight still to be gained from it into the meaning of Christ's death. But that is to reckon without taking into account how the image is in fact used in the New Testament, and in particular in its two most significant contexts of use, most extensively in the Epistle to the Hebrews and most conspicuously in accounts of Jesus' baptism where reference is made back to the sacrifice of Isaac. Both contexts can in fact be used to challenge the direction in which the metaphor was subsequently developed, in effect hardened into a requirement imposed on others such as soldiers and women.

In Hebrews Jesus is presented as breaking down the barriers that the Old Testament had assumed prevented ordinary individuals from achieving direct access to God. Recall the hierarchical structure of the Temple at Jerusalem. Only the outermost court was accessible to Gentiles, with the next court as far as women could go. Even male Israelites had to watch in their own courtyard while beyond priests offered animals in sacrifice on their behalf. Then, even that priestly caste was not allowed within the inner Holy of Holies. Instead, the High Priest alone had this privilege once a year on the so-called Day of Atonement. No, says the author of the epistle, Jesus has, as it were, knocked down all those walls, and now allows each and every one of us direct access to God as our Father.[6] In particular, Gentiles and women can now also exercise the same privileges as male Jews. In other words, gone is the demand for some sort of mediating offering imposed by God on others and in its place has come direct access for all: soldier and wife could alike stand proudly before God without the 'pride' of others, as in Wilfred Owen's phrase, demanding something more.

But it is perhaps the paralleling of Jesus' commissioning with the sacrifice of Isaac in the Father's words 'This is my beloved Son' at Jesus' baptism that presents the more complete response to the two types of challenge with which we began.[7] Modern preaching on Genesis 22 tends to focus, as in the original version of the story, on the father Abraham's dilemma, but by the time of Jesus and still more so in subsequent Jewish and Christian history this had moved firmly elsewhere, to what it had meant for Isaac (now assumed to be of an age capable of making an independent judgment), and a similar trend can be seen in the writings of the early Church Fathers as the parallel with Christ is developed.[8]

Given that in the end Isaac was not required to make the supreme sacrifice of his life, the point of that parallel cannot be that Isaac and Christ had to die, but rather a *life* so wholly dedicated to God that, although such a sacrifice might be entailed, more fundamentally, it was a life made completely holy, the literal meaning of the Latin word *sacrificium*. So Christian sacrifice, understood correctly, has nothing to do with leaders of nations offering up their youth in sacrifice or husbands expecting their wives to live their lives vicariously through them. Instead, it is all about self-sacrifice, a life no less than death wholly dedicated to God. Of course in Jesus' case such dedication did lead to a death of excruciating agony but it is important to emphasize that the point in the image of sacrifice should be seen not to lie in the agony but the self-dedication from which it stemmed.

In short, Jesus' life no less than his death can be described as a sacrifice, one of complete self-dedication to God, from which joy could emerge no less than pain, as in his appreciation of the beauty of flowers, peace on mountain tops and partying with friends and 'sinners':[9] so, certainly a terrible death as the culmination of such dedication but also a life no less wholly dedicated to God in the totality of what that might mean.

Beauty

To describe beauty as itself an image or metaphor rather than a particular kind of description of the relevant image may seem odd, but with its application to cross and crucifixion something odd does in fact happen. The actual object and event are themselves transformed and that is perhaps one reason why of the three images considered here it is probably beauty that in the contemporary world is found the most puzzling and perplexing. Moreover, not only do people find it hard to see what could possibly be meant, there is the suspicion that it would seem to come perilously close to describing what ought to be condemned, the infliction of pain, as somehow in itself a good thing. Yet earlier generations often took a different view. Nowhere is the contrast more evident than at the beginning of the sixteenth century with a High Renaissance painting such as Raphael's Mond Crucifixion and the Northern Gothic of Grünewald's Isenheim Altarpiece.[10] For Grünewald Christ's suffering cannot be too strongly emphasized since it demonstrates the Saviour's total identification with all the terrible depths into which human beings may fall. But Raphael takes a quite different view. Not only does the beauty of Christ's body remain unaffected but also angels can be seen dancing under the arms of the cross as they gather blood for communion chalices.

To most Christians of today Grünewald seems profound, and Raphael merely pretty and artificial, and on first reflection that seems exactly right. Not only does Grünewald seem to present the event as it must have happened but also he effectively picks up on how Isaiah anticipates that death ('he had no beauty, no majesty to draw our eyes'),[11] and so appears to be more consonant with Scripture. In addition, such a way of thinking obviously provides a very powerful gospel message, of Christ coming alongside us and wholly identifying with human misery. But it worth pausing to observe that, despite initial impressions, Grünewald is not in exactly the same tradition as the savage realism of more recent treatments like Mel Gibson's film *The Passion of the Christ* (2004). Balancing the depiction of Jesus' acute agony are pointers to a different reality not only in connections made with the hospital patients who were intended as the primary viewers of the painting but also in indicators of some more permanent significance for the suffering, with the deceased John the Baptist brought back to life to make a connection with the Eucharist.[12] In other words, Grünewald does not hesitate to use the visual equivalent of metaphor in surprising images to go beyond literal depiction into some wider theological significance. So the question of what might be entailed by the use of metaphor is by no means confined to Raphael.

Nor will it do to object that Raphael, unlike Grünewald, is deploying purely pagan imagery derived from Platonism. Admittedly, by the time of the Renaissance this was the primary source of inspiration, with physical beauty seen as a pointer to moral and spiritual, and beauty in general a guide to truth. Even so, using beauty to inform understanding of the cross long antedates the Renaissance, and indeed is to be found in some surprising places. Thus, for instance, the famous Anglo-Saxon poem *The Rood* in which the cross is declared beautiful and now adorned with jewels even finds its way onto the most famous standing cross in Scotland, the eighth-century Ruthwell Cross in the south-west where part of the poem is carved in runes on one side.[13] Another early example is Venatius Fortunatus's familiar hymn, 'Sing my tongue the glorious battle' that in its original Latin spoke of a 'faithful cross, among all trees uniquely noble, none in blossom, foliage or fruit your equal', sadly elided by most contemporary hymn editors presumably on the ground that the notion would be too difficult for contemporary singers to comprehend.[14]

That earlier tradition connects not so much with Platonism as with another, more biblical image for the cross, and that is the theme of victory, illustrated by that same hymn of Venatius Fortunatus which describes the cross as 'the victor's trophy'. It is a theme familiar from John's Gospel, not least in Christ's final words from the cross, 'it is finished'.[15] These are not, as they can so easily sound in English, merely remarking upon the completion of a particular purpose but rather provide a firm declaration of permanent accomplishment, the Greek perfect tense being more appropriately translated perhaps as 'All has now been accomplished'. Even so, that may still sound quite far from any notion of beauty but here we need to reckon with the rather different conceptions of beauty that pertained in the Hebrew and Jewish world as distinct from the Greek.

The latter was concerned with notions like balance and proportionality whereas the Hebrew *kabod* and its nearest Greek equivalent *doxa* were much more a matter of 'glory' or 'splendour', the Hebrew term literally meaning what 'weighs' upon or has a profound impact on the percipient. Used over 300 times in the Bible, it is an image particularly associated with the presence of God in the Old Testament and with the story of Jesus in the New, with his birth, resurrection and ascension all finding the term deployed,[16] as also occasions in which disciples see Christ in a new light.[17] Somewhat surprisingly, the actual word does not occur in accounts of the transfiguration,[18] whereas it does in relation to the crucifixion, with John repeatedly asserting that this is where Christ's glory was to be found, as at the point of Judas' betrayal: 'When he had gone out, Jesus said, "Now the Son of Man is glorified, and in him God is glorified".'[19]

All this might seem to argue decisively in favour of John finding beauty in Grünewald's portrayal of the crucifixion rather than Raphael's, but matters are not quite that simple. It is after all in John that Jesus is portrayed as most in control, with the verse already quoted, for example, replacing the cry of dereliction found in Mark and Matthew, or again, even as glory is found at the point of betrayal, it is John who emphasizes more than any of the other evangelists that it is a betrayal which takes place with the full knowledge of Jesus.[20] So it is not implausible to argue that elements in Raphael are as much in John as are ideas that one might draw from Grünewald. Indeed, given the fact that the disciples in John find Jesus' glory at the miracle of water into wine at Cana, one might argue that Raphael's depiction of the 'splendour' of the blood of the cross transformed into wine is not all that dissimilar.

But what John thought is not of course quite the same issue as how such competing ideas of beauty might be received today. Even as late as the nineteenth century, the poet and priest Gerard Manley Hopkins found no difficulty in applying the Platonic model, and so insisted that not only was Christ beautiful during his earthly life but would be still more so in heaven, where he argues that the scars from his wounds must have disappeared.[21] But nowadays we are less confident. Such a view seems to endorse precisely the kind of privileging of one kind of individual over another that Christ came to overthrow. It is a question that is posed with particular force by one contemporary artist, Marc Quinn, in the statue he erected in 2007 on one of the plinths in Trafalgar Square in London.[22] Alison Lapper, his sitter, as well as being pregnant with child at the time, was also bereft of arms and had truncated legs, both the result of a condition known as phocomelia. Quinn's question to those passing by was why should Alison not also be considered beautiful in her own right and without reference to some general abstract ideal or Greek standard of feminine beauty, not least when so much of the beauty in Greek statuary that we admire in museums is now similarly truncated.

While such reflections might initially appear to suggest that we are once more pulled back to a more Hebraic notion, it is as well to remind ourselves that it is not the suffering as such that creates the splendour but who was suffering and, more importantly, how he suffered. In fact, what I would propose these reflections demonstrate is that modern difficulties with applying the notion of beauty to the cross lie in assumptions about pre-determined set answers, whether these be pagan or Christian. To be beautiful, Christ and his cross, it is believed, must conform either to conventional Platonic accounts or to relatively unexamined assumptions about the Hebrew *doxa*, whereas the metaphor's real power lies not in any set answer but precisely in its ability to challenge us to reflect more deeply on what beauty is, and where it can truly be found.

Penalty

More conservative Evangelical Christians still commonly maintain that a penal view of atonement is the only position ever found in the New Testament, and indeed the attempt is often then made catch all other images within its ambit. Yet the penal account only achieved such dominance relatively late in the day, particularly under the influence of Calvin. In his view all human sin incurs divine wrath, and as such the punishment justly due can only be avoided by someone totally innocent paying a corresponding heavy penalty instead. Expressed like this, there is thus a marked difference from Anselm's position. Anselm had insisted that only a perfect life offered freely in death was required by way of recompense, not suffering as such, whereas for Calvin the fact that Jesus suffered so dreadfully adds, he believed, to the plausibility to his account. Seen through God's eyes human sin is terrible and so must meet with a correspondingly dreadful penalty.[23]

Before addressing the specific biblical passages to which appeal is made, it is as well to note what probably appeals most, and that is the relative simplicity of the view. Yet it is a simplicity that conceals a troubling complexity, for it depends on an individual believing, first, that their sin is sufficiently serious to deserve such an awful death and, second, that it is still justice if someone else pays the penalty rather than the individual who has done such deeds. But on the latter point, surely the reason why we all admire Sydney Carton going to his death on the guillotine in place of his friend in *A Tale of Two Cities* is not because justice was thereby served but rather precisely because he acts to avert the consequences of an unjust penal system that the new French Republic was now imposing.

On the question of guilt the issue is more complicated. On the one side, it is of course true that we are often far too indulgent to our own failings, treating them less seriously than they deserve. Studdert-Kennedy (the 'Woodbine Willie' of the First World War), has a poem that makes this all too clear:

> When Jesus came to Birmingham, they simply passed Him by,
> They never hurt a hair of Him, they only let Him die,
> For men had grown more tender, and they would not give Him pain,
> They only just passed down the street, and left Him in the rain.[24]

Sometimes it is non-believers who have a livelier sense of the evil within us than do Christians. Certainly that was true for the greatest British painter of the twentieth century, Francis Bacon. Although a convinced atheist, he was obsessed by the crucifixion, and it is an image that appears repeatedly in his paintings.[25] From his own perspective, it was a useful device for indicating the meaninglessness of human existence, of the terrible suffering that can emerge for no very obvious reason. But we can also read him asserting how deep evil runs in human beings, an evil that often remains totally indifferent to others's suffering. So in one adaptation he has cars passing by, in another drinkers at a bar observing the tortured body, while in a third Christ utters a dreadful scream from the cross even as the figure above (more like a dog than a human being) proves powerless to help.[26]

Yet, if such evasion of culpability may be set on one side, there is also something troubling to be put on the other, and that is the way in which this particular approach has encouraged guilt-obsessed individuals under which the gospel message, so far from bringing liberty, has actually created a new kind of prison. This is because, wherever such an approach is prevalent, in order for the message of forgiveness to be appropriated, a strong consciousness of sinfulness must first be inculcated. Sometimes, of course, there are no deleterious consequences, and indeed a marvellous sense of release is the result, as in Charles Wesley's great celebratory poem on his conversion.[27] While Wesley does not hesitate to use the language of appeasement, what primarily comes across is his huge sense of relief as in the words:

> I woke, the dungeon flamed with light,
> my chains fell off, my heart was free,
> I rose, went forth, and followed thee.[28]

And no doubt numerous Methodists have been encouraged towards similar experiences, as they sang the poem as a hymn.

Yet that has not always been the case. Perhaps nowhere have the problems with this approach been more clearly indicated than in the spate of child abuse scandals that have occurred in recent years, for, sad to relate, it is more often the abused who feels guilty and soiled rather than the abuser. Somehow they feel that there must have been some evil lurking in them that led on the abuser. But, equally, if we spread the net more widely, there is no shortage of other sorts of individual in the contemporary world, who have been traumatized by an exaggerated sense of guilt and for whom the only release seems to be escape from the Church rather than a deeper entering into its life.

Yet all such problems might have been avoided had metaphor not been turned into dogma, as can be seen from careful consideration of the two types of passage to which appeal is most commonly made. Take first Romans 3:25 (with the related passages in 1 John 2:2 and 4:10) where the term 'propitiation' is used in the King James Bible, as indeed it had also been in the Latin Vulgate. The reason for thinking that in the Greek original we find ourselves in the presence of a metaphor and not some particular theory of the atonement is because the two related words do not mention a doctrine at all but simply refer in the one case (Romans) to the Mercy Seat in the Temple, and in the other (John) to the action that took place there.[29] That is to say, it was the place where sacrifice for the people's sin was symbolically offered on the Day of Atonement through the symbolic sprinkling of blood on the furniture. In other words, the image is too brief and too dense to suggest any precise parallel, but at most that Jesus' death was intended to achieve reconciliation with God just like that original offering, and that is why modern versions of Scripture usually translate very much more loosely.[30]

Again, much the same can be said of the other key passage to which appeal is commonly made, 2 Corinthians 5:21, where according to the King James Bible Paul appears without qualification to endorse substitutionary atonement, in declaring that God 'hath made him to be sin for us, who knew no sin'. But once more what is offered is really a dense image that could legitimately be developed in more than one possible direction. Comments from a contemporary of Wesley, the Anglican divine, William Law, may be used to indicate why Jesus suffering divine wrath against sin cannot be the passage's most natural expansion:

Now will the Scriptures, which tell us that the love of God sent His Son into the world to redeem man from that hellish wrath that had seized him, allow us to say that it was to extinguish the wrath that was got into God himself...? No, surely; but to bruise, alter, and overcome an evil in nature and the creature, that was become man's separation from the enjoyment of the God of love .... And is not this sufficiently telling us what that wrath was and where it existed, which must be atoned ...? It was a wrath of death, a wrath of hell, a wrath of sin, and which only the precious, powerful blood of Christ could change into a life of joy and love.[31]

In other words, as many a modern translation seems to imply, the point is not that Jesus was in any sense regarded as a substitute for the sinner but rather that he became one with our sinful condition;[32] that is, divinity entered into every aspect that speaks of the terrible consequences of sin which inhibit the ability of human beings to lead life to the full. So like us Jesus experienced divisions in his family, petty jealousies among his friends, opposition from his fellow countrymen, oppression from occupying forces and so on – all the ire in sin that sets one human being against another. And yet on the cross all this was overcome, with him able to promise one of the thieves dying with him a better life, able to forgive those who had put him there, and even be seen by one of those responsible, the centurion, as who he really was when he declared him Son of God. And so, then, likewise with us, Jesus opens up to us a path that can get beyond all the destructive consequences – the wrath – that necessarily follows from human sinfulness.

Conclusion

In this chapter I have explored only three of the many images used in the New Testament and later Christian tradition to make sense of Christ's life. While I stressed that all such metaphors could be used to complement one another even where apparently conflicting,[33] the three I took for more detailed examination have been so extensively criticized in modern times that many have concluded that they are no more capable of effective use. My counter stance was that the fault lay not in the metaphors in themselves but in the tendency of their advocates to set them in stone as doctrines rather than allow the richness onto which they can open properly to flourish as their original application had first suggested.[34]

Notes

1 Not, though, a uniform pattern even as late as the middle ages. Bonaventure, for example, used different theories in different places without worrying whether they were inconsistent: Christopher Cullen, *Bonaventure* (Oxford: Oxford University Press, 2006), 147–148.
2 E.g. Psalm 18:2.
3 E.g. Psalm 17:8; 91:2.

4 The *War Requiem* was first performed in 1962. It is one of the many places in which the text of Owen's poem is available.

5 For the key scene, see Hendrik Ibsen, *Four Major Plays*, trans. by James McFarlane and Jens Arup (Oxford: Oxford University Press, 1981), 78–86, esp. 84.

6 Cf. Hebrews 9:6–15.

7 Although Psalm 2:7 and Isaiah 42:1ff. play their part, most commentators also assume an allusion to Genesis 22:2.

8 For references and a more extensive discussion, see my *Tradition and Imagination: Revelation and Change* (Oxford: Oxford University Press, 1999), 237–260, esp. 251ff.

9 Matthew 6:28–29; 14:23; 11.18–19.

10 Raphael's Mond Crucifixion is in the National Gallery in London, the Isenheim Altarpiece now at Colmar in France. For an image of the former, see www.national-gallery.org.uk/paintings/raphael-the-mond-crucifixion.

11 Isaiah 53:2 (NEB): one of the Suffering Servant songs.

12 The figures in the side panels with boils and arrow blows were intended to allude to the patients' own suffering and its parallels with that of Christ. John the Baptist is depicted as physically present at the crucifixion. For an excellent discussion of the details of the painting, A. Hayum, *The Isenheim Altarpiece: God's Medicine and the Painter's Vision* (Princeton, NJ: Princeton University Press, 1989).

13 That connection has made some prefer an attribution to Caedmon rather than Cynewulf but the truth is we simply do not know: Albert S. Cook, ed., *The Dream of the Rood* (Oxford: Clarendon Press, 1905), 6–7. For discussion of the Cross itself, Brendan Cassidy ed., *The Ruthwell Cross* (Princeton, NJ: Princeton University Press, 1992).

14 The difference is well illustrated by contrasting more recent hymnbooks with even the Scottish Presbyterian *Church Hymnary* of 1927, where such language is retained (108, v. 4.).

15 John 19:30.

16 Birth: John 1:14; Luke 1:14. Resurrection: Luke 24:26; Romans 6:4; 1 Peter 1:21. Ascension: 1 Timothy 3:16.

17 E.g. Luke 2:9, 14; John 2:11; 2 Corinthians 4:6.

18 Though the imagery of splendour does.

19 John 13:31 (REB); cf. John 12:23, 28.

20 Note the gradual build-up in 13:1, 3 and 21.

21 Sermon for 23rd November, 1879; e.g. in W.H. Gardner, ed., *Gerard Manley Hopkins: A Selection of his Poetry and Prose* (Hardmonsworth: Penguin, 1953), 137–139.

22 See http://marcquinn.com/exhibitions/solo-exhibitions/marc-quinn-fourth-plinth.

23 See e.g. John Calvin, *Institutes of the Christian Religion*, II, xvi, 6.

24 The second stanza of his poem 'Indifference': included in James D. Morrison, ed., *Masterpieces of Religious Verse* (New York: Harper & Brothers, 1948), 195.

25 For an example in the Tate, see http://www.tate.org.uk/art/artworks/bacon-three-studies-for-figures-at-the-base-of-a-crucifixion-n06171.

26 For images of each of these, as well as some further thoughts on Bacon's use of the crucifixion, see Rina Arya, *Francis Bacon: Painting in a Godless World* (Farnham: Lund Humphries, 2012), 59–83.

27 21 May 1738. 'Free Grace': the poem and hymn that begins 'And can it be that I should gain'.

28 From the fourth stanza. The fifth contains the line 'quenched the wrath of hostile heaven'.

29 The Greek term in Romans is *hilasterion*, while in the other two cases it is *hilasmos*.

30 For example, 'a sacrifice of atonement' in the RSV, 'a means of expiating sin' in NEB.

31 Quoted without reference in W. R. Inge, ed., *Freedom, Love and Truth* (London: Longmans, Green and Co., 1936), 100–101. The topic is raised numerous times in his writings: see *William Law*, ed. Paul G. Stanwood (New York: Paulist Press, 1978) in Classics of Western Spirituality series.

32 As in the NEB: 'God made him one with the sinfulness of men, so that in him we might be made one with the goodness of God.'
33 As with light and shade mentioned at the beginning of the essay.
34 The inspiration for these reflections first came from an invitation from Bob Gillies, the Bishop of Aberdeen and Orkney, to deliver a series of sermons at the Three Hours service on Good Friday, 2015 in his cathedral in Aberdeen.

Part IV

Heaven and our Communal Destiny

Introduction

Readers may be surprised to discover that none of the following essays addresses the question of eschatology in terms of 'a new heaven and a new earth': very much the dominant approach in contemporary theology that conceives final human destiny as occurring simultaneously with the dawn of a new form of material existence. This is not because I wish to decry the legitimacy of such an element in Christian belief, but it is to challenge whether such an emphasis should be bought at the cost of acknowledging heaven as a present reality. Admittedly, there were quite a number of wrong turns in the past in the way in which theology envisaged heaven but, as I attempt to demonstrate in what follows, none of these defects is fatal. Purgatory, for instance, need not be tied to notions of punishment and heaven should not be seen as denying the material aspect that helps constitute human identity in this life.

More importantly, despite what advocates of the new emphasis claim, their position is in my view far more culturally conditioned than its more traditional alternative, and in at least two ways. First, it buys into modern difficulties in conceiving of any other form of reality than a material one. So, however much ideas of heaven were once influenced by Platonism (and the extent of that influence is contested in what follows), these ideas can *now* be seen as firmly counter-cultural, and so as offering their own quite distinctive message. But, secondly, the dominant current view can equally be seen as conceding too much ground to contemporary individualism since it offers a future prospect where all the redeemed are restored to full life at one and the same time, and so without any clear sense of the social relations that once made them the distinctive human beings that they in fact once were. By contrast, the traditional picture sees not only the living and departed in current interdependence on one another but also even Christ himself functioning as such a social being in heaven. Yet, if the jettisoning of the more traditional account is in general the pattern both within Christian circles and more widely, one interesting deviation is the survival of earlier conceptions in more popular media, and in a way that at least sometimes takes the notion seriously, for example in films such as *What Dreams May Come* (2003) or *The Lovely Bones* (2009). What this may possibly suggest is that elements of traditional Christian belief can sometimes be better preserved outside the practice of the faith than within it.[1]

The first essay in what follows as much concerns this life as the next, in that it seeks to persuade more Protestant readers of both the legitimacy and usefulness of identifying particular individuals as saintly. Next, purely philosophical considerations are used to argue for a preparatory state. Although elements of continuity with the traditional notion of Purgatory are observed, major differences will also be detected, including the absence of features that helped precipitate the Reformation. Finally, both theological and philosophical arguments are deployed to argue for the existence and importance of heaven as a present reality.

Note

1   A key point made in a recent St Andrews doctoral thesis from Timothy Allen, *Heaven and Imagination* (University of St Andrews, 2016).

11 Why 'Saints' Matter

Initially, some readers may find it odd that a consideration of the importance of saints is offered as tribute to Vincent Brümmer, formerly Professor of the Philosophy of Religion at the University of Utrecht, on his eightieth birthday.[1] After all, the specific term as such scarcely finds a mention in Brümmer's own writings, and that would of course be true in general of the Reformed tradition to which he has remained so faithful throughout his life. Nonetheless, three factors pull in the opposite direction. First, although the term except in its standard abbreviation is largely absent, much of his work has in fact been concerned with analysing the religious experience of those close to God whom others might well label as saints.[2] Second, his writing and practice have been consistently ecumenical in their scope, and so a topic that attempts to bridge differences between Geneva and Rome and written by an Anglican would seem not entirely inappropriate. Finally, however, and most importantly, it is my hope in what follows to emulate in some small way the model of careful analysis, sound scholarship and measured reasoning that has been so characteristic of his contributions to theology.

In using 'saints' in this narrower sense let me concede at once that I thereby depart from New Testament usage, where such holiness or sanctity is seen as the vocation and aspiration of all and the term therefore applied indifferently to Christians of all kinds on more than sixty occasions.[3] Nonetheless, no one would deny the existence of conspicuous sanctity. So the issue at stake is not the fact as such but whether there are advantages or otherwise in identifying such a narrower group. I shall begin by rehearsing three objections with possible responses before exploring three positive arguments on the other side. As will become clear, my argument as a whole is cumulative.

Three Arguments Against Singling Out Saints

(1) The first is that any such focus inevitably detracts from a proper sense of the uniqueness of divine holiness, and thus brings with it the usurpation of functions that rightly belong to God alone, among them, most obviously, an intercessory role. That this is a problem by no means unique to Christianity will have become obvious to Brümmer on his lecture visits to Iran; so it is worth pausing briefly to observe how the issue affects Islam.

Although Arabic has terms that parallel the Catholic hierarchic distinction between 'saint' and 'blessed' (*wali* and *tahir*), there has in fact been a long history of opposition to all such differentiations that continues to this day. Notoriously, the inherent dangers were observed as early as the Persian al-Hallaj's claim to identity with God.[4] However, thanks to writers such the philosopher al-Ghazali and the poet Farid ud-Din Attar more moderate approaches eventually prevailed.[5] Even so dangerous claims to a mediatorial role might be said to be implicit in the very architecture of saints's shrines among the Shi'ites of Iran,[6] while the marabouts of North African Sunnis could also be seen as exercising a not dissimilar role even while still living, although even as early as Ibn Khaldun's early-fifteenth-century classic history Shi'ites are blamed for thus leading Sunnis astray.[7] In contemporary Islam, the influential Wahhabi sect of Saudi Arabia is particularly forceful in its objections. For them the uniqueness of God (*tawhid*) is thereby fatally compromised.

So, generalizing, the potentially problematic character of saints might be said to be inherent in any monotheistic religion. Yet there is no doubt that the problem is intensified within Christianity, with Christ's unique mediating role with the Father now also seen as under threat. Instead of the prayers of Christ being sought, saints may be asked to intercede, and may indeed be viewed as more friendly and sympathetic. The nadir of such an approach is often identified as occurring in medieval attitudes to the Virgin Mary. Yet, in recalling that history it is important to remember that the primary fault lay with an inadequate conception of Christ as a stern judge reluctant to forgive.[8] A more balanced conception of the Saviour would have made desperate flight to gentler intercessors unnecessary. It was partly to correct such misconceptions that the Second Vatican Council insisted upon the removal of so many saints's images from churches. Equally, much modern Roman Catholic theology has sought to place the two types of sanctity (wider and narrower) in closer relation to one another. A particularly good example is to be found in Elizabeth Johnson's attempt to set the existence of persons of special sanctity within a strong doctrine of the *communio sanctorum*, the sharing of the entire Christian community in such a vocation.[9] Their primary purpose as exemplary (not intercessory) is thereby underlined and maintained.

(2) A related objection concerns the way in which the identification of the possibility of such singular sanctity may lead not only others astray (towards assuming a mediatorial role), but also even the individuals themselves so identified. It could so easily encourage pride on their part, rather than a sense of humble service under divine grace. This seems to be the heart of Dietrich Bonhoeffer's objection. He describes how initially he was greatly impressed by a French pastor who had spoken of his desire to become a saint, but on further reflection he took a quite different view:

> I discovered later ... one must completely abandon any attempt to make something of oneself, whether it be a saint, or a converted sinner, or a churchman (a so-called priestly type!), a righteous man or an unrighteous one, a sick man

or a healthy one. By this worldliness I mean living unreservedly in life's duties .... In so doing, we throw ourselves completely into the arms of God, taking seriously, not our own sufferings but those of God in the world.[10]

Nor will it do to say such arrogance has never befallen those whom the Church has identified as saints. On the contrary, as the dying words of Polycarp testify, the deliberate search for martyrdom was a conspicuous feature of the earlier Church, while in subsequent centuries where such an option was no longer available there was usually still a focus on heroic virtue and so on the necessity for extreme and at times horrific forms of asceticism and self-abasement.[11] It was abasement that could all too easily turn into a sense of satisfied self-achievement, as can be seen in the life of St Thérèse of Lisieux. Sadly, her appropriation of contemporary teaching on the doctrine of the treasury of merit led to a rather depressing counting of her own good acts, even their conscious balancing against the wrongs or suffering of others.[12]

All this might suggest that any talk of saints in the narrower sense is best discouraged, but my earlier reference to Paul's wider usage belies the fact that even in his writings the distinction between the two types of saint is already being made. Although Paul's most famous reference is to the imitation of Christ, surprising as it may seem, more commonly he refers us to his own example.[13] 'I urge you to become imitators of me'; 'You yourselves know that you ought to imitate us'; 'Brethren, join in imitating me'.[14] Such formulae may be taken to imply that identification of good in oneself need not necessarily be wrong, and indeed a constant denial might well soon lead to the sort of hypocritical false modesty that is so often parodied in literature.[15] It seems as though aspiring saints must walk a narrow tightrope that on the one hand avoids a false estimate of their own condition and on the other any haughty assumption that this has all been achieved from their own resources.

(3) A final objection arises from the way in which extremes so often generate their opposites. Where sanctity is acknowledged, there is often a regrettable tendency towards the production of its dualistic opposite, in the demonization of individuals on the other side. This is perhaps the well nigh inevitable result of the way in which the lives of the saints have commonly been told in the past. In effect, their life stories have been portrayed as a struggle between two types of supernatural force, one for good and the other for evil. St Antony of Egypt, for example, does not battle alone in the desert but with demons.[16] Again, those who held power in the Roman Empire and opposed the martyrs were more often than not demonized for their role in such a struggle. Especially in fictional accounts, a simple execution was seldom enough. Instead, the saint's opponents were envisaged as adding numerous gratuitous tortures, so cruel and callous is all that is opposed to them taken to be.[17]

Sadly, it is possible to detect this kind of problem within the New Testament itself. In the Book of Revelation the world is essentially divided into two opposing camps, with all views different from that of the writer placed firmly on the other side. Indeed, even Paul is implicitly treated in the same way, since those who take a position like Paul's on food offered to idols are consigned to Satan.[18] Again, faults that had once been freely admitted in earlier versions of admired lives either disappear altogether or else are projected onto others. Within Scripture itself the most conspicuous of this trend is found in the treatment of King David. Detailed comparison of his story as told in the writings of the Deuteronomic School of historians and in Chronicles demonstrates the desire to exonerate David from all, or almost, all sin.[19] Gone is all reference to his adultery with Bathsheba as also the key role played by the northern tribes in his rise to power, and in their place comes an almost exclusive focus on Jerusalem as the eventual home for the Temple.

It is a pattern that continues into later history. Within the Jewish tradition Jacob, for example, becomes the model *tzaddik* or righteous one who has been carefully schooled in the ways of rabbinic thought.[20] Within Christianity even as customarily careful a historian as Bede succumbs to the same sort of temptation. In light of the fact that he supported the centralizing Roman policy that was adopted at the Synod of Whitby in 664, it is fascinating to observe how, apart from Oswald's relations with St Aidan, minimum attention is given to the positive role of the losing Celtic faction in his account of St Oswald's life. So, for instance, Oswald's invocation of St Columba at the battle of Heavenfield (recorded by our earliest source Adomnan) is omitted, while little is made of the fact that the defeated Britons were also led by a Christian, Cadwallon. As others have observed, there must have been some rough edges on Oswald, were he to have any chance of survival in the type of royal courts that *Beowulf* so vividly portrays for us.[21] Yet none of this survives into Bede's account.

This tendency to create a world of pure black and white, of crude contrasts between undefiled goodness and unremitting evil, is among the most glaring deficiencies in the history of western spirituality that need to be confronted by the modern Christian. Not that the motives were necessarily wholly bad. Presumably, one thought may have been that, since the saints were intimate with God, it could not but be the case that divine holiness would inevitably be clearly reflected in the life of the saint. But the wrong kind of intimacy was presumed, one in which God would simply override any contrary beliefs or elements of moral blindness. As both Judaism and Christianity have wrestled in more recent years with the fallibility inherent in their own histories, they have at last come to see that God does not quite work like that. Instead, God gives human beings the necessary space to come to see the truth for themselves, and that means accepting limitations both in the community history as a whole and in the lives and attitudes of specific individuals. So, just as in the case of Scripture if we are to learn fully from its pages we must acknowledge its shortcomings no less than the profundity of its insights, so in the individual case as much can sometimes be learnt from the flawed side of the saint as from his or her undoubted holiness.

Fortunately, this is increasingly being recognized in the way in which biographies of the saints are now being written. In my own case it is a recurring theme in one recent book of mine that attempts to explore Church history through the lives of the saints.[22] It is also sometimes evident in the very title chosen by an author for such a work, as in Simon Tugwell's *Ways of Imperfection*.[23] If Joseph Heller goes too far in his provocative re-telling of David's story,[24] what he does indicate is how spiritually challenging the imperfect can be no less than the perfect. Such changes in perspective constitute a welcome development, as it makes the possibility of learning from the lives of the saints more feasible. Instead of august figures fundamentally different from ourselves and so with a particular entitlement to the divine ear, they are now to be seen standing in solidarity alongside ourselves, imperfect just as we are. The difference lies rather in the degree to which they consistently strove to move towards perfection in a life lived under divine grace. The traditional Protestant objection that saints are put on the wrong side of the dividing line between God and the rest of his creation is thus very effectively undermined. They bridge the gap precisely because they so obviously at one and the same time stand on both sides of the divide.

Three Arguments for Assigning Saints a Key Role

In suggesting that it is their exemplary rather than intercessory role that makes saints important I have already begun to move to more positive considerations. Just as I noted three types of objection to the concept, so here too I want to pursue the issue through three more positive arguments.

(1) The first attempts to answer the objection that to speak of them as exemplary sets them up as a barrier that the ordinary Christian must still cross before a more direct relationship with God and Christ becomes possible. Is not Jesus' own example enough? In the most obvious sense that must of course be true, since Jesus remains the standard for the Christian against which all human morality must be judged. Even so, the admission does not of itself entail that help is not needed in mediating such standards into what are often quite different human scenarios. So it is as a bridge between Christ and us in a quite different sense that I want to advocate the relevance of saints's lives here: that they can enable us to see more easily how a Christ-like life might be lived in situations quite different from the original context of Jesus' own life.

Such a strategy may already be in play even as early as Paul. Certainly, that is one possible explanation of why, as noted above, Paul so often chose to refer directly to his own example rather than that of Christ. Whether Paul's motivation or not, with the advance of the centuries the problem has undoubtedly increased proportionally, as the imaginative distance between the setting of Jesus' life and that of his followers has grown. Not only is martyrdom no longer an issue for most of us, there are also huge differences in standards of living and resultant options, in choices of life-style, in engagement with other cultures and ideas, even in life-expectancy itself.

Elsewhere I have identified three types of distance that encouraged focus on the lives of saints as a way of bringing the example of Christ closer to the sort of lives Christians now lead: what I called there metaphysical, spatial, and temporal distance.[25] 'Metaphysical' refers to Christ's unique relationship with his Father, and the difficulty of converting such absolutes into the more ordinary conditions of human life. The obsession of the early Church with martyrdom may be used to illustrate one version of the tensions encountered, the monastic ideal seen in the Middle Ages as a higher (and not different) calling another. By 'temporal' I alluded to the changing cultural conditions that have confronted the Christian community across the centuries. Modern capitalism, for instance, hardly presents exactly the same challenges as ancient agrarian societies. With all of us increasingly conscious of a single interdependent world, spatial distance might seem very much less an issue in our own day. Yet for most of human history the distant was seen as strangely alien. That was one reason why not only were local saints cultivated but also sometimes even those who were formerly distant were now brought close by the removal of their bones to a more immediate locality.[26]

Despite the strength of these concerns the Church proved surprisingly slow to respond, with little recognition given to the fact that sanctity was a possibility for laity just as much as for those called to the religious life. Even then female religious had significantly more of an uphill struggle towards recognition than men, while acceptance of married women in this role remained rare. Indeed, the latter seemed only to gain admission if they had the added advantage of royal birth, and so an already existing band of powerful advocates. That helps explain exceptions such as Queen Margaret of Scotland (d. 1093) or Elizabeth of Hungary (d. 1231). Not that male royalty had it that much easier, since their hands were usually seen as polluted by war. This probably explains why King David I of Scotland was not exalted to such ranks despite his undoubtedly devout life.[27] More successful was Louis IX of France. That had much to do with the fact that he was monarch of a more important country, and played a key role on behalf of the Church in the Crusades.[28] What little thought was given to what holiness might mean in the conduct of ordinary warfare is well illustrated by the fact that King Oswald's attempts to advance the kingdom of Northumbria had to be re-presented as a battle on behalf of Christianity. That way, he could be declared a martyr, although he actually died in the course of an ordinary battle.[29]

In more recent times the papacy has attempted to correct such faults, and now there is a much more representative spread of types of vocation and life.[30] Other churches have done likewise, as in the Church of England's modern calendar.[31] Even so, it should not be thought that such a search for a greater range of mediated examples is entirely a modern phenomenon. Instead, in earlier history alternative strategies were commonly adopted that relied, significantly, largely on the imagination. The lives of legendary saints were adapted to speak to conditions that were not directly addressed elsewhere. One astonishing case is how the issue of pregnancy was dealt with: Margaret of Antioch's legendary struggle with a dragon was used as an analogy for what in the past was often a highly dangerous moment in women's lives.[32] A small but significant illustration of its widespread application is in Jan van Eyck's famous Arnolfini marriage portrait, in which a small carving of Margaret and the dragon is to be found by the bedside.[33]

On my view it is also here in such considerations that the elaboration of Mary Magdalene's life story is to be found, and not, as so many modern feminists allege, in suspicion of, or hostility to, women.[34] Although the composite tale that combines various women in the New Testament and extends this beyond into ministry in France was undoubtedly sometimes used negatively to denigrate women, this was by no means its primary or most common application.[35] Instead, the elaborated fictional tale gave readers and hearers of Scripture the opportunity to observe a sinner's growth in holiness across the various New Testament incidents, as the composite woman was observed progressively deepening her faith and understanding in her developing relationship with Christ: first receiving his forgiveness, then learning at his feet; identifying with him in his death on the cross, then discovering the new life offered in his resurrection.[36] Medieval Christians found in Mary Magdalene someone ordinary like themselves growing in holiness, and so the promise that the possibility might also be their own, whether their own besetting sin was sexual or otherwise. The point of the sexual aspect was thus its very ordinariness, not woman as temptress, however much that theme might intrude elsewhere. Perhaps one example of that earlier attitude may suffice, St Anselm's prayer to Mary Magdalene:

> Most blessed lady, I the most wicked of men do not touch once more on your sins as a taunt or reproach but seek to grasp the boundless mercy by which they were blotted out .... Draw for me from the well where I may wash my sins ... For it is not difficult for you to obtain whatever you wish from so loving and so kind a Lord, who is your friend living and reigning.[37]

Some readers may regret, even despise, the resort to fiction upon which the power of Mary Magdalene's story depends. They should not. Even today such means remain the most common form of moral reflection among the population at large. Think, for instance, of the key contribution TV soaps have made in allowing viewers to explore and wrestle with some of the major moral issues of the day, gay relationships among them.[38] It is of course possible to argue that all that is happening here is a reflection of already changing social values. But it is not without significance that the first television treatments of such issues occurred before opinion polls were reporting a majority sympathetic to gay relationships. The scriptwriters do thus appear to have played a key role in helping viewers to explore how they might appropriately regard family members or colleagues at work similarly situated.

Equally, Christians have sometimes found it easiest to explore moral dilemmas in contexts such as war or sexual ethics through the medium of the novel. So, for instance, some of Graham Greene's works seem to have fulfilled just such a function for Roman Catholics struggling in situations where moral absolutes seem hard to apply.[39] Again, novelists like R.C. Hutchinson helped an earlier generation over the preservation of integrity and sanctity in the face of the conundrums of conflict and war.[40] That conceded, something of course would still be lacking, were the imaginative never to find reflection in parallel real lives. So the better way remains that such matters be pursued through actual historical examples, if at all possible, which is where the notion of saints would continue to have relevance.

(2) That admission links with a second major argument for the importance of saints in theological reflection. This is the contribution they might make to the question

of evidence for the existence of God. Apart from professional philosophers, few now give credence to the traditional arguments for the existence of God. They seem at most to raise the possibility rather than push an open mind decisively in one direction or the other. One philosophical theologian (admired by Brümmer) who used the saints to tip the balance in just such a way is the former Warden of Keble College, Oxford, Austin Farrer.

> Such a life, then, is evidence; and what other evidence could you hope to find? We have no inspection, no insight into the works of nature, which could conceivably let us through them to a vision of anything that lies beneath .... The only being we can know from within is our own; we are forced, however inadequate it may be, to take it as a sample of the rest, and judge the world from man. And man knows God only by yielding to him; we do not know the fountain of our being, so long as we are occupied in stopping it with mud. So the saint is our evidence, and other men, of course for the glimpses of sanctity that are in them.[41]

Discounting the customary male-orientated character of the language of the day, what most strikes us now in Farrer's discussion is his ready admission of the powerful impact one such individual had made on his own life, and the inevitable consequence this entails in selecting some individuals over against others. As he observes in a memorable phrase, 'the evidence of faith is incorrigibly aristocratic'. More recently, Rowan Williams has moved in a similar direction. Quoting St Ambrose's remark that 'it did not suit God to save people by arguments', he goes on to indicate the key role played by others in shaping belief or otherwise in the truths of faith: that sometimes even 'the very angst and struggle they bring to their relation with God is a kind of argument for God'.[42] In particular, he offers the intriguing observation that sometimes people 'take responsibility for making God credible in the world', as appears to have been the case with Etty Hillesum, a young Jewish woman sentenced to Auschwitz, who wrote that she felt called to 'bear witness to the fact that God lived, even in these times'.[43]

The point is that, where sanctity is of a truly heroic kind, it seemed simplest to accept the saint's own account of what has made this possible, the aid of divine grace. Sometimes of course individuals do appear able to maintain a similar witness to the good without reliance on faith, but for the Christian the unrecognized hand of grace will still usually seem the best explanation for such persistence, however much the individual may insist on an alternative explanation. How plausible such an account might be is too complex a question to enter on here. Suffice it to say that it seems supported by the individual Christian's own experience of divine guidance, for this too is often only discovered in retrospect.

(3) Finally, and perhaps surprisingly to some readers, something needs to be said on the way in which the idea of saints can help strengthen our sense of social interdependence. Much contemporary Christian theology has been preoccupied with the apparent disintegration of western societies into narrow, self-centred individualism,

and various counter-strategies have been proposed, among them a revived social doctrine of the Trinity.[44] Thus far I may have conveyed the impression that attending to the lives of the saints is part of that individualism, all just a matter of personal piety, each individual modelling his or her life on that of another (the saint), however much each might find their ultimate rationale in the life of the Saviour himself.

Yet such a formulation ignores the essentially social character of human identity, something that must carry implications for our understanding of the person of Jesus both as incarnate and as now exalted to heaven. Whereas for most of Christian history theologians assumed the existence of special infused knowledge in the incarnate Lord, biblical criticism has now compelled recognition of a more complex reality in some form of kenosis, even if the more precise formulations of the nineteenth century failed to gain any wide acceptance.[45] There was a real shaping of Jesus by his own culture and surroundings that would have included important contributions from others, among them not only his human parents, disciples and friends but perhaps also the local rabbi, the Syro-Phoenician woman and so on.[46]

Here I allude to that strange incident (Mark 7:24–30) because it was possibly this encounter that moved Jesus decisively towards a more positive appreciation of Gentiles. The passage is one in which pagans are described by the diminutive for dogs. Although the Greek (*kunaria*) is occasionally interpreted as a diminutive of affection, more probably, it seems to me, it was an unthinking use by Jesus of a typical Jewish term of abuse.[47] The woman's response then provoked Jesus towards a re-think. At any rate, that might be one possible reason why remembrance of the rather puzzling exchange was preserved: it was seared on Jesus' own consciousness. Whether true in this particular case or not, my general point holds. The social shaping of Jesus' identity would have been expressed in the fact that, as well as giving, he also received, precisely in order to give more deeply. Indeed, one might say that it was Jesus' acceptance of the very definite cultural setting in which he found himself that gave his ministry such power. Audiences heard what he had to say in terms of, and within, frameworks with which they were already familiar. Nothing was wholly *de novo*, but built upon an already familiar base.

While such dependence might well have ceased with the end of his earthly life, and that is often how the issue is treated (with resort once more to infused knowledge), I wonder if such an approach does not after all undermine the basic claim of the Ascension, which is of humanity permanently exalted to heaven, not of humanity now effectively absorbed into the divinity. Certainly, we are happy to think of Christ continuing to be dependent on humanity to act on his behalf in this world. Thanks to their use in many collections of prayers, words attributed to St Teresa of Avila are now quite familiar:

> Christ has no other hands but your hands to do his work today; no other feet but your feet to guide folk on his way; no other lips but your lips to tell them why he died; no other love but your love win them to his side.[48]

While of course applicable to all Christians, such comments would be especially true of saints. Interdependence is thus demonstrated not just in the fact that they are found performing actions on Christ's behalf but, more profoundly, in the distinctive contribution they make in adapting that message to the specifics of their own lives.

But such patterns of interdependence I would argue continue not only with respect to this world but also in the very nature of Jesus' existence in heaven. That may seem an extraordinary claim, but it makes good sense once we start to reflect more deeply on what it might mean to assert the permanent exaltation of Christ's humanity to heaven, as the doctrine of the Ascension asserts. Given that human beings only flourish in the presence of others like themselves, it is hard to see why Christ should be treated as an exception. Donne's 'no man is an island' is more than a merely contingent fact.[49] It points to an underlying ontological reality. So, even if now no longer dependent on others for his development and knowledge, Jesus would still be dependent on them for his full flourishing as the social being all humans are. One obvious implication is that Christ could not possibly, therefore, be heaven's only current human occupant. To talk of the presence of the saints in heaven should thus not be seen as their fitting reward but rather entailed by Christ's own exaltation to heaven. The Ascension thus speaks of the realization of a corporate social reality: of the presence of the body of Christ in more senses than one.

The modern fashion in theology is to downplay or even reject entirely talk of heaven as a present reality and to substitute biblical talk of a final culmination of the human story in a new heaven and a new earth. But this is by no means the only biblical position. While expected imminence of the world's end meant that not much attention was given by New Testament writers to the topic of heaven,[50] the beginnings of later attitudes are already there.[51] That is why I disagree with scholars such as Tom Wright who wish all the emphasis to be on the eschaton. So worried is he by the Church's traditional position on the saints that he has even proposed abandoning All Saints' Day and its associated hymns,[52] something that would have worried John Wesley, so scarcely just a conventional Catholic/Protestant dispute.[53] While Wright is quite correct in objecting to the way in which saints were sometimes treated as more like influential patrons ready to act for their clients before the divine King,[54] he errs badly in my view in ignoring this more corporate dimension to the Christian faith.

Of course the resurrection was a unique event, but that does not mean that it is without more immediate implications for others. In the more distant past this was expressed through the doctrine of the harrowing of hell, with Christ conceived of as releasing Adam and the saints of the Old Testament into the new life that he came to bring.[55] But the saints of the new covenant also have their place. There is nice irony in the fact that on the front cover of Wright's major work on the resurrection a painting by Titian is used to suggest that Christ rises alone,[56] whereas, if taken into conjunction with the two side-panels, a quite different story emerges. Seen as whole with various saints in these side panels, the triptych effectively indicates that others too now share in the exaltation of Christ to life with his Father in heaven.[57]

The suspicious minded may think that such observations are but a prelude to the invocation of saints in precisely the form to which Protestants have traditionally taken exception but nothing could be further from my intention. Once this strong social interdependence is stressed, it becomes clear that the saints can accomplish nothing on their own. Their invocation would thus not be a matter of some special influence they might have over Christ but rather clear acknowledgement of this essentially social dimension to our humanity. Just as we ask our friends and local church for their prayers in times of special need, so the wider Church beyond the grave may be invoked. While it is pointless to speculate in any detail how and in what form such a petition might be communicated to them, what we can say for certain is that such knowledge would need to be mediated. Only God could know directly what occurs in this world and only God could grant what the petitioner requests. So, such prayers would remain held firmly within the corporate reality that is the body of Christ, and not just a matter of a purely personal relation between two individuals, the petitioner and his or her favourite saint.

Conclusion

Not all clauses in the Apostles' Creed are equally clear. So, for example, the article that speaks of Christ's descent into hell was once taken to allude to the release of the Old Testament saints from their waiting, to share now in salvation from Christ, whereas in contemporary theology it is more commonly understood, as it was in Calvin, to express the extreme limits to which Christ's suffering went,[58] and that dispute is reflected in uncertainty over the Latin's correct form at this point.[59] In a not dissimilar way, *communio sanctorum* is ambiguous. Although usually rendered into English as 'the communion of saints', the Latin could equally mean 'a sharing in holy things'. Yet that very ambiguity could be the article's strength, for it is by participating in the Church's reading of Scripture and the sacraments that we are drawn closer to one another (the wider sense of saints) and also to saints in the narrower sense, as we aspire through divine grace to emulate those who have preceded us in following in the steps of Christ.

Notes

1 Originally published as part of as special Festschrift number of the South African Dutch Reformed Theological Journal, *NGTT* (*Ned Geref Teologiese Tydskrif*), 53, supp. 3 (2012), 13–24, and used here with permission.

2 E.g. mystical union in Vincent Brümmer, *The Model of Love: A Study in Philosophical Theology* (Cambridge: Cambridge University Press, 1993), 57–79; *amicitia Dei* in Vincent Brümmer, *Brümmer on Meaning and the Christian Faith: Collected Writings of Vincent Brümmer* (Aldershot: Ashgate, 2006), 295–302.

3 It is possible that the usage derives ultimately from the Book of Daniel's identification of the elect with 'the saints of the most high' (7:18, 22, 25, 27).

4 A mystic, he was tried for heresy and put to death in Baghdad in 922.

5 Attar's *The Conference of Birds* is a classic work of Persian spirituality. For a brief historical survey of attitudes within Islam, F.E. Peters, *A Reader on Classical Islam* (Princeton: Princeton University Press, 1994), 307–357.

6 Resting on a cube symbolising the earth, they are topped by domes indicative of heaven, while in between is an octagonal drum, used to represent the transition from this world to the next.

7 Ibn Khaldûn, *The Muqaddimah: An Introduction to History*, 2nd ed., vol. 3, trans. Franz Rosenthal, Bollingen Foundation, vol. 43 (Princeton: Princeton University Press, 1967), esp. 83–86, 92–93, 99–101.

8 See further, David Brown, *Discipleship and Imagination: Christian Tradition and Truth* (Oxford: Oxford University Press, 2000), 250–260.

9 Elizabeth A. Johnson, *Friends of God and Prophets: A Feminist Theological Reading of the Communion of Saints* (New York: Continuum, 1998).

10 Dietrich Bonhoeffer, *The Cost of Discipleship*, trans. R.H. Fuller (London: SCM Press, 1963), 69.

11 Catherine of Siena (d. 1380) ate her own vomit, St Margaret Mary Alacoque (d. 1690) scratched the name of Jesus on her breast.

12 While such practices were even advocated in earlier twentieth-century biographies, the feature is downplayed in more recent treatments.

13 For imitating Christ, Philippians 2:5–11; cf. Romans 15:7. The paucity of such references of course parallels the infrequency of appeals to Jesus' teaching: only explicit twice, at 1 Corinthians 7:10 and 1 Corinthians 9:14.

14 1 Corinthians 4:16; 2 Thessalonians 3:7; Philippians 3:17 (RSV). For imitation of Paul and Christ combined, 1 Thessalonians 1:6.

15 As with Uriah Heep in Charles Dickens's *David Copperfield* and Gilbert and Sullivan's Poobah in *The Mikado*.

16 Central to St Athanasius' account in his *Life of Antony*. Admittedly, that may well have been how Antony himself experienced the struggle, with hunger inducing hallucinations of devils, but one suspects a degree of literary license on Athanasius's part, not least to draw a parallel with Christ's own temptations.

17 So, for example, St Catherine of Alexandria's famous torture on the wheel before her beheading or St Sebastian's attack by arrows before being clubbed to death (he survived the former thanks to the solicitations of the widow Irene).

18 Contrast Revelation 2:14–16 and 19–23 with 1 Corinthians 6:12ff.

19 Two actions seen as sins are still recorded, though both are made less significant. There is the undertaking of a census (1 Chronicles 21:1), now blamed on Satan rather than on directly on divine judgment (2 Samuel 24:1) and there is the transfer of the ark from Kiriath-jearim by non-Levites (1 Chronicles 15:13) but with David's dubious motive for desiring possession of the ark now omitted (2 Samuel 6:12).

20 For similar transformations in Abraham, Isaac and Joseph, see David Brown, *Tradition and Imagination: Revelation and Change* (Oxford: Oxford University Press, 1999), 208–271.

21 For the battle, Bede *History* 3.2. For reflections on the changing story of Oswald, Clare Stancliffe and Eric Cambridge, ed., *Oswald: Northumbrian King to European Saint* (Stamford: Paul Watkins, 1995); for Bede and *Beowulf*, 39–41, 71–75.

22 David Brown, *Through the Eyes of the Saints: A Pilgrimage through History* (London: Continuum, 2005).

23 Simon Tugwell, *Ways of Imperfection: An Exploration of Christian Spirituality* (London: Darton, Longman and Todd, 1984; Springfield, IL: Templegate, 1985). Tugwell's focus, though, is rather different from mine. He is less interested in identifying faults in the saints as in picking up from their writings recognition of a continuing battle with sin.

24 Joseph Heller, *God Knows* (New York: Alfred A. Knopf, 1984).

25 Brown, *Discipleship and Imagination*, 66–79.

26 Technically known as *furta sacra*, they were commonly justified at the time in terms of some perceived neglect by those in their previous location: Brown, *Discipleship and Imagination*, 71–72; Patrick J. Geary, *Furta Sacra: Thefts of Relics in the Central Middle Ages*, revised edition (Princeton: Princeton University Press, 1990).

27 Writing probably one year after the king's death, St Aelred of Riveaux tried hard to advance his cause, and Archbishop Laud included him in his Scottish Prayer Book of 1637. For the various factors that pulled in opposing directions, Richard Oram, *David I: The King Who Made Scotland* (Stroud: The History Press, 2004), esp. 145–165, 203–225.

28 The seventh and eighth Crusade. For details, Jean Richard, *Saint Louis: Crusader King of France* (Cambridge: Cambridge University Press, 1992), esp. 85–152, 293–329. Yet the book does end by conceding that Louis was 'the greatest peacemaker that the thirteenth century had known' (332).

29 Probably at Oswestry in 642.

30 John Paul II created more saints than all previous popes combined.

31 *The Alternative Service Book* of 1980 also attempted to be thoroughly ecumenical, in including Counter-Reformation and Non-Conformist saints (e.g. Teresa of Avila and John Bunyan). *Common Worship* (2000) went even further in including Newman, who had deserted the Church of England for Rome in 1845.

32 For further discussion of her legend, see Brown, *Discipleship and Imagination*, 83–85, 89–93.

33 Surprisingly, even whole books devoted to the painting take little or no account of the image: cf. Edwin Hall, *The Arnolfini Betrothal: Medieval Marriage and the Enigma of Van Eyck's Double Portrait* (Berkeley and Los Angeles, CA: University of California Press, 1994); Linda Seidel, *Jan Van Eyck's Arnolfini Portrait: Stories of an Icon* (Cambridge: Cambridge University Press, 1993), 119–123.

34 For a detailed presentation of this view, see Brown, *Discipleship and Imagination*, 31–61.

35 Gregory the Great is largely responsible for the western integration of the various Gospel women into a single figure. In his defence it needs to be noted that even the evangelists seem to have adapted Jesus' anointing to their own purposes (Ibid., 40–43), while the name of Mary Magdalene is mentioned by Luke almost immediately after his own account of the anointing of the penitent sinner (8:1–2).

36 'Learning at his feet' because Mary Magdalene was also identified as the sister of Martha and Lazarus. This is not as implausible as it might initially sound, as in John (12:1–8) their sister is identified as performing an anointing at their home village of Bethany, precisely the place chosen by Mark for his anonymous anointing (14:3–9).

37 My translation: *Oratio* 16, excerpts from 10–26 in Anselm of Canterbury, *Opera omnia*, vol. 3, ed. F.S. Schmitt, (Edinburgh: Thomas Nelson, 1946), 64–65.

38 *Eastenders* featured the first TV gay kiss, while *Emmerdale* included discussion of the possibility of a priest blessing a lesbian couple's union. Even the longest running British soap, the more conservative *Archers* featured one of the principal families agonizing over how to respond to a son entering into a civil partnership.

39 For an introduction, Roger Sharrock, *Saints, Sinners and Comedians: The Novels of Graham Greene* (Notre Dame: University of Notre Dame Press, 1984).

40 As in novels such as *The Unforgotten Prisoner* (1933) that deals with revenge and reconciliation in the aftermath of the First World War, *Testament* (1938) that explores the Russian revolution, and *The Fire and the Wood* (1940) that examines some of the dilemmas associated with the rise of Nazism.

41 Austin Farrer, 'Narrow and Broad', in *The Truth-Seeking Heart: Austin Farrer and His Writings*, ed. Ann Loades and Robert MacSwain (Norwich: Canterbury, 2007), 184–189, esp. 187.

42 Rowan Williams, *Tokens of Trust: An Introduction to Christian Belief* (Norwich: Canterbury, 2007), 20–6, esp. 20, 21. The quotation from Ambrose is from his *De Fide* I, 42.

43 Williams, *Tokens of Trust*, 22; K.A.D. Smelik, ed., *Etty: The Letters and Diaries of Etty Hillesum, 1941–1943* (Grand Rapids, MI: Eerdmans, 2002), 506. For further discussion of Farrer, Williams, and Hillesum on the evidential value of sanctity, see Robert MacSwain, *Solved by Sacrifice: Austin Farrer, Fideism and the Evidence of Faith* (Leuven: Peeters, 2013).

44 With Jürgen Moltmann setting a pattern in his *The Trinity and the Kingdom: The Doctrine of God*, trans. Margaret Kohl (London: SCM, 1981) that many others followed.

45 Although Aquinas did eventually admit growth in Jesus' empirical knowledge (a matter on which he changed his mind; contrast *Summa Theologiae* III.9.4c with the earlier

III *Sent.* d14.a3), he was always insistent that the beatific vision was infused right from the moment of Jesus' conception (ST III.9.2, q10). For nineteenth-century kenoticism, *Divine Humanity: Kenosis and the Construction of a Christian Theology* (London: SCM; Waco, TX: Baylor University Press, 2011).

46 See David Brown, 'The Glory of God Revealed in Art and Music: Learning from Pagans', in *Celebrating Creation: Affirming Catholicism and the Revelation of God's Glory*, ed. Mark Chapman (London: Darton, Longman and Todd, 2004), 43–56.

47 Cranfield is among those who defend the alternative view, assuming here an untypical Jewish reference to pets. See C.E.B. Cranfield, *The Gospel According to St Mark: An Introduction and Commentary* (Cambridge: Cambridge University Press, 1959), 248.

48 Probably derived indirectly from Evelyn Underhill's (1913) translation.

49 'No man is an Island, entire of itself, every man is a piece of the Continent': part of his *Meditation* 17.

50 For imminent expectation, e.g. 1 Corinthians 7:29; 1 Thessalonians 4:15–17.

51 E.g. in Luke 23:43; 2 Corinthians 12:2; Philippians 1:23.

52 N.T. Wright, *For All the Saints?: Remembering the Christian Departed*, (London: SPCK, 2003).

53 John Wesley's entries in his *Journal* for All Saints' Day, 1756 and 1767 are especially revealing.

54 Cf. Wright, *For All the Saints?*, 3, 16.

55 Based on Matthew 27:52 and 1 Peter 3:18–20, the theme was developed and popularized in the *Gospel of Nicodemus*. To this day it is still the most common way of representing Christ's resurrection in Orthodox icons.

56 N.T. Wright, *The Resurrection of the Son of God* (London: SPCK, 2003).

57 I discuss the painting and the issues involved at rather more length in Brown, *Through the Eyes of the Saints*, 11–19. For an illustration of the complete painting (still in its original location in the church of Santi Nazaro e Celso at Brescia), see Filippo Pedrocco, *Titian* (New York: Rizzoli, 2001), 127–129.

58 As in Hans Urs von Balthasar, e.g. *Mysterium Paschale* (Edinburgh: T & T Clark, 1990), 148–188. For Calvin, *Institutes of the Christian Religion* Book II, ch. xvi, para. 9–11.

59 'Descendit ad inferna' seems to have been the original form ('he descended to the depths'). But this was eventually modified in the Roman Breviary to 'ad inferos' ('to those below'), presumably to indicate more clearly that the descent was to the departed, not to the place of the damned.

12 No Heaven Without Purgatory

If Purgatory is given a role at all in modern conceptions of the afterlife to be at most of the kind found in Hick and Rahner,[1] in providing a for those of whom it might be argued that they have had no proper this life. Apart from its intermediate character, however, this account in common with the traditional conception, whereas it seems to n sophical reasons, partly conceptual and partly moral, compel assent very much more like the traditional view. This I take to have had features: (a) that it was a place of moral preparation (not trial) for thos and decisions had already destined them for Heaven and (b) that this aration involved some kind of purgatorial (i.e. purifying) pain that necessary consequence of the rectification of moral wrong-doing. Thre in defence of (a) are offered below. These will help to provide an approp work for the brief defence of (b) which then follows. For convenience arguments may be labelled the temporal argument, the identity argum self-acceptance argument.

The Temporal Argument

The temporal argument is in some ways the most complex, and so I shall take it first. Set out schematically, the argument might run thus:

(1) A human being at death is clearly morally imperfect.
(2) But essential to the definition of Heaven is that human beings are in a state of complete moral perfection.
(3) Therefore, either there is an abrupt transition between the two conditions or an intermediate state exists to effect a gradual transition.
(4) But there is no way of rendering such an abrupt transition in essentially temporal beings conceivable.
(5) Therefore, an intermediate state of Purgatory must exist, if Heaven exists.

The structure of the argument is presumably uncontentious apart from (4), which contains the key to the entire argument. My claim is that such an abrupt transition to moral perfection in essentially temporal beings is not the sort of claim to which clear sense can be attached, and so conceptually we have every reason to believe that, if Heaven exists, then so must Purgatory. So far as I can see, there are only two ways in which the abruptness of the transition might be rendered comprehensible. Both involve temporal considerations; hence the name of the argument.

The stronger of the two in terms of its challenge to temporal considerations is the claim that any worry about the abruptness of the transition is meaningless since Heaven in any case involves a totally different perspective on time. Humanity can there partake in God's timelessness, and so it is meaningless to speak of any temporal measure of change as having relevance. All of a person's life will be instantaneously and simultaneously present to them. So all the necessary correctives can be present to him or her in that same instant.[2] Several philosophical challenges to the coherence of the notion of timelessness have recently been offered.[3] There is no need for me to repeat them here. They are of a purely formal kind, whereas a more interesting objection that achieves the same purpose is the claim that change, and thus temporality, is essential to meaningful human existence.

For justification of this one might refer to Bernard Williams's article on 'The Makropoulos case'. In it he compares the prospect of a changeless future life in Heaven to the prospect of a future life that is held before Elina Makropoulos in Janáček's opera of the same name. She has taken an elixir of life and for the past three hundred years has been permanently aged forty-two. As Williams puts it: 'Her unending life has come to a state of boredom, indifference, and coldness. Everything is joyless: "in the end it is the same", she says, "singing and silence". So she refuses to take the elixir again and dies.'[4] The point is that for human beings interest would seem to be inextricably linked to change and development. So Heaven would be boring for human beings unless there was change.

Williams believes that this is sufficient to jettison the notion of Heaven. But there he is quite wrong. For it is possible to postulate the type of change required from within the resources of the Christian tradition. The fourth-century Cappadocian Fathers so emphasize the infinite nature of God that the conclusion is drawn that our attempt to comprehend him will never come to an end. Thus Gregory of Nyssa in his *Life of Moses*, after arguing that to impose any comprehensible limit on God would make him necessarily finite, goes on to deduce from this that

> this truly is the vision of God: never to be satisfied in the desire to see him. But one must always, by looking at what he can see, rekindle his desire to see more. Thus, no limit would interrupt growth in the ascent to God, since no limit to the Good can be found nor is the increasing of desire for the Good brought to an end because it is satisfied.[5]

Gregory Nazianzen offers us a dramatic image in one of his sermons, when he describes God as 'like some great Sea of Being, limitless and unbounded ... which escapes before we have caught it, and takes to flight before we have conceived it'.[6]

In other words, taking up their suggestion, one can conceive of Heaven as an endless process of development, not, of course, in the moral sense, but in terms of our ever-increasing understanding of God. For as beings of finite intellect, we will never completely grasp the infinite riches of God. So Heaven can with complete legitimacy be conceived of as an endless voyage of discovery, as it were, that inevitably involves change for us, rather than as an essentially static condition. Later in the same article[7] Williams complains that even endless purely intellectual activity would be unfulfilling, since of itself it lacks anything specifically individualistic and personal. It cannot matter who does it. I seriously doubt whether the proposed relationship with God can be seen as sufficiently intellectual to fall foul of this objection, but even if it were to do so, this conception of Heaven could still be reinforced by specifically personal projects, such as the development of relationships with other human beings in Heaven.

But if we never can become changeless, timeless beings and in consequence even Heaven has to have a temporal character, it becomes reasonable to expect that God will effect the moral perfection appropriate to Heaven by methods appropriate to our essentially temporal condition. If that is so, then the question arises whether any major change, including this change to perfection, can ever be effected in a temporal being like ourselves except gradually. It is at this point that the second way of attempting to render comprehensible the abruptness of the moral change becomes relevant. For an objector to the doctrine of Purgatory might well concede the incoherence of a timeless Heaven but reply that even a necessarily temporal being like humanity could meaningfully be subject to such radical change. Indeed, he may claim that there is no shortage of instances.

How plausible one believes these apparent counter-examples will depend on a number of factors, among which will be personal experience, historical assessment, and moral theory. Certainly, I find it impossible to take seriously any of the usually quoted illustrations. Thus in respect of dramatic religious conversions, the abruptness of the change is surely more apparent than real. Certainly, where detailed historical evidence is available, this is clearly substantiated, as, for instance, in the case of Augustine. His entire life story, as recorded in the *Confessions*, can be read as leading up to the dramatic denouement in which he hears the words in the garden: '*Tolle, lege.*' With St Paul we have no such advantage, but it is interesting to note that writers as varied as Jung and Bornkamm, when writing about his conversion, have postulated antecedent contributory causes.[8]

But, of course, that is not the end of the argument. For the response may be made that, while it takes time to come to a decision for the good, once that decision has been made, everything else can then quickly fall into place. That being so, given that the prospective entrant to Heaven has already *ex hypothesi* made the decision in principle for the good, there can be no conceptual difficulties in envisaging everything else quickly falling into place, once he or she is confronted with the full revealing light of the divine presence. But, yet again, this claim must surely be challenged. For all our experience of this life surely tells us that, while dramatic changes of direction do undoubtedly occur, just as they have antecedent causes, so also there is no dramatic wiping out of the past, but only a slow overcoming of previously ingrained habits.

To give a non-moral example, there is no doubt that one can suddenly give up smoking; there is a conversion; but it takes a long period of resistance before the urge to smoke finally disappears. In other words, the past lingers on for a long time, despite the change of direction. There is no reason to suppose that the situation is any different on purely moral questions. Deeply ingrained tendencies of thought will remain to tempt individuals long after they have ceased to act according to those dispositions, and indeed occasional lapses may still occur as a result, as Paul seems to acknowledge in a famous passage.[9]

To this it may be objected that to compare our moral characters to an addictive habit like smoking is to introduce a highly misleading analogy. At most, it may be said, what I have drawn attention to is a common empirical fact, not a deep universal truth about human nature and moral endeavour. It is now that one's conception of human morality becomes relevant. If this is conceived merely in terms of external compliance to rules, clearly not only instantaneous change of direction but also instantaneous goodness is easily conceivable. But, traditionally, Christian morality has been interpreted in much more profound terms. Only when moral action arises spontaneously from an ingrained, natural disposition or habit, in short only when a virtue is present, may that person properly be called good. Nor, of course, though we cannot argue the matter here, need this be seen as an especially contentious or specifically Christian premise. The insight is at least as old as Plato and Aristotle, that a person may not properly be called good unless that goodness has been imprinted upon the essential self, one's character traits or habits.

But the very notion of such a habit suggests practice, and practice implies time, time in which to practise overcoming the opposing habit, time in which to practise reinforcing the new. I conclude, therefore, that not only is human nature essentially temporal, our capacity for moral perfection is likewise. No clear sense thus attaches to the claim that a human being could become instantaneously virtuous, morally perfect, and so, if God is to respect our nature as essentially temporal beings, God must have allowed for an intermediate state of Purgatory to exist.

The Argument from Identity

My second argument for (a), the argument from identity, may be set out schematically thus:

(1) We know and can identify ourselves only through continuity with our past.
(2) Therefore, the more dramatic the contrast in character between a person A at time x and person B at a subsequent time y, the more likely is the latter individual B to doubt whether he could in fact be the same person as person A at time x.
(3) But Heaven with its perfection of character constitutes such a dramatic contrast to our earthly existence.
(4) Therefore, unless there is an intermediate stage between earth and Heaven, the resurrected individual could have no reasonable grounds for believing himself to be the same person as the person to whose earthly existence he allegedly corresponds.

(5) Accordingly, to save the coherence of the doctrine of Heaven, an intermediate state of Purgatory must be postulated.

The general point of the argument is best seen by indulging in a thought experiment. Imagine someone looking like you and having your present 'memories' waking up tomorrow in your bed, but with at least one significant difference: he is morally perfect. It is very doubtful whether he would regard himself as the same person as you. He is much more likely to see himself as a different person who, somewhat strangely, has been substituted into your body. The reason for supposing this is the lack of significant connections between his character and yours. He would be unable to understand how he has become the type of person he now is. Thus, for example, through his 'memory' he would know of previously existing strong desires, but would be totally unable to account for their present absence. To give a trivial example, he will remember that you could never resist a second helping of blancmange, but will have no such inclination himself nor any understanding of how the previous overwhelming urge in the presence of the jelly has now totally gone. Likewise, he will 'remember' that you always got irritated in the presence of X, but experience no such irritation himself nor have any understanding of how such irritation was overcome.

But the difficulties are not confined to the disappearance of what were once conscious temptations. This new individual will also see as wrong what he will have no 'memory' of having regarded as wrong at the time. All those self-deceptions you once indulged in he will view with disdain, for example, the times when you thought you were right to be angry when deep down you were just being spiteful. Thus it is not just the individual's orientation towards the future that will be totally different. He will also have a transformed attitude towards your past. Attitudes that your memories tell him he endorsed at the time he will wish totally to reject and yet be unable to account for what has brought about the transformation.

The most natural reaction for an individual in this situation would surely be for him (or her) to experience at the very least a profound identity crisis, the most natural resolution of which would be for him to refuse to identify with the foreign 'memories' that he finds so alien to his present character. The greater the contrast, the more natural it would be for him to seek an alternative explanation, for example that he has somehow acquired telepathic powers in respect of the past behaviour of another individual who merely physically resembles himself. But to such a conclusion from our thought experiment at least two types of objection might be raised.

The first is that the way I have told the story by initially describing the two individuals as distinct biases the reader towards the desired conclusion. In fact, it may be said, I have made a simple logical mistake; for, if they are memories, logically it must be the same person. But that is precisely why I used inverted commas. For my point is that 'memory' of itself cannot provide sufficient assurance of identity. As David Lewis puts it in 'Survival and Identity', 'what matters in survival is mental continuity and connectedness',[10] but here there is a glaring absence of 'connectedness'. Certainly these 'memories' will provide me with access to apparent knowledge of what a body like mine has once done. But I cannot reasonably be required to acknowledge the body as mine until I see sufficient connection between the past actions of that body and my present character.

A second type of objector might accept that 'memory' of itself is insufficient, but suggest that 'connectedness' could be established through others rather than character developments, just as sometimes happens in cases of amnesia when we accept the explanations of others regarding intervening connections. So in the case of the moral gap between death and Heaven the proposal would be that God could fulfil this role by providing the individual with an explanation of what has happened, which will make all the difference. But I fail to see why it should. Certainly some meaning could be attached to the announcement that a divine decree has put an end to all those temptations which one had been consciously struggling against. But it is extremely hard to see how one could personally identify with an announcement that much of what one had not even regarded as wrong was now to be seen as a heinous crime. If it is to be part of one's identity, it surely has to be in some sense a personal discovery, and that takes time. Moreover, even with conscious temptations the amount of meaning that can be attached to the proposal does seem strictly limited. One will undoubtedly experience relief at the absence of former temptations, but it is hard to see why one should definitively identify with the person who once had them when, so far as one's present consciousness is concerned, they were simply effortlessly overcome. In short, there is a lack of meaningful connectedness, and therefore insufficient grounds for identifying with the person one allegedly once was.

The Argument from Self-Acceptance

It remains now to say something about my final argument, what I called the argument from self-acceptance. Schematically, it is very simple:

(1) God always desires a free response, with complete self-acceptance from the individual of the divine will.
(2) But Heaven by definition can provide no opportunity for completing the process of self-acceptance.
(3) Therefore, an intermediate state of Purgatory must exist, if Heaven exists.

In my first two arguments conceptual considerations were dominant: in the first that the marking of time by gradual change is indispensable to intelligible human existence and in the second that continuity of memories without continuity of character is insufficient to justify belief in continuity of identity. In this third argument, however, the main premise is a moral one. One could, of course, give other than a moral justification premise for (1), for example by appealing to the key role played by free will in theodicy or in modern synergistic (i.e. co-operative) views of grace.[11] But this would merely throw the problem a stage further back, of why free will should be so valued in such cases. So it would seem best to face the issue directly, by observing that (1) is not just the most satisfactory explanation of the existence of evil in the world and so forth, but represents a basic demand of morality through respect for persons and so an integral element in any claim to perfect divine goodness.

That is to say, any person, whether human or divine, would simply have failed to give the absolute value to the other person that is his due as a person, unless whatever he persuades him to do or accept arises from that individual's own moral self-understanding and perception. Children and others not fully responsible for their actions would, of course, constitute legitimate exceptions. But, even with that said, it can hardly be maintained that such an approach has always been seen as an integral part of respect for persons. But it has increasingly so since Kant and even more so with the abandonment of paternalism and adoption of non-directive counselling. Thus the whole rationale of the latter approach is that the individual should unqualifiedly accept the decision made, not that objectively speaking it must be the right decision. Morally and psychologically, respect for persons is thus held to take precedence over an objectively right decision. But, if human beings can be expected to show this much respect for individual human dignity, then *a fortiori* we must expect this of the all-good God. Divine respect for persons will be such that God prefers them to come to right decisions voluntarily by trial and error through their own mistakes rather than ever compel a decision upon them, and this is in fact precisely what the so-called free will defence maintains is happening in respect of our earthly existence.

But, while the basic thrust of this argument is thus very widely accepted, the objection will probably be raised that the situation in Heaven is very different. For there, it will be said, since *ex hypothesi* the individual has already made a basic decision in favour of divine goodness, by implication self-acceptance of whatever final adjustments to character are required has already also been given. In one sense this is, of course, true. But even so, morally, the implications are questionable. Certainly in the human case respect for persons would seem to demand that even where we know that such assent would be forthcoming, it should none the less be explicitly obtained. Nor is this a mere function of politeness. It is a matter of demonstrating that the individual is valued in his own right.

Thus it seems clear that God is under a moral obligation to see that the individual concerned personally endorses each aspect of the transformation of his or her character. That being so, the existence of Purgatory is a legitimate deduction from the goodness of God. Thus, if we accept the language of synergism, just as the individual's earthly life has been a co-operative venture with God, so will this voyage of self-discovery that constitutes the transition to Heaven. The decision to redeem those parts of the personality that are hitherto unredeemed will be a decision of both God and the individual. To suggest otherwise would be to place God's respect for individual personal dignity at a lower level than the highest standards set by God's own creation. Indeed, there is even a strong moral argument for saying that the individual's first confrontation with God after death should be as he or she is, warts and all. For only then can God properly be said to have accepted the individual for what he or she is as a whole, rather than merely for what the individual can allegedly instantaneously become.

Purgatory and Pain

What the three arguments given above have attempted to demonstrate is that moral development in an intermediate temporal context is an essential postulate if sense is to be made of the otherwise unintelligible gap between the imperfection of death and the presumed perfection of Heaven. However, to fully substantiate my claim that both the main features of the medieval view are still defensible, what remains now to be done is that some grounds be offered for (b), in particular for speaking of purgatorial pains in respect of such an intermediate state. But that such a preparatory process will be a mixture of pain and joy surely goes almost without saying. There will be joy because of certainty about one's ultimate destination in Heaven. But there must also be pain. For no sense can be given to any notion of moral development that is bereft of it, since being pained at discovery of the wrong one has done would seem integral to any properly moral recognition that it was in fact harm-doing. So inevitably there will be pain as we come gradually to a realization of all those occasions when, had we been more open and receptive to the divine will, we could have avoided hurt to others and to God. Indeed, many occasions on which we harmed others profoundly, we will become aware of for the first time. But perhaps most traumatic of all will be the pain of self-discovery, the hurt of discovering ourselves as we really are – with far more warts than we ever imagined.

That such pain could be a consequence of a loving respect for persons is acknowledged in writers as different as T.S. Eliot and St Catherine of Genoa. The former, in a well-known passage in the *Four Quartets*, comments: 'Who then devised the torment? Love. / ... We only live, only suspire / Consumed by either fire or fire',[12] while Catherine, writing shortly before the Reformation, declares that: 'Having come to the point of twenty-four carats, gold cannot be purified any further; and this is what happens to the soul in the fire of God's love.'[13]

A critic may well respond that the very mention of love rather than justice as the moral basis for such painful self-discovery puts me at an enormous distance from the medieval view, and so I cannot properly claim continuity with it. It must be conceded that in many ways this is true. So, for example, I do not wish to imply the presence of punishment, far less that of physical pain. But to claim continuity seems to me none the less right because thereby attention is drawn to the way in which the distinction between *culpa* and *poena* on which the original medieval conceptual justification[14] was based had within it the sources for its own correction. That is why I have expressed (b) in a manner that I believe successfully encapsulates both the medieval view and my own: 'that this moral preparation involves some kind of purgatorial (i.e. purifying) pain that is a necessary consequence of the rectification of moral wrong-doing'.

To explain. On the medieval view God forgives the penitent his guilt (*culpa*) but because sin violates a divinely established order, satisfaction or reparation (*poena*) is necessary to restore the violated order. Such satisfaction is not usually completely achievable in this life, especially in the case of venial sins of which we may not be fully aware. That being so, an intermediate state is required to make up what is wanting in the satisfaction so far given in order to restore the offended divine order.

All this can perhaps be put more clearly by saying that the argument assumes a retributive theory of punishment, that every wrong committed must receive a corresponding punishment, and, of course, this may not always be possible in this life. At the Reformation objection was raised to such an account on the grounds that it detracted from the sufficiency of Christ's sacrifice, and in any case lacked biblical support. Today we might equally object to its version of the retributive theory of punishment. For, once guilt has been acknowledged, it is impossible to see what further purpose could be served in exacting punishment.

But *poena* in its widest sense means penalty rather than punishment. Taking the word in that sense, both the medieval view and my own can be seen as pointing to a necessary consequence or penalty of wrong-doing. For, if the medieval view saw retribution for any wrong-doing as a necessary moral demand, equally clearly one of the main implications of what I have said above is that, though God's forgiveness is always complete, even God cannot eliminate some of the consequences or penalties accruing as a result of our wrong-doing, namely the need for their gradual painful self-discovery. Logic forbids their instantaneous removal.

So, though my justification is obviously very different, I conclude that the medieval view was right, that there can be no Heaven for any of us without Purgatory first.[15]

Notes

1 John Hick, *Death and Eternal Life* (London: Fount paperback, 1979), esp. 414ff.; Karl Rahner, *Theological Investigations*, vol. 19 (London: Darton, Longman and Todd, 1983), 181–193, esp. 192.

2 Defended, for instance, in Ladislaus Boros, *The Moment of Truth: Mysterium Mortis* (London: Burns and Oates, 1965), 129ff.

3 Nelson Pike, *God and Timelessness* (London: Routledge & Kegan Paul, 1970); Richard Swinburne, *The Coherence of Theism* (Oxford University Press, 1977), 210ff.; Anthony Kenny, *The God of the Philosophers* (Oxford University Press, 1979), 38–48.

4 Bernard Williams, *Problems of the Self* (Cambridge: Cambridge University Press, 1973), 82.

5 Gregory of Nyssa, *Life of Moses*, Classics of Western Spirituality (New York: Paulist Press, 1978), 116, para. 239.

6 Gregory Nazianzen, *Oration* 38, Library of Nicene and Post-Nicene Fathers, 2nd series, vol. 7 (Grand Rapids, MI: Eerdmans, 1974), 346, sect. 7.

7 Williams, *Problems of the Self*, 96–98.

8 Bornkamm suggests that the catalyst was arguments with Hellenistic Christians in Damascus (Günther Bornkamm, *Paul* [London: Hodder & Stoughton, 1971], 23), while Jung bases his interpretation on the fact that 'fanaticism is only found in individuals who are compensating secret doubts' (C.G. Jung, *Contributions to Analytical Psychology*, trans. H.G. and Carey F. Baynes [London: Routledge and Kegan Paul, 1928], 257).

9 Romans 7:15.

10 David Lewis, 'Survival and Identity', in *The Identities of Persons*, ed. Amélie Oksenberg Rorty (Berkeley, CA: University of California Press, 1976), 17.

11 As, for example, in John Oman's classic, *Grace and Personality* (Cambridge: Cambridge University Press, 1917) and reprinted in many other editions since.

12 T.S. Eliot, 'Little Gidding', in *Four Quartets* (London: Faber and Faber, 1944), IV, 42: the fire of judgment or purification.

13 St Catherine of Genoa, *Purgation and Purgatory*, Classics of Western Spirituality (London: SPCK, 1979), 80.

14 As, for example, in Aquinas, *Comm. in Lib. IV Sent.*, dist. xxi, qu. 1.

15 I am very grateful to David Cook, Oliver O'Donovan, and Janet Soskice for helpful, critical comments on a previous draft. This chapter originally appeared in *Religious Studies* 21 (1985), 447–456. I am grateful to the journal and its publishers, Cambridge University Press, for permission to reprint with some small alterations.

13 Heaven and the Communion of Living and Departed

Since the Second World War there has been a marked shift of focus in theological writing about post-mortem human existence. Discussion has largely focused on the resurrection at the end of time, and with it the promised renewal of creation. As with most historical change, there is no single explanation for why heaven as a present reality now receives so little attention.[1] Clearly relevant is the re-discovery of how strongly eschatological is the New Testament itself, as is the ecological crisis and the Church's attempts to respond to it.[2] However, it can be surmised that difficulties in talking intelligibly about such a state have also played a significant role. The Church, Protestant no less than Catholic, had assumed that the soul could survive on its own, whereas advances in neuroscience and suspicions of Platonism as a malign influence on Christian belief have combined to call the intelligibility of such survival into doubt.[3] Equally, the associated imagery of heaven, hell, and purgatory have all come to be seen as embarrassing projections of all too fallible human concerns into the next life, with everything from crude calculations of merit to persisting class distinctions.[4] Again, even where something was still said, as in Rahner and Tillich, the retreat from more conventional positions was considerable. Tillich in effect only allowed continuing memory of the deceased in the mind of God, while for Rahner each soul is to be related to the world as a whole in a way that again seems to call into question personal survival.[5] If Barth is an exception, his exposition brought with it difficult conceptual questions, to which we will need to return.

In an essay as brief as this, I can scarcely address all such worries. So instead I want to focus on two narrower issues, both pertinent, however, to the title of this chapter: first, how such a populated reality is best conceived; second, why some sense of interchange between that world and our own is of no small importance.

Life Beyond Death: Conceiving Heaven

Although most of the New Testament's focus is on a future bodily resurrection for all, it would be quite wrong to describe belief in an intermediate state as entirely an alien product, the result of Platonic dualism. No doubt the initial idea came from Hellenism, but resurrection too was in that sense a foreign import, in the latter case from Zoroastrianism.[6] Both, however, came to be adapted and modified within the contours of Jewish belief. Certainly, the most conspicuous debate during Jesus' lifetime was between the Pharisees' assertion of resurrection and the Sadducees's denial. But readily available were also quite a few writings that advocated immortality of the soul as an alternative (e.g. Wisdom 2:23–4; 4:11–15; 6:19; 1 Enoch 103:4; 4 Maccabees 10).[7] Indeed, it has even been suggested that belief in immortality may have come first as a way of declaring that, despite the tortures imposed on the bodies of Jewish martyrs, their souls would survive.[8] So it should come as no surprise that occasionally the New Testament itself also seems to presuppose such a reality, perhaps most obviously, Christ's words to the penitent thief (Luke 23:43: cf. Matthew 27:52; Mark 12:25; 2 Corinthians 12:2). Nor should we be surprised that in consequence in the subsequent history of the Church the two beliefs were combined. Add to this imminent expectation of the end of the world as a reason for the prominence of the resurrection hope, and there ceases to be any good biblical reason for refusing to take seriously some form of conscious prior post-mortem existence.[9]

Indeed, perhaps the real surprise to emerge from the history of the Christian tradition is the extent to which belief in immortality was seen as the easier option, even among those who could not be accused of any natural sympathy with Platonism. So, for example, Calvin appears to have thought that resurrection of the body was in the fact the more difficult position to sustain. Given its Calvinist background similar considerations may underlie the strident insistence of the Thirty-Nine Articles on how Christ's Ascension is to understood: 'Christ did truly rise again from death, and took again his body, with flesh, bones, and all things appertaining to the perfection of Man's nature, wherewith he ascended into Heaven.'[10]

But, irrespective of belief in the Empty Tomb, this cannot be quite right. Not only must heaven be a different order of reality from the material flesh and bones that make up this world but also the New Testament is quite clear that the eventual restoration of all things is of a physical world radically transformed, with no more sea, sun or moon (Revelation 21:1 and 23). The different capacities of Christ's resurrected body also points in the same direction. While it was still a body that could partake of food (Luke 24:42–43), it was also now one that could appear and disappear at will, walk through doors and so forth (e.g. John 20:19). It was also one not always immediately recognizable (Luke 24:31), and, even when recognized, it could produce a quite different reaction from the past, in the immediacy of worship (Matthew 28:1). In contemplating the future resurrection of the dead, Paul points in a similar direction: their new bodies will be as radically unlike as seed and eventual grain (1 Corinthians 15:37).

Against this it is often argued that unless we can speak of the transformation of Jesus' actual mortal body (and thus eventually of own own), we will be left without any justifying grounds for talk of it being the same person who lives beyond death. Indeed, this is sometimes taken to be the underlying truth behind the story of the Empty Tomb.[11] But to my mind the contrast between the two states as envisaged is just so vast that it is far from clear why on this scenario it is not in fact a new body that is being produced rather than in some sense the old one continued. Just saying it is the same body when it lacks so many of the features that would betoken continuity (occupying the same space, being subject to the same physical laws etc.) suggests more a commitment of faith than any obvious rational grounds. If that is so, apparent fundamental disagreements on this issue such as those between Marcus Borg and Tom Wright may not run quite as deep as either side suppose.[12]

So it is a mistake to suppose that conceptual difficulties are easily resolved by postponing everything until the end of time. Not only does it look as though the eventual resurrection body will function in a quite different way, apart from the need for self-recognition and recognition by others there is no reason even to suppose that it must resemble its predecessor.[13] Any objection that the lives of souls in the immediate after-life would bear little resemblance to how they have lived here would therefore seem beside the point. So far from providing a jarring interval before a similar identity is once more taken up, such discontinuities appear inevitable. Thus no course ahead is without its problems.

Nonetheless, it is often noted, with some justification, that talk of the soul surviving on its own has become especially difficult in modern times.[14] Developments in neuroscience have demonstrated such close interdependence between body and mind that it is hard to see what sense could be given to the idea of the soul as naturally continuing beyond death. So it is perhaps not surprising that even among defenders of dualism there has been a retreat from claims to immortality.[15] Such retreat in any case squares more easily with New Testament thinking, within which life beyond death is consistently treated as a gift and not as any kind of possession. Indeed, even in the case of Christ himself he is repeatedly described as raised from the dead rather than himself rising: he too depended on the gracious act of his Father (e.g. Romans 6:4; 1 Thessalonians 1:10). So it would seem entirely appropriate that a similar supposition is applied to ourselves.

Although increasingly subtle attempts are made to defend some version of materialism in which mind and brain are in effect equated, all founder on the lack of equivalence of meaning between mental predicates and neurological descriptions of firings in the brain.[16] So, although dependent on brain and body for successful operation in this world, it is possible to conceive of God securing the mind's or soul's operation in some other way in the next life. One way of doing this is to think through how a world consisting of purely immaterial souls might function. Perhaps the most intriguing attempt made in modern times was by the philosopher H.H. Price after his return, late in life, to the practice of the Christian faith. Beginning with the objection that such disembodied existence would be altogether too intellectual for most of us, the picture is gradually filled out until it comes to bear an uncanny resemblance to ordinary, physical existence.[17] Dreams, for example, are used to model how such a world without material sensations might still include feelings and a sense of spatial location. Again, telepathy between like-minded souls is suggested as a way of overcoming isolation, while even bodily expression finds its place in the notion of an image-body.

In their enthusiasm to defend resurrection of the body, some Christian philosophers have declared all such accounts incoherent. One reason given is the resultant lack of continuity in human identity (only memories survive), but insistence on material causal interconnections would seem to me a mistake.[18] The resurrected body as commonly envisaged is also likely, as noted above, to have great difficulties in meeting any such a test. Of course, such looseness opens the logical possibility that the souls in the next life are merely identikits rather than actually the same person. But, if God guarantees a one-to-one correspondence, that would seem enough for most of us to regard the new reality as indeed a continuation of ourselves. In other words, it is our sense of self that is ultimately the determining criterion for interest in such a future rather than the rather wooden tests that philosophers sometimes impose.[19]

Yet there are other related difficulties that might still pull us after all towards a more material-like conception. That is the question of what would happen to those mental aspects of ourselves that are most bodily dependent, our emotions and self-expression. Price's appeal to our dream world is not altogether convincing, partly because such experiences are parasitic on memories of earlier bodily experiences and partly because such reality as they do have is to a degree still dependent on current bodily sensations, as borne witness, for example, by the cold sweat experienced on emerging from a fearful dream. Significantly, in order to fill out their descriptions of the intermediate state, much medieval discussion ended up giving in effect to souls many attributes that only really make sense in the presence of a body.[20] So an alternative approach is to think, as of course with Christ himself, of the soul already being given a sort of body, though still of a different kind from that provided in the final resurrection. Such an assumption runs deep even among some of the more Platonic of the Church Fathers, and is to be found as late as Ralph Cudworth.[21] However, given the major role now played by science in shaping our conceptions, it is perhaps scientific analogies that will prove most fruitful here, provided, that is, they are not taken too literally.[22]

The heart of who we are is a bit like the information-bearing pattern, the ideas or 'program' that constitutes the software of a computer: strictly speaking something non-physical. Certainly this needs some hardware in order for it to operate at all, but it need not necessarily be anything like our present computer. So it is likewise, then, with our 'souls'. God retains the memory of that pattern until he re-establishes it in some appropriate 'hardware' either immediately after death or at some later stage. But at least in respect of the next life he does so in a world not physically contiguous with our own. The heaven where the resurrected Christ now is, is, as it were, 'a parallel universe' existing alongside our own world, but with a body so physically unlike the body he had in this world that it shares none of the same matter. Whether the final 'new heaven and the new earth' do is a question that need not concern us here.[23] If readers prefer a literary analogy for the relationship between the two worlds, they might like to might draw on C.S. Lewis's children's classic, *The Lion, the Witch and the Wardrobe*. Recall the door in the wardrobe and the way in which it linked two worlds. Perhaps the eucharist is rather like that, with the resurrected Christ drawing alongside our present world to interact with it but at the same time in no sense physically and temporally contiguous with it.

Communion with the Departed

Although a full-blooded conception of the communion of living and departed may have developed more slowly within Christianity than was once thought, it is important to stress at the outset that without acceptance of some such notion, it is not just our relationship with the rest of humanity that is affected but also with Christ himself.[24] Luke's rather pedestrian account of the Ascension (Luke 24:51; Acts 1:3–11) can easily mislead us into supposing that the Ascension is only peripheral to Christian belief: just a way of marking the end of the resurrection appearances. But if we turn from description of the event itself to associated imagery then we discover that, so far from being rare, the notion of ascension runs right through the New Testament. It is, for instance, an image repeatedly found in John (e.g. 3:13; 6:62), in Paul (Colossians 3:1; Ephesians 4:10) and elsewhere (e.g. Hebrews 4:14; 1 Peter 3:22). What the passages share is emphasis on exaltation (sometimes very obviously under the influence of Psalms 110:1): that our own humanity has been exalted to the right hand of God in a new estimation of human value and worth. There is also a new availability to the person of Christ. In telling Mary Magdalene to stop clinging to him because he is not yet ascended (John 20:17), we must not vainly suppose that Christ is merely rebuking her for slowing down the next stage of his work. Rather, what he is offering is a promise: to be with her always if she will but allow him the necessary space to be who he really is: both human and divine, both God and exalted humanity.

It is important to note that it is within precisely such a context that conflicts in interpretation over the nature of Christ's presence in the eucharist should be set. In considering those disputes, what was at stake is often misunderstood. Simply by definition God is 'omnipresent', present everywhere. So the issue has nothing to do with questions of divine presence. Rather, it was a matter of how Christ's resurrected humanity is mediated to us, for, however transformed his body, it will still be limited to one space rather than another if it remains truly human and thus finite. So it was felt that a miracle was necessary for its presence to be felt in numerous eucharists occurring simultaneously throughout the world. Transubstantiation was thus introduced as one way of explaining how this is possible: Christ's human body and its related spatial dimensions are there 'by natural concomitance' (association) rather than literally.[25] Calvin's notion of our souls being briefly caught up to heaven by the Spirit to relate to Christ in that realm is but another.[26] But the key point, however expanded, remains the same: the human Christ continues to make himself available to us for our transformation. The eucharist is thus not just about encounter with God (often the modern reductive way of 'explaining' the sacrament) but equally encounter with the humanity of God in Christ, a humanity there to forgive, to heal, to release into new life.[27] Fortunately, a less literal understanding of 'body' makes the notion more comprehensible.

Under the ultimate inspiration of Barth, some have sought to go further.[28] In particular, T.F. Torrance argued that the relational character of modern physics allows us to think of Jesus' resurrection permitting a new relationship to space and time.[29] From his own eternity he now becomes accessible not just to every place but also to every moment of our own successive moments of time. It is a conception that has been endorsed by much recent writing on the theology of the Ascension, as well as more generally.[30] However, the position is not without its difficulties. Even leaving to one side the scientific claims (which are contentious), the more basic problem is that it seems to require us to abandon Christ's involvement in one key element of the human condition, and that is its temporal character. To be human is to have to think and act sequentially. So, if the human nature of Christ is caught up into divine timelessness, there is a heavy penalty to be paid: a Saviour perhaps better able to relate to this world as a whole but failing to carry into heaven an essential part of what it is to be human. Even more problematic would be any attempt to argue that each individual on death can be seen to enter the eschaton immediately precisely because its ultimate reality is non-temporal (or not temporal in our sense). Certainly, the language sounds impressive, but the cost is in effect human identity absorbed into the divine rather than a true flourishing and celebration of humanity in its most fundamental features.

It is precisely in order to preserve that identity that it seems to me so important that we talk of other human beings alive with Christ in the here and now. Were the rest of humanity assumed to be 'asleep' till the end of time and only Christ to be alive, his humanity would in effect have become a quite different sort of reality and so have effectively ceased to be representative of our own. To be human is to be a social being, not only in the sense that human identity is heavily shaped by others (family, friends, teachers, and so on) but also that without such support and friendship human beings are unlikely to flourish. That is no doubt one reason why from the early centuries onwards his Mother and others crucial to Jesus' own story have always been assumed to be present with him. Talk of his larger Body should therefore not be taken to imply an end to normal humanity but rather its perfecting in a realized community of love.[31]

Those who prefer to delay such possibilities to the eschaton rightly observe that, if the dead are sleeping, there is no interval that might otherwise speak of frustrated longings. That is true, but what is thereby ignored is the resultant impact on those still living. Prayers for the dead can appropriately be concerned just as much with benefit for the living as for the departed in a realistic recognition of how far short they have fallen no less than those who have gone before them. There is so much unfinished business at death: the wrongs never publicly owned, the quarrel never reconciled, the sheer nastiness and spitefulness that at times afflicts most of us, with some issues affecting one party but perhaps most both. It is scarcely gospel or 'good news' to be told of some distant hope of reconciliation, when an alternative, more immediate prospect seems a realistic possibility: in the Church's prayers now reaching out to those beyond the grave in ways that can bring for both living and departed great healing and peace. So, for example, the living can ask forgiveness of those whom they have wronged in this life and know that it is accomplished in that other life beyond, just as the living can pray for others who have done them wrong and know too that in this other world such wrong will be blotted out. Under the watchful eye of Christ, prayers such as these will help effect mutual reconciliation, and so draw the community closer into the one Body that is Christ's.

It is a truth that modern Protestant liturgies are beginning once more to enter-
tain as Reformation suspicions of prayers for the dead continue to decline, though
it is worth noting that individuals were seldom as extreme as the official teaching
of their churches.[32] The point in any case is not that an individual's ultimate destiny
can still be altered but that the person is now entrusted to God's continuing care.
Yet, even so, the Church's current understanding of such prayers is still not entirely
satisfactory since so little thought is given to the mutuality inherent in all such relationships of the kind suggested above: that it is as much the living as the departed
who are in need of forgiveness for the harm they have done. So commending the
departed to God is not just a matter of entrusting them to God's care but also peti-
tioning that through that care they may be enabled to reach out to the living in a
more complete and wholesome way. Some may object that this seems to imply that
God's forgiveness is not enough. Certainly, where individuals remain unreasonably
recalcitrant it must always be possible in the last resort to rely on divine forgiveness
alone. Yet at the same time it would seem odd to talk of a fully reconciled community if the individual actually wronged has not also extended forgiveness. So part of
the point in praying for the dead is to ask God to draw the wronged party (living
or departed) into the divine circle of love such that attitudes are transformed and
moves made that were once thought impossible.

Equally, care needs to be exercised in thinking what might rightly be entailed
by asking for the prayers of the saints. The point is not that God is more likely to
listen to godly people like them rather than to the average petitioner. Admittedly,
that very sanctity must mean that the individual is in some sense closer to God, but
there is too much contrary evidence in Scripture to suggest that this entails more
likelihood of being heard. Instead, God reaches out indifferently to all.[33] The point
is surely not that the saints are in a better position to influence God but that they
are in a better position to know the divine mind, a quite different thing. In other
words, because prayer is essentially about trying to align our wills with God's own
ultimate intentions for the world, asking the prayers of those fully attuned to that
will is more likely to draw our own wills in a similar direction.

Conclusion

Perhaps the most obvious objection to the account offered above is that it seems
to deprive the New Testament's stress on the eschaton of its central importance.[34]
Certainly, one key aspect was removed in Benedict XII's decision to place judgment immediately after death; but hope for a transformed world remains, as also
the gathering of all into one common world.[35] Even for the departed who are now
with Christ much must remain incomprehensible until the appropriate moment
in the historical unfolding of divine purpose makes all clear. To see that this so, it
is only necessary to reflect on how much the Church has got wrong in the past.

It is so very easy to tell a story of Christian doctrinal development in which
increasing specificity about heaven, hell, and purgatory resulted in an all too inevitable collapse of belief, as their structure was found to be based on projections onto
another reality of heavily time-bound assumptions. Best to leave well alone in a

healthy agnosticism many might well say. But, if I am right in this chapter, far too high a price is being paid. Not only is the larger communal identity of the Church in a pilgrimage shared by living and departed lost, but also the larger role once claimed for Christ's human nature in our salvation. As Christopher Wordsworth's Ascension hymn expressed it in the language of the time:

> Jesus reigns, adored by angels;
> Man with God is on the throne.[36]

So praying for the departed and asking for the saints' prayers, so far from being optional extras, can be argued to be integral to the Christian vision, as the living are drawn into not only a lively sense of shared community with the departed in the body of Christ but also the common vision of an ultimate resolution at the end of history that will be more fully theirs in the next life.[37]

Notes

1 In one recent search for an explanation, this turns out to be virtually equivalent to explaining decline in religious belief more generally: so Jeffrey Burton Russell, *Paradise Mislaid: How We Lost Heaven—And How We Can Regain It* (New York: Oxford University Press, 2006).

2 With the former concern clearly prominent in the writings of a New Testament scholar such as N.T. Wright, but with the latter also playing a major role in a theologian such as Jürgen Moltmann.

3 Immortality of the soul was affirmed at the Fifth Lateran Council in 1513: Heinrich Denzinger and Adolf Schönmetzer, *Enchiridion Symbolorum*, 36th ed. (Freiburg: Herder, 1976), 353–354. It is also endorsed in the Calvinist Westminster Confession of 1647 (ch. 32).

4 Well illustrated in the survey offered by Colleen McDannell and Bernhard Lang, *Heaven: A History* (New Haven: Yale University Press, 1988).

5 For Paul Tillich, *Systematic Theology*, III (London: SCM, 1962), 394–423; for Karl Rahner, *On the Theology of Death* (New York: Herder and Herder, 1971) and Marie Murphy, *New Images of the Last Things: Karl Rahner on Death and Life After Death* (New York: Paulist, 1988).

6 Elevated exposure of the corpse in Zoroastrian practice did not in fact indicate contempt for the body but rather the desire that it benefit from the purifying rays of the sun: Alan F. Segal, *Life after Death: A History of the Afterlife in Western Religion* (New York: Doubleday, 2004), 173–203, esp. 187–189.

7 Contrast Krister Stendahl, *Immortality and Resurrection* (New York: Macmillan, 1965) with the much more varied pattern argued by George W.E. Nickelsburg, *Resurrection, Immortality and Eternal Life in Intertestamental Judaism* (New York: Oxford University Press, 1972).

8 James Barr, *The Garden of Eden and the Hope of Immortality* (London: SCM, 1992), 53–56.

9 As in 1 Corinthians 7:29: 'the time is short.'

10 4th Article of 1563.

11 So Francis Watson, 'He is Not Here: Towards a Theology of the Empty Tomb', in *Resurrection: Essays in Honour of Leslie Houlden*, ed. Stephen Barton and Graham Stanton (London: SPCK, 1994), 95–107.

12 Marcus J. Borg and N.T. Wright, *The Meaning of Jesus: Two Visions* (London: HarperCollins, 1998), 111–127. Cf. William P. Alston and Sarah Coakley, 'Biblical Criticism and the

Resurrection', in *The Resurrection: An Interdisciplinary Symposium on the Resurrection of Jesus*, ed. Stephen T. Davis, Daniel Kendall and Gerald O'Collins (Oxford: Oxford University Press, 1998), 148–190.

13 Even the most conservative interpretation of such hopes must reckon with children now living as adults and the bodies of the elderly returning to their prime.

14 E.g. Wolfhart Pannenberg, *Jesus – God and Man*, trans. Lewis L. Wilkins and Duane A. Priebe (London: SCM, 1968), 87.

15 E.g. Richard Swinburne, *The Evolution of the Soul* (Oxford: Oxford University Press, 1986), 305–306.

16 Patricia Smith Churchland, *Neurophilosophy: Towards a Unified Science of the Mind-Brain* (Cambridge, MA: MIT Press, 1986), 317–323.

17 H.H. Price, *Essays in the Philosophy of Religion* (Oxford: Clarendon Press, 1972), 98–117.

18 As in Peter Geach, *God and the Soul* (London: Routledge & Kegan Paul, 1969), 17–29; Peter van Inwagen, *Material Beings* (Ithaca: Cornell University Press, 1990); Dean W. Zimmerman, 'The Compatibility of Materialism and Survival', *Faith and Philosophy* 16 (1999), 194–212.

19 Personal identity may in any case be a much looser concept than that usually still found among philosophers of religion; cf. Derek Parfit, *Reasons and Persons* (Oxford: Clarendon Press, 1984).

20 As in the ascription of physical pain to souls: Caroline Walker Bynum, *The Resurrection of the Body in Western Christianity 200–1336* (New York: Columbia University Press, 1995), 155.

21 For examples from Origen, Synesius of Cyrene, Hilary and Augustine, see my *Discipleship and Imagination: Christian Tradition and Truth* (Oxford: Oxford University Press, 2000), 126–127; for Origen's acceptance of subtle bodies, Brian E. Daley, *The Hope of the Early Church: A Handbook of Patristic Eschatology* (Cambridge: Cambridge University Press, 1991), 55–56; for the Neo-Platonic notion of astral bodies, including Cudworth, E.R. Dodds's edition of Proclus, *The Elements of Theology*, 2nd ed. (Oxford: Clarendon Press), 313–321.

22 The objection has been raised that in the scientific case parallel universes do not interconnect, and so there can be no continuity between the body here and there. That is true, but in the analogy there is continuity in the immaterial basis of both bodies as determined by God. See further Philip Francis Esler, *New Testament Theology: Communion and Community* (London: SPCK, 2005), 246–249.

23 With our present universe inherently subject to decay (the second law of thermal dynamics) and some biologists arguing that all forms of life have time limits built into them ('telomeres' that entail that a cell can only divide a finite number of times), it is hard to see how it could in any sense be the same matter.

24 It has been argued that in the early centuries the Church only took an interest in the elite dead; so Éric Rebillard, *The Care of the Dead in Late Antiquity*, trans. Jeanine Routier-Pucci (Ithaca: Cornell University Press, 2009).

25 Thomas Aquinas, *Summa Theologiae* 3a.76.1.

26 John Calvin, *Institutes of the Christian Religion* 4.17.24.

27 Discussed at greater length in my *God and Grace of Body: Sacrament in Ordinary* (Oxford: Oxford University Press, 2007), 403–421.

28 For the key references and a brief discussion, Wolfhart Pannenberg, *Systematic Theology*, 3 (Edinburgh: T & T Clark, 1998), 586–607.

29 T.F. Torrance, *Space, Time and Resurrection* (Edinburgh: Handsel, 1976), esp. 159–193.

30 Douglas Farrow, *Ascension and Ecclesia* (Edinburgh: T & T Clark, 1999), esp. 262–267; Gerritt Dawson, *Jesus Ascended: The Meaning of Christ's Continuing Incarnation* (London: T & T Clark, 2004). More generally, Anthony C. Thiselton, *The Hermeneutics of Doctrine* (Grand Rapids, MI: Eerdmans, 2007), 574–581.

31 This point is argued at rather more length in Chapter 11, above.

32 Robert James Edmund Boggis, *Praying for the Dead: An Historical Review of the Practice* (London: Longmans, Green and Co., 1913); Ralph, Houlbrooke, *Death, Religion and the Family in England 1480–1750* (Oxford: Clarendon Press, 1998). Anglicans like John Aubrey, John Evelyn, and Samuel Johnson all prayed for the departed, whilst Jeremy Taylor and Thomas Ken believed that the dead prayed for us.
33 The whole biblical story from Abraham to Paul illustrates the point, as do Jesus' parables about divine concern for the lost.
34 E.g. Pannenberg, *Systematic Theology*, 3, 576–577.
35 In the bull *Benedictus Deus* of 1336.
36 From 'See the Conqueror Mounts in Triumph.'
37 This is an abbreviated version of an article first published as 'Communion of Living and Departed', *The International Journal for the Study of the Christian Church* 10 (2010), 244–256, and is republished with permission of the editors and publishers, Taylor and Francis.

Index